T0374968

"Whether reflecting upon the scourge of pandemic, the spread of political violence, or the possibilities inherent to new digital technologies, many today narrate our age as 'unprecedented.' Yet, perhaps the insistence that human society faces disaster as never before exhibits how deeply we have become strangers to ourselves as mortal creatures. In *Mortal Goods*, Ephraim Radner shows how a wide spectrum of political and ecclesial viewpoints today treat calamity as a bug that mortals can fix rather than as a component of God-given creaturely life itself. Combining scholarly gravitas with a stark realism about the joys and sorrows of human life, Radner dares to peek under the veil of our self-congratulatory tales, testifying to God's gracious work of redemption within our mortal limits. At once groundbreaking and deeply traditional, *Mortal Goods* is a wonder, a gift from one of the most creative theologians writing today. Whether or not one concurs with Radner's conclusions, readers hungry for fresh insights on modern responses to mortal calamity will be deeply enriched by this volume."

—**J. Todd Billings**, Western Theological Seminary, Holland, Michigan; author of *The End of the Christian Life*

"In a polarized age when edifying discussions about religion and politics are in short supply, Ephraim Radner asks us to rethink what we mean by 'the good life.' It begins with a self-imposed challenge to write a letter to his children about what makes life valuable. The letter he eventually pens, after pondering various God-given mortal goods (earthly gifts, like being part of a family, that constitute our brief lives in the world), is worth the price of the book—and has the potential to reorient, rehabilitate, and redeem our present political morass."

—**Kevin J. Vanhoozer**, Trinity Evangelical Divinity School

"What is our Christian duty in public affairs? Many of us imagine that we're called to put our shoulder to the wheel of progress. Radner argues otherwise. We are called to honor the beauty of creation and to ameliorate, as best we can, the burden of life after the fall. Supposedly high ideals are invitations to despair. Radner shows that we need a politics of finitude, one that is grateful and not grudging. *Mortal Goods* is a must-read in our difficult times."

—**R. R. Reno**, editor, *First Things*

MORTAL GOODS

REIMAGINING
CHRISTIAN POLITICAL DUTY

Ephraim Radner

Baker Academic
a division of Baker Publishing Group
Grand Rapids, Michigan

Published by Baker Academic
a division of Baker Publishing Group
Grand Rapids, Michigan
BakerAcademic.com

Printed in the United States of America

Library of Congress Cataloging-in-Publication Data
Library of Congress Cataloging-in-Publication Data
Names: Radner, Ephraim, 1956– author.
Title: Mortal goods : reimagining Christian political duty / Ephraim Radner.
Description: Grand Rapids, Michigan : Baker Academic, a division of Baker Publishing Group, [2024] | Includes bibliographical references and index.
Identifiers: LCCN 2023030382 | ISBN 9781540963802 (paperback) | ISBN 9781540967411 (casebound) | ISBN 9781493444618 (ebook) | ISBN 9781493444625 (pdf)
Subjects: LCSH: Christianity and politics.
Classification: LCC BR115.P7 R23125 2024 | DDC 261.7—dc23/eng/20230831
LC record available at https://lccn.loc.gov/2023030382

Baker Publishing Group publications use paper produced from sustainable forestry practices and postconsumer waste whenever possible.

24 25 26 27 28 29 30   7 6 5 4 3 2 1

To R. and J. Reno and to our families

Contents

Acknowledgments

My thanks to *First Things* magazine, *The Living Church* magazine, Austin Graduate School of Theology, Wycliffe College's Scripture and Theology Colloquium, Church of the Resurrection Capitol Hill (Washington, DC), Christ Church (Georgetown), St. John the Divine (Houston), and *St. Andrews Encyclopaedia of Theology* (https://www.saet.ac.uk/) for the chance to share and work out some of the ideas in this book. Thanks are due as well to friends, colleagues, and students with whom I have had the good fortune over time to talk about these matters; and to my father, an unconscious sparring partner over the years. I am especially grateful to my wife, Annette, and children, Hannah and Isaac, whose gifts represent the focus of many of my main arguments here.

Introduction

For thus saith the LORD that created the heavens; God himself that formed the earth and made it; he hath established it, he created it not in vain, he formed it to be inhabited: I am the LORD; and there is none else.

Isaiah 45:18

I never had a clear desire to write this book until I made an effort, a couple of years ago, to write a letter to my two adult children and son-in-law about the kind of life I wished for them and prayed that they might have. I tried to write it bearing in mind things I had learned, often at great cost but also with much joy, about my own life. I was getting older; I had been ill; COVID was upon us. I wanted to share my faith, certainly, but not in an immediate way. I was more interested in communicating a sense of what makes life valuable.

I actually wrote the letter and sent it to them. The letter speaks of several elements that go into what I consider to be "the good life," one that I would want for them: our particular, embodied being as women and men; our life in families and as families; our toil to live and sustain this; our life with neighbors; our friendships; our suffering and our joy. Only then, the church. All these are "goods"—the goods that are part and parcel of mortal life, the life God has given us and that, in a sense, must be who we are if we are not to be God. Tending these goods is our vocation, our "service" or "offering" to God—*avodat Hashem*—who is the giver of these goods.[1]

The letter was fine, sort of. Perhaps a bit deflating: *That's all?*, one might have responded. *Just our bodies, families, work, friendships, sorrows, and delights? Then you die?* I realized that the letter needed some cultural context, as it were. I'm not sure I ever did a great job teaching my children about these goods as *truly good*, the good and the goods that go into our service of God, our creator. What has kept me from doing so? How do our environments in our day and place conspire to obscure this reality of meaning and purpose and instead give us other meanings and purposes that have so sapped especially younger people's hopes today?

The present volume is meant to reflect on the political landscape in which the Good Life, in Christian terms, can be more or less helpfully pursued. As a result, this book is about how Christians might more faithfully and realistically imagine their *political* vocation, though "political" will turn out to embody no more than the conditions necessary for a father to write a letter to his children. Thus, the book is about earth, not heaven. It does not treat, except in a passing way, the resurrection, eternal life, or the beatific vision. Neither, as we will see, does it treat of grand political theories and civic landscapes. Earth is the space where politics is done, but it is an earth inhabited by people who struggle simply to live a few years and to live in a way that honors these years as God's gifts, nothing more. I believe we need to reimagine and restrain the grand political hopes that churn up the soil of our lives and to think more modestly, more rootedly, within that soil's own ground.

To be sure, the Christian tradition rightly connects earth with heaven in an essential way, especially when it comes to politics. The connection is frequently given in the form of a conditional. At its simplest, perhaps most simplistic, it goes like this: *If* you or I, or we, do *this* here on earth, then the shape of our existence in heaven will be *that*. The condition is usually, in fact, given in the form of an imperative: You or I, or we, *must* do this *so that* in heaven *that* might be the case. Both the conditional and the imperative mimic much secular political thinking—if, then; we must, so that—which is based on calculations, instrumentalities, predictions, probabilities. That the paradigm is held in common between the church and the enemies of the church should perhaps make us suspicious of the paradigm itself.

For myself, I actually do hold to the paradigm after a fashion, with its connections, conditions, and imperatives alike. But I find them so obscure in their details, so complex and difficult, that the application of the paradigm to calculations, instrumentalities, predictions, and probabilities seems useless. Indeed, throw into the paradigm's parts the reality of human sin, divine judgment, forgiveness, grace, and the glory of the cross and thus of a certain kind of human suffering, and it seems clear that the whole connection between earth and heaven can only be affirmed, never parsed. If anything, we should resist seeing earthly politics and heavenly reward as bound to a common paradigm, precisely because the former is bound to infect our understanding of the latter, while in fact it is the latter that must inform the former. Let heaven push back upon the earth with its own energies; and let the earth be our concern, though with the hope of heaven's power. Even this order has its problems, however: it can either turn into another version of striving and an instrumental version of the first set of conditionals and imperatives (*if* or *since* heaven is this, *then* you must do that on earth); or it turns the earth into some evanescent shadow of heaven (or of "the future" in some modern theological euphemisms). So perhaps what is best to say is this: let the earth be simply the earth, as created by the Lord God Almighty, King of the Universe, whom neither heaven nor earth can contain (1 Kings 8:27).

The argument of this volume is simple enough. If "politics," in a general way, refers to the deliberate judgments and decisions ordering our corporate existence, then our Christian calling is to limit our politics to the boundaries of our actual created lives and to the goods that stake out these limits: our births, our parents, our siblings, our families, our growing, our brief persistence in life, our raising of children, our relations, our decline, our deaths. These mark the goods of our lives along with the acts that sustain these goods, like toil and joy, suffering, prayer, and giving thanks. Christian politics is aimed at no more and no less than the tending of these "mortal goods." That is the argument, and its exposition follows a cumulative reflection on some of the bits and pieces of human debate and experience that have clustered around and, more often than not, obscured the elements of this argument over time. The category of "mortal goods," in fact, forms the main focus of the volume as a whole, and its definition will emerge only in the course of this reflection. Given that the theological value I will be giving the category of "mortal goods" is both enormous and counterintuitive precisely in theological terms, we can only get at what a "mortal good" is by dwelling with, rather than by formulating, its impinging character. On this score, Scripture will provide a constant, orienting tug at the discussion, on the presupposition that, without Scripture and its defining terms, we are in any case left with nothing but the centerless infinity of someone like Giordano Bruno's universe, one in which human life is but a floating point in an endless sea of aimless and ultimately isolated entities.[2] It is the God of earth and heaven who provides that center both by speaking it forth and by ordering its form through his Word.

Christian Political Indifferentism

From the perspective of political theory, my argument falls within the category of "political indifferentism"—that is, the notion that politics is mostly
a matter "indifferent" to core human interests. In a broad way, my views
cohere with some of the main arguments of the great twentieth-century
French Protestant thinker Jacques Ellul, whose elaborated discussions of
the "political illusion" were shaped by his pointed studies of the socially
transformative power of contemporary technology and its "technocratic"
application to large societies.[3] The complicated challenge of organizing
these increasingly intricate societies, Ellul argued, has involved a bureau-
cratization of life that has rendered the category of "democracy" an empty
vessel and transferred decision-making to a range of other, often morally
distorted and distorting, corporate forces. Ellul had little optimism that this
situation was reversible, and he concluded that our dependence on political
solutions to social and moral problems was, literally, an "illusion." From a
Christian perspective, in any case, Ellul argued that we should reorient our
practical hopes more realistically and focus on matters more directly tied to
the divine power that alone will properly transform the world, if mainly on
an eschatological horizon. I would place far more emphasis than did Ellul
on demography as divinely providential in its stark demands. Demography
describes the life-constraints that God and human action place upon individuals and peoples, from which only secondarily flows the technological
development Ellul worried over. Furthermore, divine (in the sense of created) demography relativizes the existential need for the eschatological shift
Ellul, and many others, proposed. Still, most of Ellul's political analyses are
ones I would accept, along with what became, toward the end of his life, a
fascinating form of biblical figural reading.

But an emphasis on divine demography significantly reorients my own
reflections here with respect to positive political commitments, however
chastened. I believe that our created frame ought properly to order our practical values in a substantive manner. Thus, the indifferentism I commend
coheres with the traditional application of this category to certain strands
of Christian thinking in particular, except in a crucial area that I will mention in a moment. Karl Marx was among the first to speak of Christians as
political indifferentists. In a short essay of 1873 entitled simply "Political Indifferentism," he attacked his near contemporary Pierre-Joseph Proudhon's
practical political reticence with the charge of bourgeois class self-interest.
Proudhon was a remarkable and influential social theorist. But for all his
insight into the dynamics behind the oppression of the laboring classes,

he counseled against activist revolution. Coercive violence, he argued, was counterproductive, upsetting the social applecart in ways that could only end up harming workers. In this worry, Marx notes, Proudhon was simply following an age-old "Christian" tendency to shy away from politics altogether and let rulers continue to oppress. Marx ends his critical essay with dripping sarcasm aimed at the self-interested hypocrisy of Proudhon's restraint:

> If the early Christians, who also preached political indifferentism, needed an emperor's arm to transform themselves from oppressed into oppressors, so the modern apostles of political indifferentism do not believe that their own eternal principles impose on them abstinence from worldly pleasures and the temporal privileges of bourgeois society. However we must recognize that they display a stoicism worthy of the early Christian martyrs in supporting those fourteen or sixteen working hours such as overburden the workers in the factories.[4]

The term "indifferentism" had previously been attached mostly to matters of religious belief, by an individual or a state. But Marx's use of the phrase "political indifferentism," and in particular its putative early Christian paradigm, seems to have stuck. Early twentieth-century historians of political theory, such as Columbia University's William Archibald Dunning—whose allegedly racist studies of American Reconstruction may or may not have been related to his larger historical survey—provided an influential outline of Christian political indifferentism. From Jesus through the early Middle Ages (and despite Constantine), as Dunning outlined the framework, Christians prioritized spiritual over earthly goods and power.[5] Marx would have agreed, whatever his and Dunning's different explanations. More recent scholarship has sought to upend this standard view almost completely, although in quite diverse ways.[6] Most of these attempts, however, seem to reflect modern political concerns projected backward in a way that seems so obvious as to suggest the almost iron grip of academic and cultural ideology upon critical reasoning. There is, in fact, little to indicate that either the New Testament authors, in their variety, or early Christians held any driving political vision based on their faith; and where any political vision asserted itself, self-interest of one kind of another, or the *longue durée* of restructured social habits, brought on as much by demographic turbulence as by anything, is a sufficient explanation. The eighteenth-century historian Edward Gibbon, in his monumental *The History of the Decline and Fall of the Roman Empire* (1776–89), is a far more convincing reader of this material than are many modern scholars, who seem overly eager to discover various contemporary modes of political action lurking in Jesus, Paul, Irenaeus, and Augustine. Such modes are not there.

That Christian political indifferentism was an actual theoretical tradition until the modern era named it as such seems unlikely. But the de facto reality of most people's lives—the lives of those within the church as much as anywhere—meant that the indifferentist attitude's practical shape was long compelling. In the sociologist Peter Berger's lucid analysis, only after the sixteenth and perhaps seventeenth centuries in Europe did individuals consider their lives in terms of choice-making. For most people and for most of the time, life and its social forms have been "givens" into which one is born and which one assumes and navigates as best one can according to standards internal to the fixed character of physical and social existence.[7] This has been most evident in so-called peasant societies, which involve subsistence agriculture but also artisanry (something we will discuss in later chapters). Even nonpeasant roles, before modernity, were for the most part externally framed for and imposed upon individuals. Few individuals "decided" to be silversmiths or weavers. They were born into such trades. While noticeable change obviously took place in terms of social arrangements, it was usually sudden, often disturbing (disease, famine, violence), mostly thrust upon a person, and rarely calculated and strategically pursued. Who made political decisions and what those decisions might amount to was, before Europe's modern era, outside the scope of both interest and influence for the vast majority of a given population. That some have linked, if only in form, early Christian political attitudes to Epicurean responses to the inescapable assaults of the world upon individual well-being is a matter, surely, less of the genealogy of ideas than of the common lot of human life: we can change a little, but not much. The social force of "mortal goods" arises in this context of steady changelessness.

Modern rearrangements of social order, including the mitigation of immediate existential threats for whole nations, have opened up to many more individuals the field for the strategic calculation of political goals and execution. With more energy, more time, and more resources available to the average person in our modern societies, more and more of us are encouraged to participate in the great task of bettering our lives. While the efficacious consequences of this are probably illusory, the illusion itself stirred up debates about the value of political engagement from a Christian perspective. Søren Kierkegaard, in the nineteenth century, explicitly insisted on Christianity's political indifferentism since his religion's focus upon the "higher" realm demanded, by default, "subservience" to earthly authorities. By contrast, he writes with disapproval, "Now, everything is politics, and the clergy itself is the first to rush to Parliament."[8]

Kierkegaard's attitude is hardly winsome, though it sounds rather Pauline. Revolutionaries—for example, in Russia's Bolshevik upheaval in the early twentieth century—were eager to accuse Orthodox Christians of political indifferentism, which had by then turned into an accusation of profound immorality. The resurgent post–World War II American evangelicalism of Carl Henry (rightly or wrongly) accused earlier fundamentalists of political passivity.[9] Less virulent, though perhaps with as much passion, was Reinhold Niebuhr's argument against Karl Barth's supposed political indifferentism, which would seem (according to Niebuhr) to leave the world to disintegrate in the clutches of evil men, all on the basis of a purported commitment to the transcendent perfection of God. Such a commitment, Niebuhr claimed, mistakenly leaves every human effort at social betterment pointless and indeed necessarily perverted: "The Barthians are very critical of present society but they are also very critical of every effort to improve society. They regard it as necessary but dangerous; dangerous because moral and social activity might tempt men to moral pride and conceit and thus rob them of salvation. If the Barthians are socialists, I think it is not unfair to them to say that they don't work very hard at it." Niebuhr, by contrast, thinks it is not only worthwhile but morally necessary to "strive" for the attainment of "relative goods" within society.[10]

Much of the present volume is concerned with this category of relative goods. I will be arguing that, defined in very specific ways with respect to life, the so-called relative goods of generation, family, and generational nurture in the faith (matters that inevitably concern the lives of neighbors) are hardly "relative" at all in mortal terms. In fact, these elements constitute the absolute good of mortal life itself, as it is given. While the earthly absolutizing of mortal goods does not imply *no* politics for the Christian, it certainly points to an antiprogrammatic orientation. This does indeed cohere with aspects of Barth's attitude—and his thinking, along with Ellul's, has certainly influenced my own.

Barth, of course, was deeply involved politically, although the bases and forms of his commitments remain debated. The Barmen Declaration (1934), which he helped draft in protest of Nazi political hubris, has achieved the status of a kind of hypostatic exemplar of Christian moral-political integrity. Yet there *is* a kind of indifferentism at its core. Its assertions press more to the side of church-state separation, in my reading—the freedom of the church *from* politics—than anything. One could read the Declaration (8.15) as a rejection of political power itself. But because forms of human "lordship" seem to reach the level of idol, and thus create "lords" who may try to supplant the lordship of Christ, Barmen announces that the church is called to a posture of resistance that must finally be politically entangled. At the same time, the purely human powers of political order are not rejected by Barmen, at least not in themselves, and this is emphasized in typical New Testament terms (divine authority and order). Barmen commends "resistance" then, primarily with respect to state usurpations of ecclesial life and confession. These are cases when a human "lord" attempts to direct the affairs of the true Lord.

But exactly how to resist, outside of the internal ordering of the church's life, is not clear. And why should it be? The Christian's political engagements cannot be any less ad hoc than that to which such engagement responds. Barmen calls these the "arbitrarily chosen desires, purposes, and plans" of the political actors of the moment (8.27).[11] These are all but the vagaries of human corporate self-organization, by consent or force, vagaries which themselves follow no rule but the winds and eddies of a time far larger than any one human life. As the Christian historian Herbert Butterfield remarked at the close of one of his most popular volumes, "We can do worse than remember a principle which both gives us a firm Rock and leaves us the maximum elasticity for our minds: the principle: Hold to Christ, and for the rest be totally uncommitted."[12]

"Uncommitted," of course, is not the same thing as "passive"; nor does political indifferentism as I embrace it imply quiescence. Christians do all kinds of things in the world in which they live that may or may not give rise to utilitarian consequences. In many contemporary societies, Christians vote for political representatives or leaders. They may give money to campaigns. They may volunteer to promote political parties or causes or to take roles within their local system of governance. But what they should not do is imagine that any of these actions achieve their highest or even their penultimate purposes. These political habits, choices, and deeds are, literally, pastimes, activities that provide stimulation to oneself or others on perhaps multiple levels, but without long-term or even immediate ameliorative benefit, except by chance. To think anything else is to commit oneself to that which not only has no ballast but which will probably obscure or even subvert the deeper goods that constitute human life as the ultimate gift of God to the creature.

This may seem a perverse claim. If it did not, it would mean that one has been raised in a contemporary social and cultural vacuum, one in which the dynamics of today's common life, with its relentless valorization of "bettering the world" (and oneself), simply did not exist. I have had to try hard to pry myself loose from this culture, and my own life and instincts have been wrapped in contradictions over this. Still, ours is a culture whose ameliorative values, furthermore, are not random. Governance of communities can, after all—and often does—involve injustice, oppression, corruption, and incompetence as well as simple mistakes in calculation and execution. Given this reality, politics as it gives rise to and enables particular forms of governance must surely be a necessary duty for any human actor who lives with others. The argument of this book, however, is that the immoral burdens of governance require more than standard—that is, contextually customary—political engagement only when they threaten the mortal goods that constitute the absolute gifts of human createdness.

Types of Politics

Perverse as this argument may be in contemporary cultural and practical terms, it is not religiously and existentially implausible. In exploring this topic, it may be useful, then, to define certain terms as they will be used or implied in what follows.

First, I will frequently speak of something called "Christian politics." This is a broad and malleable category, as I use it. It could mean "what Christians themselves think they should be doing politically," or perhaps "what some Christians think they should do" on some basis or other. On this level, "Christian politics" is best examined historically, in either social or "history of ideas" categories. I will do a bit of this. But I will also be using the phrase "Christian politics" prescriptively—often by contrast with these other usages. Here, I will mean simply and exclusively "the tending of mortal goods." This latter, prescriptive sense may well involve the second category I now mention, but often not at all.

For, second, Christian politics also presupposes something else, in distinction from it: what I would call "normal politics." I define "normal politics" as playing one's role in whatever system of governance one finds oneself living within, according to the rules of the system (which may include rules on reshaping that system and its laws). These rules may envisage constant change or they may assume stasis. They may assume broad and popular engagement or they may assume the engagement of only a few. "Politics" here is a broad term for whatever it takes to put in place and to maintain or perhaps reform a given system of governance. While Christians, as I have said, may well engage in normal politics, they will do so for a host of reasons, only one of which, rarely, will be motivated by their specifically *Christian* political concerns (in my definition, the tending of mortal goods). In a basic way, Christians *should* view normal politics with indifference (and such an indifference would reflect a more prescriptive "Christian politics"). I will mention some reasons Christians may wish to engage in normal politics later in the volume, but by and large I mostly want the reader to imagine how this might play out, on the basis of the prescriptive sense of Christian politics itself that will gradually emerge within the book.

There is a third category I need to lay out as well, one I will call "abnormal politics." Christians engage abnormal politics when they are pressed by some threat to their mortal goods to take on a political role that either stands outside their normal political functioning within whatever system of governance they happen to find themselves, or that moves beyond individual political avocations. Abnormal politics, for Christians, emerges as an imperative to action on their part when there arises a need to reorder the system of governance *for the sake of* mortal goods. If this sounds revolutionary, it may well be. But the Christian's abnormal politics has no grand strategic end in mind; it is ad hoc and limited, and thus its "revolutionary" character is focused and transient and aims at preventing harm, protecting life, and assuring a realm of peace in which the integrity of mortal goods can be faithfully attended.

Abnormal politics is also almost always engaged in the midst of and through the means of catastrophic realities. I am writing this in 2022, in the middle of the Russian war against Ukraine and her peoples. I know personally some of those caught up in this conflict. Their stories and evident struggles rend the heart. However this war ends, it is a war that demonstrates close at hand the way that abnormal politics seems to arise, but also how such politics is hardly clear or clean, let alone even useful, ultimately. Ukrainian soldiers are taking up arms—I would say necessarily—to protect their families. Yet in the process, as one Ukrainian Christian leader said, "Our humanity is slipping away" and "our souls are dying." Abnormal politics is a kind of limit, the driven encounter with which is always bound up with death. "The necessary" is not always the same as "the good." Nor is the good very often the same as the useful.

Let me take one example. I have already mentioned the generally cohesive nature of "peasant" existence, for all its diversity in time and place, and one might look at historical examples of, for example, medieval and early modern European "peasant revolts" in the light of abnormal politics.[13] Disagreement among historians about the causes of these diverse uprisings remains profound. But in at least some instances it seems clear that actual subsistence, in the face of onerous taxation, famine, and poverty, was at stake in what were mostly limited and local demands for change in the governmental and social structures of the moment. In some cases, these demands were met; and in many cases the consequences of the uprisings themselves may have been worse than the problems they sought to address, something that marks a hovering question mark over the shape of all abnormal politics. Yet at the center of these moments of political abnormalcy, most commentators recognize, stood the press for survival rather than ideologically articulated political strategies. These uprisings were framed within the religious petitions of desperate individuals and their families, whose capacity to navigate a dangerous world relied not only on material goods but on the imaginative frameworks—a certain Christian faith and its conditions—that provided value to their vulnerable existence. Both local and broader impositions of arbitrary political power within such an existence do indeed elicit Christian political response. Political indifferentism, that is, has its limits.

Mortal Goods

The benchmark for Christian political engagement is the integrity of what I call "mortal goods," the sustained realities and possibilities of birth, growth, nurture, generation, weakening, caring, and dying. These are the goods I want to share with my children. These goods, in their persistence or in their vulnerability, define the compelling limits of the various categories of politics I have just mentioned. So I will claim. I realize that, in a modern perspective, such a claim must seem morally stunted. But that is only because such a modern perspective has confused the spiritual and material aspects of "the good" in a constantly shifting and thus misleading fashion. The parable of the good Samaritan in its material aspect has become a paradigm for contemporary moral purpose, politically executed: the alleviation of physical suffering. At the same time, the parable's traditional spiritual meaning within the Christian tradition has been transferred to just this moral purpose of pain mitigation, providing the latter with a grand symbolic reach that can take in values like inclusion and tolerance of difference. These values are, of course, devoid of the soteriological meanings that once informed the parable's significance in the first place. But because they are viewed as primarily pain-resisting values, they have a transcendent force. From this arises a morally inflated—indeed, voracious—politics that insatiably demands more and more action in order to reshape social life in accord with the figures of victims, Levites, and Samaritans, figures that refer to all aspects of bodily and psychological struggle. This material-spiritual confusion has meant that Jesus's counsel to "be a neighbor" becomes an unending social upheaval: there must always be a beaten traveler to be encountered; there are always callous and prejudiced Levites to be called out; and we are ever pressed to become Samaritans, marginalized in our inner righteousness. The dynamic of such a reading is emotionally and socially unsustainable, and the practical default lies in identifying the obvious: everyone becomes a victim somewhere along the line, and everyone else becomes a victimizer; and the truly good person is ever further down the road. These judgments are, in some measure, always accurate given the nature of human life. But "judged" in just this way, the essential responsive expression of a mortal good, thanksgiving itself, is swallowed up by death.

By contrast, my stress on the benchmark of mortal goods is meant to limit these voracious moral demands, politically pursued, to just a few items whose actual enactment will vary by circumstance. We become Samaritans only as we walk our particular roads outside the Great City, and only in this or that encounter along the way. Everything is close to us, for we can never travel far, given our unsteady gait and the few days we are given. What is nearby, however, is filled with wonder and demand and can in fact be enumerated, if not always predicted, in its detail. We know who we are as creatures of God, and we know with whom we have to do in our lives. We are mortal; and only within this mortal life and its forms does goodness lie.[14]

The notion that politics is best conceived of in terms of pursuing or even possessing certain goods is traditional enough, for Christians as much as anyone. But a stress on a Christian politics of specifically *mortal* goods is rare. Instead, Christian politics of "the good" has always had the soul mostly in view, somehow disengaged from the human person's mortality. One can take, as a recent example, Simone Weil's influential *The Need for Roots* (posthumously published). The book is a fertile discussion of a decent society in which the human soul can flourish, and was written in the shadow of World War II and Europe's unraveling.[15] Weil provides a list of "goods" necessary to such a society and its inhabitants, including order, liberty, responsibility, obedience, honor, and truth. These are all goods of the soul, as it were, but they are ordered politically because they constitute what "has to happen" for the good of the soul, and in this sense for the good life. Weil spends a good deal of time discussing how contemporary social life—in the cities, countryside, and nations of 1940s Europe—restricts or even dislodges these "roots." But Weil's list, for all its political orientation that by definition involves calculations and the ordering of bodily life and relations, is deliberately aimed at something other than any of these concrete elements. Bodies are for the sake of the soul, however essentially, but in a way that demands, heuristically, that the soul's life determine the body's.

There is something eerily *un*rooted about Weil's approach, spectral, ethereal. To conjure up these goods, to reroot human life, seems to demand two alternatives: either coercive social enforcement—something she rightly shies away from—or the dissolution of mortal goods into some sphere beyond human life altogether. How else take hold of the soul's proper good? This has been sensed by many and is surely wrapped up with Weil's own frustrated death, which some have attributed to a form of self-starvation, as distant from the value of a mortal good as possible.

That said, I think that Weil's approach to politics in terms of "goods" and their social furtherance makes sense. It's just that any list of goods must itself be more concretely "rooted," with roots that lie in aspects of our created existence more basic than the principles of liberty and honor. Spiritualizing politics is a danger, even (and perhaps especially) among adamant contemporary materialists. Why not admit that "just" to live is a good, and thus just ordering common life for the sake of survival founds the political good? I agree that, taken without qualification, such an admission says too little for the Christian. The Christian asserts that "to live is a good *because God has given me life*, and this God-given life is what I am." This qualification infinitely enriches the admission, and properly so: it grounds the consequential political good in God's creating gifts, ones explicated by Scripture itself. But this grounding also means, not that the straightforward goods of living are thereby shown to be delusions in favor of some greater good, but rather that they can be properly appreciated as divine gifts in their own right. The admission that life is God's gift is itself, as I will explore in this volume, an offering of thanks. The admission that "to live is good" is thus a proclamation: "O LORD, our Lord, how excellent is thy name in all the earth! who hast set thy glory above the heavens" (Ps. 8:1).

The Shape of the Book and the Children It Serves

The book's main argument, to repeat, is that Christian politics ultimately serves, as one instrument among many, to secure the Good Life, constituted by the mortal goods God gives us. The outline of how I pursue this argument is straightforward, though its progress will be cautious. My reflections aim at a final (and revised) letter to my children about the Good Life, and I introduce the volume with a historical meditation on why parents write such letters in the first place. But because I am aiming at a word to my children, some of what I write will be quite personal; for I am after what is most personal of all, my life and theirs.

Taken as a whole, the rest of the volume is divided into two parts. In the first, I will explore the character of the Good Life, given the inescapable limits of our created existence. Short chapters sketch this life in terms of our service of God offered through the "mortal goods" that constitute our persons as creatures. As the discussion unfolds, I will also then reflect on how such an offering can be fulfilled within the boundaries that define our lives. Here I move to a second and larger section, where particular issues in political discussion arise: responsibilities, possibilities, expectations, calculations. These issues are then looked at in the perspective of our lives' actual course, their ups and downs and indeed significant and sometimes final upendings and catastrophes, of which our deaths are but one figure. The political indifferentism as well as the occasional revolutionary impulses of the Christian faith find their character unfolded in this context of a human life's small but often jagged compass, whose capacity to achieve resolutions of common purpose within the overwhelming complexities of reality is mostly frustrated.

The reader will quickly perceive my discomfort with progressivist hopes. While I will attempt some brief indications of concrete political responses to this and that reality of our world, this is not a "how to" guide on voting, policy advocacy, or activism, let alone political theory in the tradition of much "political theology." Such discussion is hardly worthless (though something that demands a radical modesty). But I am aiming more at reimagining the framework in which such discussion takes place. Since much of the political engagement we are called into as Christians in our service of God is limited and ad hoc, uncertain and often overwhelmed, the moral, let alone practical, certainties that form the staple of modern political discourse are simply inapplicable to the reality of our human existence in any deep way. Instead, while I can point to this or that happenstance that might compel our concern, in the end I can only turn to my children and tell them what to cherish as the goods of their lives. That is what I am after. How exactly they shall do that—with the few years they have been granted and with the fragile frames that carry them and with the calibrated respirations of their times and, finally, with the love they hold for those given them in their small compass of encounter—will itself become the offering of "something beautiful for God."

This book is aimed, in its conclusion, at formulating a letter to my children. Whatever human creation is in its fullness, the image of God in which we are made is at least the replenishing fullness of generation given by the life of male and female joined together and giving birth, the act by which human creation is itself rendered "good" (Gen. 1:26–28, 31; 2:18, 24). That our children (or we ourselves, our parents' children) kill one another, wander away and are lost to us, or simply order an existence that drifts beyond our touch (Gen. 4:1–17) is clearly the outcome to some sorrowful rending of the world's being and thus of our own. Yet the rending—of which the fall is a distorted reflection rather than a cause—itself points to the divine purpose at our origins. Its very ache makes of the letters written to our children both a plea and an act of thanks that, given who we are, mark our lives as "good." To speak in these terms and to have these aims orients this volume's political interest fundamentally. If political indifferentism seems perverse in our era, surely so too seems my eventual focus on the household (which of course limits that indifferentism, as I have said) as the seat of Christian politics. Does not framing Christian politics in terms of the household—of parents and children and the responsibilities of generation and nurture, shaped by their difficult times and places—pervert the purity of the gospel itself, dragging it into the realm precisely of Genesis 4's familial disorder, siblings killing siblings, parents mourning their children, procreation flowing out of loss rather than of fullness? True enough. Yet, for all of Genesis 4's initiating knottedness, this world of siblings, parents, struggle, death, longing, and generation lays out rather clearly the realm within which the goods of mortal life reside, the place wherein "began men to call upon the name of the LORD" (Gen. 4:26).

Not in heaven, but on earth; not generally, but specifically; not in attitudes but in the imposed responsibilities of being born, giving life, and dying; not in mortality's elision or sublation, but in its suffering for good or ill. The great contrarian and social philosopher Ivan Illich worried that the "ethos" of the household, subsequent to Jesus, so engulfed the true "love" preached by the gospel—and with a decisive quickness, as the Pastoral Epistles show—that the gospel itself was rapidly corrupted. The good Samaritan, one of Illich's favorite paradigms of the gospel's substance, seems to have little to do, he insisted, with the obligatory struggles of feeding one's relatives and village.[16] Christian politics cannot therefore be located primarily in the household, and love cannot be politicized.

I am almost convinced by the purity of vision that arguments like Illich's embody—but not quite. The politics of the household are complicated, to be sure. But the cultural histories related to household politics are easily and often unfairly caricatured, as Illich himself discovered when attempting to trace their integrity in terms of men and women, an experiment that was mostly greeted with the angry prejudices of his readers.[17] The Christian depoliticization of the household has often been driven, after all, by an anti-Judaism, however unconscious: the *novum* of the gospel, preached by the desexualized Jesus, finally shatters the old socially oppressive systems of Israel, which never understood the freedom of grace that lies at the heart of God. I could not disagree more. The ethos of the household, taken in a distilled sense, *is* the church's life, largely because the church's life in its practical enunciation exists in order to manifest the grace of God as the God who has made us and calls us, just within the forms of created existence that constitute our births and deaths. There is no other "place" where God is glorified (and heaven is not a "place" in any case).

Life can obviously become a fetish or idol, as Illich and Giorgio Agamben have noted (and as arguments, by especially Agamben, in the COVID pandemic have recently asserted).[18] But God is the God of our lives, and these two realities—God and human life—cannot be pried apart conceptually, as the ill-conceived distinction, not only by Agamben but earlier by C. S. Lewis, between *bios* (mere biological existence) and *zōē* ("real" life, deeper, meaningful, spiritual, true) has tried to do.[19] Our lives, just in their "biological" (that is, created) limits, are mortal, and this reflects God also, but in a way that does nothing to grant us metaphysical or moral maps to our common being, except in the most basic ways. We cannot escape the fact that inscrutability clothes the Lord God, King of the Universe; and the incarnation, death, and resurrection of Jesus, while they manifest in the flesh this transcendent person of God, do not thereby dissolve God's incomprehensibility (cf. Paul in Rom. 11:33–36), but rather render it most clearly as a gift to embrace or be embraced by, rather than to run from. This life, given us by our parents and bequeathed to our children somehow by us, is our one way into the mystery of God. The God-man, Jesus of Nazareth, has made that clear and established it as a promise. While Christian politics may concern mortal goods, the receipt of these goods unveils the mystery of the Christian God.

This book is about earth, not heaven.[20] "The earth is the LORD's, and the fullness thereof; the world, and they that dwell therein" (Ps. 24:1). But its stress on mortality does not therefore signal a simple focus on "immanent" concerns over transcendent ones. This would be to seriously misunderstand the perspective being offered here, which is founded on the claim that our created existence, because created by God, is always *about* God somehow. Yes, all that politics can and should do for the Christian is to engage the tending of mortal goods, realities that exist within the immanent domain of mortal life, given in natality, generation, decline, and death. But mortal goods neither exhaust God nor create life's meaning, which is in fact only God's to give and use, and thus it partakes, in a real fashion, of God's inexhaustible being. There is little talk of heaven in this book, nor of the great eschatological transformation promised by God in the Scriptures, delivered somehow in his Son, and enacted in our liturgies. Is mortality a "gateway" to these things, as many have argued? Perhaps. But, in my argument, the steady focus upon mortal goods is less daring in its scope, although it does not deny that such a vision is possible and even desirable. Rather, mortal goods reveal God simply in their being given. That revelation is fundamental to human created being and its purpose. Take this divinely revelatory essence of mortality away, and any further horizon is smudged or even erased from view. God is indeed the creator of the heavens. He is also creator of an earth which he made for habitation (Isa. 45:18), a thoroughly postlapsarian reality (cf., e.g., Gen. 4:16; 11:2) that comprehends the kind of mortal life that we in fact enjoy and suffer. We know this Lord, the Lord of heaven and earth both, exactly where we dwell.

If there is scriptural ballast to this political orientation, it is perhaps Ecclesiastes—that most political book of the Bible, written by the most politically experienced human author of the Bible. Ecclesiastes provides the proper equation of toil with the transient "breath" ("vanity") of human life itself (Eccles. 2:22–23; cf. Ps. 39:5), yet shows us how this equation is somehow reflective of the very "works" of God (our vain human works [Eccles. 2:11] nonetheless reflect the beautiful works of God [3:11]; cf. 4:4). Politically and otherwise, "Let us hear the conclusion of the whole matter: Fear God, and keep his commandments: for this is the whole duty of man" (12:13).

This book is about the basics, because only these basics can offer the possibility of something more; and just these basics have been degraded and dismissed in our time, thereby obscuring all that could ever be "more" for a desperately hungering creature. So I would tell my children.

Part One

THE GOOD LIFE

One

Letters to Our Children

By thee have I been holden up from the womb: thou art he that took me out of my mother's bowels: my praise shall be continually of thee. . . . Cast me not off in the time of old age; forsake me not when my strength faileth. . . . O God, thou hast taught me from my youth: and hitherto have I declared thy wondrous works. Now also when I am old and greyheaded, O God, forsake me not; until I have shewed thy strength unto this generation, and thy power to every one that is to come.

Psalm 71:6, 9, 17–18

"Politics" generally refers to those judgments and decisions that are deliberately made to order our corporate existence. In one way or another, this always turns out to involve our children most fundamentally: how they are formed, what they choose to do, what will happen to them, who they think they are. That is how it should be. But if that is so, then the springs of our political life are drawn from deep parental desires, something this initial chapter will reflect upon.

Like every parent, I want, sometimes desperately, my children to live well. We teach them how to live, for better or worse, by the course of our lives with and without them: how we act with them and others, how we speak to them and about others, how we carry ourselves in this or that situation, sometimes when we are far away. While it is right to assume that our children must finally achieve a responsibility for their own lives, we recognize that we have given or withheld from them resources to carry

3

this out. I have watched, over the past six decades, the world change around me, mostly for the worse as far as I can tell. All these changes confuse my instinct to cast blame for particular ills. The dynamics of social change are too complicated to chart individual causalities. I certainly cannot blame my children, in cases where I do not approve or understand, for thinking and acting as they do within the current of these changes: they have been taught, and by a far wider community than their parents. I, along with others, have given them certain tools, but not others. My children are responsible for their own lives. But so am I.

It would be nice if we could all just think through our lives rationally, and thus simply teach the skills of thinking well. Rationality, however, like a plant, reflects the soil and climate in which it grows and in which it is tended, well or poorly, with savvy or ignorance. With our children, especially, we at least can recognize that simple arguments we might make for what is better or worse are never really simple. Their convincing or unconvincing character is shaped by our own parental actions, long pursued, mostly unconscious and unthinking, often buried in a morass of our own unacknowledged inner turmoils. Our influences on our children, furthermore, are transformed and ordered by the wider environment that both we and they inhabit. In the gathered mass of children and their parents, over time or within the momentary demands of communal challenge, decision-making—political judgments and their execution—is not so much the working out and sum of various arguments as it is a cauldron of infinite and impossibly uncovered influences. The outcome of this churning mix is but a boiling over, in this instance or that, of some running, uncatchable liquid. I want my children to live well; I want them to have a good life in the midst of a world that is pulling and pressing in so many jostling directions. Yet nothing holds firm as a common guide, least of all my own example.

When David becomes old, "stricken in years" (1 Kings 1:1), he seems to waver in his hopes, or at least in the focus of his attentions. He lies shivering in his bed, his circulation failing, slipping away, until his attendants find a young woman to sleep close to his cold body, warming his cooling flesh under the blankets. Intrigue over the royal succession swirls around him, but he is oblivious until roused a bit by his scheming counselors, priests and prophets both who, organized by Bathsheba, press David to name Solomon his heir. As the dust is settling, David calls Solomon to him and offers him a final charge. First comes a sober and pious set of remarks: "Keep the charge of the LORD thy God, to walk in his ways, to keep his statutes, and his commandments, and his judgments, and his testimonies, as it is written in the law of Moses, that thou mayest prosper in all that thou doest, and whithersoever thou turnest thyself" (1 Kings 2:3). The bulk of his parting words of advice to his son, however, is devoted to political prudence—nay, to the settling of scores. Though David's life has now reached its limit, he urges Solomon to drag others to the same abrupt demise, if more unnaturally, and bring the old age of both his long-serving general Joab and of Saul's aged kinsman Shimei to a violent end: "Do not let his gray head go down to the grave in peace," but "bring his gray head down to the grave in blood" (1 Kings 2:6, 9 NIV). This brutal counsel, David admits, goes against his own promises of years ago, in Shimei's case, to leave him alone. Now, in a last exhalation of anger before dying, it is the time of vengeance.

It is an odd and disturbing testament that David leaves his son, especially as a foundation for political action. But perhaps not surprising, since it seems that David had long struggled over his own place as a teacher of wisdom to the young. In the Psalms we hear some tension in his sense of life and of God's place in it. With Psalm 37, he sagely asserts a kind of calm faith in the justice of the Lord, not only regarding him but also his family, and urges that others feel the same. "I have been young, and now am old; yet have I not seen the righteous forsaken, nor his seed begging bread. He is ever merciful, and lendeth; and his seed is blessed" (Ps. 37:25–26). This, from a man who saw the Lord kill Solomon's older brother at birth because of David's own murderous lust involving Bathsheba and Uriah. He had pleaded for a different outcome but then bowed before God's punishment (2 Sam. 12:15–23). The righteous never forsaken? If his own life, with all its sins, did not contradict such a claim, what were his memories of his friend Jonathan, beloved and slaughtered, in this regard (cf. 2 Sam. 1:19–27)? In any case, in Psalm 71 David's tone changes. Here he offers a desperate plea that, now in his old age, God not abandon him—at least so that he might tell others, tell the young something about God's "wondrous works" (71:17–18). It is a hope whose fruit, if his last words to Solomon are any indication, he squandered.

I can hardly do better than David, much though I might try. The venerable wish that many parents have, and teachers too, to provide our children clarity about goodness and justice by being for them an embodiment of such virtues—clearer even than we received from our own elders, we fondly imagine—rarely fades as a desire. But it is often disappointed. For "things happen," and the great examples of our lives seem too often (if we are honest) to crumble through time, at least as inspirations and models for the young. The righteous are never abandoned? I, for one, cannot demonstrate this and often doubt it. My cynicism reflects this. At best the statement needs explanation, surely, not simple assertion. Walk in the Lord's commandments, as the dying David tells his son, and this will show you how to deal with the struggles of kingdoms and nations, the rivalries and resentments of family, the best way to "keep your promises." Will it really? The books of Samuel and Kings are filled with examples of such a walk— but precisely in their mostly troubled forms and outcomes, less guides than the divine tracery of faltering capacities.

Generational Advice

Whatever the ambiguities wrapped up in a parent's desire to show a better way forward for the young, writing to youth, even to one's own children, has a long tradition dating back to ancient Greece and Rome. Some of this writing is more narrowly educational, with fathers (e.g., Cato and Cicero) providing "textbooks" for their sons on various subjects. But some is more oriented to "life lessons," to morals and character, expectations and hopes.[1] Such parental wisdom is hardly an exclusively Western practice, and there are classic (and relatively recent) Chinese exemplars, such as the nineteenth-century diplomat Zeng Guofan,[2] for whom the context of exam-taking seems to inform most moral issues, at least for boys. Last wills and testaments had themselves become, for some, helpful vehicles for moral and political instruction.[3] By the late Middle Ages and early modern period in Europe, the practice of generational counsel, often bound to the approach of death, had established itself as a genre—and in Britain a peculiar one, mixing religion, morals, and practical advice.[4]

With this book of mine I am stepping into this stream, though it is one that seems to be drying up, and with it, a whole current of political sensibility. Generational advice-giving, as a culminating exercise in personal relationships, has mostly disappeared as a formal and expected cultural task, though vestiges and new developments survive. Most advice today, in its public form, is a matter of projection and manipulation and rarely enters into the realm of personal life. Everything is about vague principles. I remember sitting around with friends, at the end of my undergraduate years, discussing what our imaginary valedictorian address would be, were we asked to give one. I don't recall the particulars offered, but we all agreed that the whole task was probably pointless and inevitably desultory. The life ahead of us was a mist; the life behind us often too painful to build motivating theories upon. We dreaded having to sit in the heat listening to the real thing. In fact, valedictorian speeches, peer to peer, are usually of an unelaborated and horizontal vision, with some finger-wagging and a little bit of the evening of scores—but mostly a "We can do it!" pep talk, whatever "it" is, though "it" is always a grand blur.

In much of the twentieth century these speeches tended to be of a modest scale, dealing in generalities. Likewise, formal commencement speeches of the past from visiting notables also had a certain restraint in horizon, even if they were usually more overtly inspirational—getting young people both to do good but also to *want* to do good and to have hope in doing good. Occasionally, a little worry might creep in, but not much. They were broad enough to take most people in but narrow enough in their moral aims to permit imaginative fervor and plausibly fulfilled righteousness. More recently, in both peer-to-peer and adult versions of the graduation speech, restraint has proved harder and harder to come by. And why not? The world that young people are entering is filled with widely publicized and burdensome demands: climate change, eliminating hate from the culture, undoing systemic injustice. Moral uplift seems to end in a tumbling movement that gathers the world, and all one's energies and resources, into its exhausting purposes.

There have always been alternatives on campus to the modern commencement speech in both its older and more recent forms. While in college I came across—I am not sure how or why—Lord Chesterfield's last letter to his godson. Chesterfield's letters to his biological son are the more famous and represent hundreds of missives that cover virtually everything. Beloved though he was, Chesterfield's son was illegitimate; and when he died before his father, Chesterfield made his godson—a distant relative— his heir. His letters to his godson, Philip, are themselves numerous and written over a long period, are mixed with French, Italian, and Latin patter, and touch upon encounters, deaths, poetry, moral habits, and family. The final personal note that we have, from 1770, is moving in its tenderness. But all these occasional letters come to a head shortly before Chesterfield's own death in 1773, when he leaves intimate conversation behind in favor of unadorned witness. With time running out, and enormous responsibilities about to be thrust upon the young man, the advice in the godfather's last communication, a kind of formal address to be delivered along with his will at the time of his death, is compressed and pointed—a paternal testament. Religious duty comes first, but the old man only emphasizes its priority and doesn't explain what he assumes is already known: without the "scrupulous" observation of religious "obligations," "you can neither be happy here nor hereafter." The point made, the rest of the long letter is about modesty, marriage, speech, demeanor, and business, with constant encouragements to avoid the temptations and pitfalls common to youth. It is all written with

Chesterfield's celebrated clarity, flair, and wit. He ends with a somewhat poignant *envoie*: "Idle dissipation and innumerable indiscretions, which I am now heartily ashamed and repent of, characterised my youth. But if my advice can make you wiser and better than I was at your age, I hope it may be some little atonement. God bless you."[5]

Whether David sought "some little atonement" with Solomon is doubtful. Israel's great leader died, it seemed, needing a redeemer more than ever before. But many parents, myself included, have wished that our older lives might claw back a little of what we have squandered. Their letters to their children have been traditionally quite different from the uncovering of great moral vistas for the world's future that we hear now at universities on sweltering summer days. Everything is smaller, though in fact the stakes seem much higher. Actions, habits, choices, and adjustments, and sometimes the gaping holes of years without communication amid a small group of acquaintances, neighbors, friends, and family—this is all a life adds up to anyway, its pieces of infinite weight, their ordering of infinite concern. We would offer wisdom, then, such as a parent can muster, and warning such as a parent knows too well: I was young once, and now I am old.

"Conduct books" represent one important genre of generational advice-giving as it developed in the publishing world of early modern Anglo-America, especially advice to young women, advice to young men, advice for mothers and husbands, for students and gentlemen. More recently, and not surprisingly, the genre has been subject to much political analysis, which has sought to uncover the ways these promulgated counsels either represented or encouraged unjustly constricted social roles. Advice, it seems, is always political. I think, however, that the term "conduct," as sweepingly applied to this genre, is somewhat misleading, and the fact that parental writings of advice have been put in the same category as broader works of social etiquette is probably perverting. Most of the parents in the early modern period who wrote to their children did so in the context of faith, first of all. Their hopes were oriented to passing on this faith. Some of the most profound "letters" were given as prefaces, sometimes even in verse, to personally prepared catechisms that parents (especially mothers) or godparents offered to their young "friends."[6] Even when not overtly catechetical, the Christian faith proved the best gift a parent could offer his or her child and was certainly the ground for all other forms of practical advice. What can a mother tell her children above all things? "Seek ye first the kingdom of God" (Matt. 6:33).[7] In the face of this deep hope, however, worries abound.

Dear Daughter,

I find, that even our most pleasing Thoughts will be unquiet; they will be in motion; and the Mind can have no rest whilst it is possess'd by a darling Passion. You are at present the chief Object of my Care, as well as of my Kindness, which sometimes throweth me into Visions, Visions of your being happy in the World, that are better suited to my partial Wishes, than to my reasonable Hopes for you. At other times, when my Fears prevail, I shrink as if I were struck at the Prospect of Danger, to which a young Woman must be expos'd. By how much the more Lively, so much the more Liable you are to be hurt; as the finest Plants are the soonest nipped by the Frost. Whilst you are playing full of Innocence, the spiteful World will bite. . . .

The first thing to be considered, is Religion: It must be the chief Object of your Thoughts, since it would be a vain thing to direct your Behaviour in the World, and forget that which you are to have towards him who made it. In a strict sense, it is the only thing necessary: you must take it into your Mind, and from thence throw it into your Heart, where you are to embrace it so close as never to lose the Possession of it.[8]

To be sure, when it comes to religion, the writer of this book-length "letter," the seventeenth-century gentleman George Savile, is interested in his daughter sticking to the established church, avoiding showy displays of emotion, and maintaining a sober morality on the basis of God's revelation. He eschews theology, which he explicitly dismisses as distracting for women. And the rest of his book covers a gamut of modest, practical, and mostly domestic matters that touch upon immediate relationships: Husband, House, Family and Children, Behavior and Conversation, Friendships, Censure, Vanity and Affectation, Pride, Diversions.

Limited though this kind of counsel may appear to be, John's First Epistle, it should be noted, covers many of the topics Savile treats, though in a kind of elevated religious register: faith in the incarnation and in God's forgiveness; acknowledgment of sin; the transitory nature of the world; victory over the fleshly passions; love for the brethren; correction of erring believers; truth and lies; idolatry; steadfastness; moral purity and obedience to God's commands; the promise of everlasting life. The letter is aimed at the old and the young, understood generationally, bound together in some kind of mutual responsibility. But the posture of John himself is one of a parent speaking to all his "children," as he calls them. They have been set upon a path that, he hopes, will lead them to see the Son of God (1 John 3:2), a hope that orders his advice toward purification and sanctity. The perspective and tone are hardly novel, though the scope of the advice offered and the conduct commended is utterly transcendental, "eternal": life and death are at the center of the epistle, but life and death that are bound somehow to God's ordering of all things, including most especially the here and now of daily life and comportment.

Savile is no Saint John; but he draws from a common well of concern, at least unconsciously. The Christian "letter to children" is, in its developing forms, usually articulated just within this vast theater of significance, though over time the theater's breadth is gradually obscured, left at best as an assumption, and often allowed simply to disappear into the shadows, in favor of the growing lists of practical counsels of direction. While Savile may well have insisted on "religion" as the main objective of any useful piece of advice to the young, it proves in fact to be only a small piece in his larger treasury (and formally shallow at that). How to get along, how to succeed, how to improve matters—all this takes over the genre more and more as the years go on, in the process exposing more and more the denuded social scaffolding upon which the religious affection of parents for their children had been previously erected. Later seventeenth- and eighteenth-century parental letters have been, as I noted, roundly assailed by modern critics, especially for their socially regressive views, about women in particular.

Still, these earlier exemplars have formed the basis for ongoing patterns of generational advice, which seem, however stunted today, to be irrepressible. Modern versions of the genre are found not only in self-help books but also in continued testimonies of hope and direction for young people in a world that, after all, remains "spiteful" and that indeed "will bite," often viciously, often with tears. How viciously? Certainly viciously enough to corrode the common life of societies and nations.

Many of the more recent testaments are overtly political, however heartfelt. The once-transgressive activist Raoul Vaneigem was still offering, in 2012, his youthful 1968 encouragements, now with the edge of an older and bitter disappointment in the corrupted and corrupting capitalist world.[9] Within the African American community, in particular, the genre persists, lit by burning moral passions and, to be honest, a certain amount of David-like resentment. James Baldwin's eloquent and pungent "Letter to My Nephew" transcends these sentiments but nonetheless keeps to a certain character-cum-political rhetoric:

> And if the word *integration* means anything, this is what it means: that we, with love, shall force our brothers to see themselves as they are, to cease fleeing from reality and begin to change it. For this is your home, my friend,

do not be driven from it; great men have done great things here, and will again, and we can make America what America must become. It will be hard, James, but you come from sturdy, peasant stock, men who picked cotton and dammed rivers and built railroads, and, in the teeth of the most terrifying odds, achieved an unassailable and monumental dignity.[10]

Maya Angelou, with a softer sensibility but nonetheless driven by an undercurrent of social imperative and exhortative uplift, wrote the popular, book-length *Letter to My Daughter* (in fact, to young women more broadly, since she never had a daughter of her own). Her sense of the vulnerability of the young is honest and accurate, and her advice in response is offered mostly as interwoven threads in the retelling of stories from her own life and encounters in ways that can be poignant as well as gently assertive.[11] Or again, consider the children's rights activist Marian Wright Edelman's various published "letters," first to her children, then to her grandchildren, and then, aiming at the web of interacting roles necessary for social health, a set of letters to parents, children, teachers, citizens, and finally to God himself.[12]

I have found Edelman's open missives, especially the earlier ones, affecting and often resonant with my own parental yearning. They combine a gracefully expressed motive of almost desperate need and steadfast hope, presented with a certain modesty of means. She commends "character" most of all—honesty, perseverance, hope, generosity—as the avenue to responsibility within the world. Yet there is also a mismatch in this combination: the whole world will be *changed*, and what we need is to keep at it in as upright a way as possible. Virtue has become a tool—and in this case a commendably necessary one—for social transformation. I can't help but hear the best of commencement speeches brought together here, but with the same nebulous inefficacy. Is this what our life before God comes down to: trying hard to make the world better, with a measure of decency? Perhaps. And Edelman's literary result surpasses most alternatives. But the content less so, unless the world and its spinning train are ordered by such earnest effort to beatitude. It is hard for me to believe it is. Just the many and often seemingly endless social and personal ills against which we are called to strain seem to make the promise less than plausible.

To Write a Letter

I keep coming back to my deep parental desire, clearly shared with many others, and it is hard to know what kind of letter to write. The ancient

Greeks, whose example is so endemic to our attitudes, were confused by just this challenge. Like Edelman, they could encourage people to never give up; yet just as often, it seems, they could admit that there are times when dying—indeed, killing oneself—makes more sense. "Giving up," that is, had its own virtue in certain circumstances. The reason for their confusion (or perhaps subtlety) is both simple and interesting: our lives are difficult, often horribly so. On the one hand, Greek popular wisdom observed, we can see others persevere, and we have managed it ourselves from time to time: Why not push forward despite the obstacles? I am no different—no weaker, no smarter—than any other mortal being in this regard. If they, then I. The nobility of such a goal, however, was founded on a certain resigned egalitarianism of incapacity, one that permitted virtue, but only a certain kind of virtue that modestly assumes the lot of humankind.[13] Thus, just this fundamental incapacity could, at times, make perseverance a dreadful and emotionally destructive foolishness: better to die in an honor overwhelmed by grief, as the wretched ending of *Antigone* displays, with its gathering up of self-murder. This can sound much like the counsel of Job's wife: "Curse God, and die" (Job 2:9). Give up. Moral and emotional egalitarianism can lead here too.

We could use a bit more of this confusion, at least in its honest admission. But perhaps only if the admission is, as in the book of Job, offered in the face of the God who created us. Without such an offering—and without such a God—endurance has little value, and failure can stoke no embers of hope. So, I would like to tell my children how hard life is. Of course they know it already, if not in themselves (they do that too, to be sure), then at least, in some adjacent way, in me. But I would also like to tell them how such a life, however hard, is beautiful, is a gift. And to do that I need somehow to express the shape of our existence as something that transcends all the "successes" and "failures" that too much advice must conjure, and having conjured it all, piles it up on the fields of our common social lives, smothering the actual gift of God itself.

The grand political version of this smothering, which seems to afflict the people of God in cycles, has been on a startling inflationary upswing in the past few centuries. The gifts of human life that are fundamental to our creation are not only increasingly invisible, but they have become the objects of outright and deliberate civil assault and destruction—biological families, biological identities, biological responsibilities. It is these fundamental gifts that parents have always sought to commend to their children, if in diverse ways, largely because they constitute the very reality of parents and children themselves, in their entwined affections and demanding obligations: the integrity of human bodies, of sexes, of toil, of family care, of eating and nurturing, of holding on and letting go in the face of the ever-encroaching and finally triumphant boundaries of survival and endings. They are gifts, however, because they are, more essentially, the framework and substance of what it means that we are created by God, creatures, objects of miraculous being who have no other claim upon our lives except that they are given from the divine hand and heart. And thus taken as well: for nothing can be freely given if it is not, in itself, something we can never own at its root. We do not possess our lives. But in both giving and taking, God's robes of grace swirl across creation. How to express all this to one's offspring, themselves essential gifts whose vulnerability informs my praise of God?

David, in Psalm 71's more desperate tone of aging anxiety, sees enemies all around him and feels acutely the possibility of divine abandonment. Although he has seen good in his life, he has also been the recipient of divinely imposed "great and sore troubles" (v. 20). God gives both. Thus, the bedrock of his hope is the fact that God brought him into existence within his "mother's bowels" and has given him life from the time he was taken from the womb (v. 6). In a psalm in which Egypt and exodus are never mentioned, the making of a baby marks the "Holy One of Israel" (v. 22), who can "quicken" and "bring up again from the depths of the earth" (v. 20). We can hope because we belong to the only one who owns life—because life is not ours but his.

One of the glaring absences in more contemporary letters of parental advice is the mention of our deaths: our deaths as parents, but also the deaths of those to whom we write. When Pope Francis promulgated, in 2019, his Apostolic Exhortation to young people, *Christus Vivit*, he offered a marvelous theological discussion of faith in Christ.[14] But when it comes to actual human experience, the document presents a more static celebration simply of being young and of the excitement (including Christian excitement) that being young involves. There is little said about the shape of the human life that young people not only are moving into but already assume. Illness and death—whether of one's family members, one's friends and peers, one's self—are never mentioned once, let alone as the framework for "youth" itself, youth that, as David says, is something that is "once" and will "now" become something else, youth that is passing.

This lacuna seems odd and disorienting. Being young is meaningful only in relation to being born and to dying, and more deeply, to being part of the lives of others for whom birth and death provide the context of one's own coming to be and taking leave—parents, spouses, children, and others. In one poem, the seventeenth-century poet Anne Bradstreet describes to her

children how she, the parent who loves them, teaches them truth through
the mortal dimensions of her own life:

> She shew'd you joy and misery,
> Taught what was good, and what was ill,
> What would save life, and what would kill.
> Thus gone, amongst you I may live,
> And dead, yet speak and counsel give.[15]

The kind of "counsel" she may have had in mind culminated in her final
letter, "To My Dear Children," falling tightly now into the genre of parental
testament.[16] Bradstreet, we know, was from a different era, when personal
health was always precarious and average life spans were almost half of
what they are today. But there is nothing unusual in the general motive she
offers for her writing: she will soon be dead, and she wishes, before she is
wholly without strength, to offer her children some "spiritual advantage"
drawn from her experience. Ancient or modern, the basic frame for such
a concern remains firmly in place. If not exactly novel, though, the "advantage" she actually provides her children seems strange to our ears: she
recounts the spiritual weaknesses of her life, its tremulous reliance upon
God, the wavering of her faith over the years, her doubts, her troubles and
inner darkness at times, her almost resented lack of divine illumination,
"sinkings and droopings," as she puts it. All this, as she explains to them,
contrasts to the "stay" that, even in these frequent and troubled periods,
God and God's Word have been to her. She has managed to survive with
some spiritual integrity.

Bradstreet lays out the back-and-forth tides of her feelings in all this—
despair and divine encouragement—in a matter-of-fact manner, as if *this*
is the expected avenue of the days that any "child of Adam" will traverse.
This, Bradstreet implies, is what it means to live for a few years as God's
creature who takes such a life seriously. And it is all good! That, she insists openly: her afflictions, sufferings, and disappointments are all good
because through them God has, each time, loomed larger and truer than
otherwise could ever be the case. If being "ground to powder"—her self-
description—can show us God, then the grinding is itself a luminescent
mercy given by God himself. So Bradstreet says. This kind of life is what
informs her approaching death and, she hopes, her final absence from
those to whom she has given birth. The gift she leaves her children is to
have known *this* existence, a divinely conditioned existence in every respect,
and not another.

Conclusion

The genre of writing to one's children with a word of guidance is a tradition, then, not born out of some mere cultural set of habits. Parents write such words, when they do, because this writing, its impetus, its catalogue of woes and wonder, is in fact how our lives are ordered, not only in their affections but in the imposed relationships of their created limits. To be created as we are is to write, to be compelled to write, to those whom we welcome into the world and leave behind us. Because we are created, and created "good," this is how the pieces have been arranged.

If so much generational advice today is political, it is also the case that all politics must bow before this imposition of created relationships, an imposition that, in this instance, is another word for grace. I must speak to my children not merely words of my choosing, but the words that reflect my need to speak to them in the first place: the story of our making and the shape of its form. It is the wise King Solomon who takes up his father's halting and ambivalent counsel offered on his deathbed and brings his own political career to its summit in his own way, a way probably more honest than David's to a certain degree:

> Remember now thy Creator in the days of thy youth, while the evil days come not, nor the years draw nigh, when thou shalt say, I have no pleasure in them; while the sun, or the light, or the moon, or the stars, be not darkened, nor the clouds return after the rain: in the day when the keepers of the house shall tremble, and the strong men shall bow themselves, and the grinders cease because they are few, and those that look out of the windows be darkened, and the doors shall be shut in the streets, when the sound of the grinding is low, and he shall rise up at the voice of the bird, and all the daughters of musick shall be brought low; also when they shall be afraid of that which is high, and fears shall be in the way, and the almond tree shall flourish, and the grasshopper shall be a burden, and desire shall fail: because man goeth to his long home, and the mourners go about the streets: or ever the silver cord be loosed, or the golden bowl be broken, or the pitcher be broken at the fountain, or the wheel broken at the cistern. Then shall the dust return to the earth as it was: and the spirit shall return unto God who gave it. (Eccles. 12:1–7)

"Remembering thy Creator" *now*, for the young, is of paramount importance because the discipline of remembering is learned early on, if it is to be used at all. Solomon, the king and statesman, does his kingly work (if he does it well) so as to maintain the conditions of such encouragement, so as to be able to say to the young, "Remember even now, before another time arrives that is also yours." This is an essential encouragement—hence its place in Scripture—emerging from the fabric of what it means to be a human being. In Solomon's person, maintaining the space and possibility and finally demand for parental guidance proves to be the goal and form of politics, where politics is even necessary, as it sometimes is.

Only sometimes. For politics, in Christian terms, thus has a modest if essential goal: to permit the birth and death of human beings in a way that expresses the generative love of parents and children, who together *are* such birth and death given as a gift. Christian politics is deeply misunderstood on any other basis than this socially ordered permission. Take as an example of these misunderstandings the way critics have read the great nineteenth-century "peasant poet" John Clare. Clare owes a great deal of his more recent rise in scholarly esteem to his passionate condemnation of the Inclosure Acts, which gradually barred the rural populace in England from common use of lands and led to the degradation of the countryside in extensive ways. These have become, in transmuted ways, central modern political concerns, and Clare has been valorized as a political poet for somehow anticipating them. But Clare's "political" profile emerged, if he is read carefully, not out of some environmentalism before the fact, nor from some economic class consciousness (though clearly he was attuned to matters that informed these modern political categories). He was, instead, concerned most intensely with a way of human interaction that bred persons of familial and local responsibility and affection. A fully human person, for Clare, was someone whose habits were formed by the common faith of those who know themselves to be, above all, *creatures* bound to the limiting graces of God's gifts, shared with the mortal texture of the land and its creaturely inhabitants.

These engraced habits were, in his view, those of toil, eating, courting, conceiving, playing, petitioning, and tending, as well as struggling with the inevitable disintegration of all of these in turn. In one letter he relates a slew of long-standing communal customs from his village, customs that were quasi-religious in nature, deeply expressive of the cycle of birth and death. Take these away, he indicates, and survival itself is threatened, a survival molded in the quite particular forms of divine fashioning. Take these away—ignore them, smother them, destroy them—and politics becomes a consuming beast. "Inclosure came and destroyed [these customs] with hundreds of others—leaving in [their] place nothing but a love for doing neighbours a mischief and public house oratory that dwells upon mob law as absolute justice."[17]

Clare's volatile personality embraced a variety of Christian commitments, ending perhaps with a vibrant but only vaguely orthodox faith. But his innate conservatism even in this area was tethered to a keen sense of what constitutes a human life, in the unadorned light of his own poverty. He explains elements from his own childhood:

> Every winter night our once unletterd hut was wonderfully changd in its appearence to a school room. The old table, which old as it was doubtless never was honourd with higher employment all its days then the convenience of bearing at meal times the luxury of a barley loaf or dish of potatoes, was now coverd with the rude begg[in]ings of scientifical requ[i]sitions, pens, ink, and paper one hour [. . .], at which times my parents triumphant anxiety was pleasingly experiencd, for my mother woud often stop her wheel or look off from her work to urge with a smile of the warmest rapture in my fathers face her prophesy of my success, saying "shed be bound, I shoud one day be able to reward them with my pen, for the trouble they had taken in giveing me schooling," and I have to return hearty thanks to a kind providence in bringing her prophesy to pass and giving me the pleasure of being able to stay the storm of poverty and smoothen their latter days; and as a recompense for the rough beginnings of life bid their tottering steps decline in peaceful tranquility to their long home, the grave.[18]

At the very end of his life, confined to a mental asylum for many years and long estranged from his own children and family, Clare turned to the child of one of his doctors, William Peel Nesbitt (the poem is an acrostic of his name), and wrote for him a small parental testament of his own, ending with these lines:

> Leave lust & sin and up to manhood climb
> Never afraid of death & hell—sublime
> Enjoyment then thy happy mind will fill
> Safe-guard of life and good for every ill
> Be good, be virtuous, for these are wise
> Inheritance, of Man that none despise:
> Take God thy Guide, and thy whole life will be
> The happy voyage to Eternity![19]

However innocuous-seeming the counsel, it was drawn from the same well as Bradstreet's, here offered in a mostly barren space filled with wrenching anguish and from which all resolving politics were banished, yet a space infused, he admits, with sublimity.

I want my children to live well. I want them, as I will explore the matter, to live a good life, perhaps even "the Good Life," as philosophers have envisaged it. To do that, however, they must be willing to inhabit a common space where God gives all, where all is taken away, and where, in the midst of this grand movement, a few clear lines of divine glory are etched, received, and followed. In what follows, I will be exploring what it might mean to join in guarding such a habitation.

Two

Evil Days

See then that ye walk circumspectly, not as fools, but as wise, redeeming the time, because the days are evil.

Ephesians 5:15–16

Toward the end of his life, in 1959, the philosopher Bertrand Russell offered his own kind of advice to the young.[1] First, he said, always try to think according to the "facts" that are before you and that you can discover; never do your thinking according to some given or accepted framework of meaning or ideology. Just the facts. Second, he said, tolerance and love are clearly the most prudent and thus the wisest way to order human relations. He was right on both counts, it seems to me. The problem is that the facts of our lives, while they do indeed suggest that tolerance and love are desirable and practically prudent in some situations, also point to tolerance and love's weakness and only occasional appearance within the ordering of common life. And this, in turn, suggests the (at best) relative value that tolerance and love embody within the navigation of the "facts."

If we wish to help our children live the Good Life, we must surely ask *where*, factually, the Good Life is to be lived. And the answer is "in the midst of evil days." Perhaps not always, nor for everyone. But it seems that this is the time in which I am now writing, and it is also so for those to whom I write: the days are evil indeed. Admitting this is not just honesty for the parent addressing a younger generation; such days must surely shape the kind of advice that one must give. This chapter is devoted to how we might begin to think about this formative honesty in a way that avoids a too-quick turn to the escape from evil days that hopes in immortality sometimes proffer.

Paul, in Ephesians, picks up a simple if stark reality and places his readers within it, but without much commentary. There *is* something paradigmatic about his claim, such that "evil days" may indeed be the lot of any Christian, any human being. "Evil" here goes back directly to Genesis 2:9, the tree of the knowledge of good and evil. Once identified, evil simply carries on through human history, coloring the human heart from its youth (Gen. 6:5; 8:21) and becoming a standard part of the human life span. "Evil" will then come to be linked with "the Evil One," the "prince of this world" (John 14:30). We cannot eliminate evil days from our lives; we cannot make evil good. Rather, we can be delivered from the Evil One (Matt. 6:13), even as we live in a world governed by his incessant busyness (Job 1:7; John 17:15). "It is an evil time" (Amos 5:13) because it is the time we live in. We cannot escape from it; we can only be redeemed within it.

Though I am now older, and perhaps should know the answer to this, I cannot say if our days today—I am writing this in 2022—are any worse for young people than they were when I was young. I grew up under the threat of nuclear war (still with us, despite our distractions) and the scars of World War II. There soon emerged, long before Communism was dismantled, revelations about the gulag, then about Mao's China. The Vietnam War was maiming individual bodies and psyches along with the national spirit. 1968 left us adrift.[2] I could go on, and should. My children were still young at the seemingly sudden outbreak of world Islamic terrorism in 9/11 and the opening up of a permanent state of war, one we still inhabit.

Everything we are dealing with now, it seems to me, is not really that different from when I was young. Pandemics? But there was AIDS even before my children were born, and I personally know more individuals who died of AIDS than I do of COVID-19 (a mark of my class as much as anything, perhaps). Ecological disaster? We didn't understand global warming six decades ago, but there were already deep anxieties over water, pollution, population, toxins, and more. "Wars and rumors of war" (Matt. 24:6)? Always. Some scholars say that things are actually quite a bit better now (though COVID may be revising some of these judgments)—but we'll get to this later. Whether all the measures we use to determine "better" or "worse" are really ones to apply in any deep way is a real question. Still, it certainly doesn't *seem* that the world has budged much, and for the young especially: "anxiety," instead, seems to be growing in recent generations, and perhaps among older folk too, which might explain the embrace, by many elderly people, of assisted suicide.

But anxiety is difficult to assess since medical and psychiatric evaluations on this score are subjective and culturally tethered in a major way. Judging the mental health of a population is always difficult. Suicides often go up in tough times, but not always, and more recently the suicide rate in North America has slowed after a long period of increase. Drug addiction similarly. But are people happier? A more substantive set of indicators may be linked to social and personal signs of rootlessness and aimlessness. Here the decline of religious commitment is clearly important. But it might not be if in fact there were some other identifiable source of meaning that was taking its place. There is not, however, and qualitative studies seem to make this clear.[3]

In fact, the network of meaningful human relations in which people have always been embedded seems to have thinned out significantly for younger people. More screen time by oneself has something to do with it, but this goes hand in hand with the decline of marriage and even partnerships, with long delays in personal attachments and a vast reduction in fertility rates. Again, these might be explained in a variety of ways, but they seem to be linked to dissatisfactions that are festering in the face of irresolution: I don't have enough money; I'm not settled; I'm in debt; and besides, why bring children into this world?[4]

So yes, the days are evil as they have always been. But today the world seems frightening in a way that is, for many, simply demoralizing and even paralyzing. This seems historically unusual, except in the midst or aftermath of destructive war. The experience of irresolution—of not "solving" the problems one can identify—appears to be growing into a larger vision of impossibility that touches on a loss of faith in family and communal identities, in legislative or broader political systems, in religious claims themselves (not just "institutions," a problem in earlier ages), in the future itself. The demand, via protest or public display, that the world listen to those who can see the deep problems of humanity but are ignored seems driven by a desperation rather than a vision.[5] I am reminded of H. G. Wells's chilling story "The Star," about a comet's sudden and unexpected appearance in the solar system and its passage near the earth. Initially, few people believe the calculations of the astronomers, but as, very quickly, the orbital, gravitational, and meteorological consequences become undeniable, there is a kind of dazed despair that quickly envelops whole populations.[6] Wells wrote the story at the turn of the twentieth century, but his quietly objective description of a spreading terror that is then fulfilled and horrifically navigated by only a few resonates still. The scientist as Cassandra, and the populace as, by stages, ignorant, terrified, and immobilized is a script that continues to play out.

To say that the days are *still* evil is not, however, meant to mimic the lugubriousness of Cassandra and her audience. I only wish to underline *where* the Good Life is lived and thus the kinds of goods it embodies. For, evil or happy, the days belong to God (cf. Ps. 31:15). Furthermore, the Good Life is thus not the same thing as or reducible to the days in which it is found. This point is important to remember, since evil days have often become the defining basis upon which a life's vocation is seen as ordered, though in several possible ways. Most of the statistical surveys standing behind my general comments above are driven by this defining assumption: the members of this or that generation order their lives according to their attitudes toward the future; hence, whether the days are happy or evil shapes social expectations and thus activities, including political activities. This is an assumption mostly framed by the outlook of modern economists, and it is now widely embraced in just those economic terms. But the assumption's roots go back much further than its cruder formulations by economists in the nineteenth century, and they are fueled quite explicitly by the consistent sense that "the days are evil."

Betterment

There have been several main lines of response to expectations about a future that unfolds in the shadow of present-day evil. Perhaps the most insistently offered direction in our era is given in the search for "betterment," for solutions to the evil of the days we are in. This has not always been the goal of politics, though this fact may seem odd to contemporary minds. Whatever the case, betterment now seems to be the dominant direction in which we aim our purpose (we will talk about this later in the book): promises in political campaigns are all about this. More deeply, there is an assumption that human life itself is properly aimed at such betterment. Where the Hebrew prophets promised a world of universal peace brought about by the hand of God, by the eighteenth century such a future was viewed as lying largely in the hands of human effort.[7]

It is now a bit of folk wisdom—used in almost every area of life, from business to church to politics itself—that our purpose in existing is to "leave the world a better place" than when we first entered it at birth. I'm not sure of the origins of this attitude, but the attitude itself seems to be linked to notions of progress that were tied to early modern hopes in intellectual research. In the early 1660s, Joseph Glanvill addressed the Royal Society, Britain's chief scientific coterie, and outlined the helpful turn that Descartes and his colleagues had provided natural philosophy: "Methinks this Age seems resolved to bequeath posterity somewhat to remember it: And the glorious Undertakers, wherewith Heaven hath blest our Days, will leave the world better provided then they found it."[8] Glanvill shared with his Royal Society contemporaries, like Robert Boyle, a general sense that the new empirical sciences, having overthrown the dogmatism of Aristotelianism, were bringing unimagined discoveries to bear—like a great "America" or "Peru"—that were simply "better" on all counts. This judgment was already congruent with orthodox religious views about moral history; one of Glanvill's contemporaries, Simon Patrick, claimed that the Son of God would not have died for any "less" a reason than "to make the World better."[9] The notion that we ourselves, like Jesus, should make the world a "better place" before we die through our religious, moral practice seems to have spread quickly in devotional literature, and by the end of the eighteenth century it was already a commonplace in sermons and instructional manuals, especially among the Methodists and Unitarians in America.

The explicit political application of this sentiment emerged in the early nineteenth century, as for instance in a resounding call to action by the British Unitarian politician William J. Fox in an 1834 article entitled "Forwards or Backwards?" Here was an entire political essay urging on the parliamentary direction taken by the 1832 Reform Act, which expanded suffrage. Fox's political vision took wing from the fact that "progression is the law of humanity." He goes on: "It is one of heaven's best blessings to have our lot cast in a period of rapid and durable improvement. There is no enjoyment like it. Even in death it is delightful to think that we leave the world better than we found it, and that the next generation will find and leave it better still."[10] This sentiment became an almost proverbial bit of wisdom. Writers across the board seemed to hold this hope, expressed in just these terms, from cultural critics like Matthew Arnold in Britain to educationalists like William Alcott in New England. By the early twentieth century, H. G. Wells was applying the idea to his Darwinian scheme of social evolution, toying with eugenics and other forms of social manipulation. He opens his manifesto *Mankind in the Making* with the claim that "every day is summed up, 'to leave the world better than they found it.' And it is from that most excellent expression that I would start."[11] "Bettering the world," as he puts it, is the practical basis of all religions and sects and ought to be the citizen's motivating desire. Most of us are familiar with the words of the Boy Scouts' founder, Robert Baden-Powell, in his "Last Message" (1941): "Try and leave this world a little better than you found it, and when your turn comes to die, you can die happy in feeling that at any rate, you have not wasted your time but have done your best."[12]

In all this meandering development of a fairly benign idea, there is little sense that things might get worse during our lifetimes, or that even the world as a whole might falter and careen out of order—common views, after all, since at least Jesus's time, as we will see. "When the Son of Man comes, will he find faith on earth?" (Luke 18:8 RSV). Or will, rather, the love of God have "grown cold" (Matt. 24:12)? Of course, the insistence in our day that we must do this or that in particular, like Fox's "going forwards," is often driven, as I said, by a sense of desperation. Journalists have been busy identifying what projects are in order for such a last-ditch snatch at "improvement." One magazine asked several thinkers about this: "The world would be a better place if everybody learned to think like scientists," said Richard Dawkins, the Oxford University evolutionary biologist (echoing in a rather more elitist way Russell's hopes). We need "universal primary and secondary education," said Wolfgang Lutz, a population expert, explaining that "new research shows that [education] generally leads to better health, higher economic growth and in the long run better government." "If we all refused to drink anything but organic, shade-grown coffee, that choice would have a major positive effect on Neotropical migrant songbirds, whose numbers are plummeting," suggested the Nobel laureate Margaret Atwood, using this as one example of how "personal choices, when multiplied, are a powerful tool for change." Other experts pressed their own priorities for "bettering the world": reducing the use of fossil fuels, implementing global health care equity, legalizing drugs, and just "being of service to others" as a "daily part of our lives."[13]

This remains the common view of our political calling, despite the pessimism that permeates everything today. Or perhaps it is partly the cause of the pessimism: it is a terrible burden to feel that one must push the world along into the greater light, let alone "save" it. The distance from H. G. Wells's politics of bettering to the suddenly paralyzing gloom and to horror's neutered bemusement in his story "The Star" is not great (the two pieces were written in the same period). The "True Activist," as one advocacy group calls itself, is unceasingly active, and thus it is not clear that some activists "inspire" so much as shame-inducingly exhaust. This may or may not be related to what Jesus has to say to Martha and Mary: the ceaseless effort of *caring* can often breed *anxiety*. The two English terms express two aspects of the single Greek root *merimna* (Luke 10:38–42).

But improvements there have been. Few would denigrate the 1832 Reform Act in Britain or the 1964 Civil Rights Act in the US. Still, "improvement" does not seem to "march forward," as the modern metaphor insists. Rather, it gleams and fades, often in a passing moment, as new shadows extend from some unexpected quarter, as in the recent pandemic and its still-uncounted millions of dead and beleaguered. If one follows the thread of actual strides "forward" made by Nobel Peace Prize recipients, one is forced to wonder as much at the failure of their efforts as at their courage. Alfred Fried (1911) was a Jewish pacifist and promoter of Esperanto. Woodrow Wilson (1919) helped found the League of Nations. Frank Kellogg (1929) coauthored the Kellogg-Briand Pact, which was signed by Germany, the US, and France and committed these nations and others to the peaceful resolution of conflict. Ralph Bunche (1950) was cited for helping resolve Israeli-Palestinian conflict. These were early recipients whose work was honored as much for the values they espoused—peace and pacifism—as for their actual achievements over time. The contemporary historiography of suspicion has, furthermore, led us to wonder more deeply about the actual values that governed the hearts of these recipients: Wilson's, for instance, given his own entrenched racism; and, of course, later recipients like Menachem Begin, F. W. de Klerk, and Yasser Arafat. One can celebrate an effort; and the Good Life might well involve such efforts. But you and I, along with billions of other human beings, will come and go with few measurable "improvements" to our credit left behind. Many of us will die with regrets after all, the sign of just the failure of "betterment," at least as we can discern it.

Goethe famously wrote, "We cannot soon enough convince ourselves how very simply we may be dispensed with in the world. What important personages we conceive ourselves to be! We think that it is we alone who animate the circle we move in; that, in our absence, life, nourishment, and breath will make a general pause: and, alas! the void which occurs is scarcely remarked, so soon is it filled up again; nay, it is often but the place, if not for something better, at least for something more agreeable."[14] We cannot outrun the sun or the moon or the stars. And while we can be redeemed from it, we cannot outrun death.

Betterment is a modern attitude born, it seems, of both inordinate pride and inordinate despair.

There are at least two other alternatives to this alternative: beatitude and distraction.

Beatitude

Before the rise of betterment as a goal, Christian theologians, especially, looked to a future that could stand outside "evil days" altogether. Redemption from evil days lay in escaping their press. This hope, drawing on ancient Greek and Roman attitudes, became early engrained in Christian discourse and set up its own difficult political perspectives. Augustine, in his early *De beata vita*—on the "blessed" or "happy" life—saw beatitude as the goal that all philosophers aim at. He sketches his own version—he wrote the text just after he had been baptized—in a deliberately religious framework. Though the work was still very much a Christianizing of a philosophical trope, Augustine kept to its basic shape all his life: the "happy life" (*vita beata*) is a life of "wisdom," which is nothing else than the "possession" of the truth, which is God himself. Hence, only the wise person is happy, and wisdom consists in "attaching" oneself only to the true things of God, not to the fakeries (*simulacra*) of material existence: there is no "excess, and therefore indigence, or misery" that the wise soul can "fear," for "whoever is happy possesses God" (*Deum habet igitur quisquis beatus est*).[15]

Augustine classically sets up a contrast between evil days and divine wisdom, not so much because they are incongruent but because the former simply has little to do with the latter. "The days are evil," Paul writes in Ephesians, and the response to that is "be wise." For Augustine this means that, ultimately, given the dragging burden of human life even as we seek to hold on to God, we must aim at an existence beyond this present life, one where our "possession" of God can be complete. This becomes a central theme of his great work *The City of God*. Evil days constitute the whole of earthly existence; and the Christian, though equipped in a way to deal with this virtuously, must nevertheless have as her goal something beyond, something that radically relativizes mortal existence altogether.

Augustine's enumerations of human misery, suffered by both the good and the evil, are famous. "Who can describe, who can conceive the number and severity of the punishments which afflict the human race—pains which are not only the accompaniment of the wickedness of godless men, but are a part of the human condition and the common misery?"[16] By the end of *The City of God* (22.22–23), he has catalogued a seemingly interminable range of human mistreatment, social ills, natural disasters and depleting demands, bodily diseases and mental anguish, loss, bereavement, and death, painful or otherwise. To a contemporary ear, these sorrows can sound extravagant in their breadth until one pauses and notes how each element that Augustine lists continues in our day, for the most part, to bedevil individual and corporate existence. For Augustine, it is only because we have a life beyond our present condition, promised to the faithful Christian, that we can pull ourselves through this life, let alone speak of true happiness as something real:

As, therefore, we are saved, so we are made happy by hope. And as we do not as yet possess a present, but look for a future salvation, so is it with our happiness, and this patiently; for we are encompassed with evils, which we ought patiently to endure, until we come to the ineffable enjoyment of unmixed good; for there shall be no longer anything to endure. Salvation, such as it shall be in the world to come, shall itself be our final happiness. And this happiness these philosophers refuse to believe in, because they do not see it, and attempt to fabricate for themselves a happiness in this life, based upon a virtue which is as deceitful as it is proud.[17]

The end of *The City of God* reiterates the theme of eternity over time, of heavenly life over earthly, of God over creation—a promised contrast that permeates all of Augustine's work, even the most practical: "There"—not "here," but in the great Sabbath of eternity—"we shall rest and see, see and love, love and praise. This is what shall be in the end without end. For what other end do we propose to ourselves than to attain to the kingdom of which there is no end?"[18]

There is far more to Augustine than this stark contrast between worlds, as we will see. But the contrast itself has, crudely or not, been persistent within the Christian tradition concerning "evil days." And, more recently, it has been heartily rejected as cheap Christian escapism. "What happens when you die" is what religion is about, according to some critics; and "going somewhere better" is what (Christian) religion offers. "Paganism," instead, "teaches that being here is the reward, and that we need to make the most of it and leave the world a better place," as the writer Michael Thomas Ford puts it.[19]

Ford isn't quite right on this point. Immortality, and attaining it, was deeply important to pagan thinkers as well, and the very term "beatitude" was used by pagan philosophers to express the experience involved in some kind of participation in immortality. But what exactly "immortality" meant varied or was simply vague in ancient Greek and Roman experience.[20] It could mean unending life continuous with present modes of existence, if at a higher level of felicity; a transmuted existence; a kind of connection with something transcendent to present human existence, and perhaps no longer personal in that sense—the Good, God, Beauty, Honor; or perhaps even "memory" among those who are living. Christians, however, in founding their views of the afterlife on the individual human soul, clearly turned immortality into a concretely personal experience somehow continuous with earthly identity. And in this way the condition of the individual "on earth" is deeply important, insofar as that condition makes possible continuity with life after death. All the important elements of such potentially formative this-worldly existence are then the focus of profound attention: ethics and virtue; acts of justice; forms of learning and knowing. A fuller and fairer reading of Augustine than I just gave shows this very forcefully: how we live *now* makes all the difference for eternity, and to this extent, eternity bleeds into the container of the present.

Here Christian and pagan thinkers overlapped. They all viewed the afterlife, whatever it was—call it immortality of some kind—as determined by today. Both Plato and Aristotle, quite differently, along with others in yet again different ways, held this view. In particular, the commitment to continuity, even if not wholly personal, meant that, for them, life today has some means of literally connecting with immortality itself. Aristotle famously lifts up the "contemplative life" (*theōria*) as this kind of bridge of continuity and participation.[21] For while "happiness" (*eudaimonia*) is the general goal of a human life for Aristotle, there is something beyond happiness that he calls "blessedness" (using the same Greek term, *makarios*, employed by, e.g., Matthew when quoting Jesus's teaching on beatitude: "Blessed are the poor in spirit" [Matt. 5:3]).

Blessedness is more "divine" than simple human happiness, Aristotle writes, and is "better" than happiness.[22] He associates this better condition with "the gods" and with the "most godlike" of human beings. But gods—or the God, as Aristotle adds—do not busy themselves with normal human virtues, such as justice (keeping contracts and so on); nor do they simply sleep. Then what? They "contemplate." Hence, human life, as it verges toward blessedness, is the contemplative life. "Now if you take away from a living being action, and still more production, what is left but contemplation? Therefore the activity of God which surpasses all others in blessedness, must be contemplative; and of human activities, therefore, that which is most akin to this must be most of the nature of happiness."[23] And since the intellect, for human beings, is that which contemplates in this godlike way, "it follows that this [activity of contemplation] will be the complete happiness of man, if it be allowed a complete term of life (for none of the attributes of happiness is *in*complete)."[24]

For pagans and Christians both, the overriding purpose of human life is bound up with something that is unchanging and thus invulnerable to the evil aspect of "evil days"—virtue, contemplation, heavenly immortality, God. Is politics about attaining heaven and the permanent? To think so is to sell one's soul to the engulfing corruptions involved with "bringing heaven to earth." Politics can only be about "the earth," not simply because this is where practical reasoning is confined but, more importantly (as I will argue), because this confinement—or rather, "gifted identity" of being earthbound—is what it means to be a creature made by God.

The days are evil, in part because good and evil are writ into the lineaments of creation, the knowledge of which is crushing, perhaps (Gen. 2), but the reality of which is inescapable one way or the other. I have no answer as to why the creation is so textured; no one does, except God. God knows why he has made creation as it is and has ended up being. If this is so, it is a horror to lose God as the source of one's life's ordering. It is also the case, however, that to say that "the days are evil" is not to say that all is lost, only that "this day" is very hard indeed, but that, because it is a day, it is also "good" as God-made (Gen. 1). One day or another, its coming and going, is God's, not as Fate, but as our Creator. And this is so not only in a "full span of life" (whatever that may be) but in any life, for any number of days. For to be a human being, we know, is to come and go (Ps. 39:4–6), and to be a created human being is to come and go as God's, exhaustively. Finally, if this day and these days are God's, just this coming and going lies at the heart of the grace by which we exist at all. (This is the secret of mortality's gift.)

Thus, as I will argue, for human beings "the Good" of "the Good Life" cannot lie only in our full possession of God or the attainment of some end—the beatific vision, say, understood as that permanent condition in which all happiness is eternally fixed in God's own eternity. Instead, the Good that we seek to live is the right ordering of God's "goods" that he has offered us, so as to know as I am known and to understand as I am understood (1 Cor. 13:12). For how *does* God know us? It is a knowledge that frames all our capacities: "For he knoweth our frame; he remembereth that we are dust" (Ps. 103:14). If this is how I know, and know in some fashion from the perspective of the one who invents the dust-bound nature of our lives—my very self—then any "possession" of God I may have can be described only in terms of a holding that is ever ordered (*not* "purposed") to being let go, or at least liable to such letting go. We could say that our possession of God is something we hold lightly, but this is both true and misleading with respect to God. In normal usage, we "hold lightly" what we know we may lose, by the very nature of the case; but also, in losing it, we recognize its lack of importance in the big picture. This cannot be true for God. We possess anything lightly because we ourselves are "lighter than a breath" (Ps. 62:9 RSV). But because this lightness is all God's, our possession of God is "all" that we are, in its reach; it is all that we touch, all that we live through, and all that shapes our lives as "coming and going." This includes just these particular evil days.

I don't mean here to marginalize the Christian tradition that sees the promised end of human life as its full enjoyment of God. I want, instead, to locate our "attainment" of this end in a sphere that is distinct from the Good Life—distinct, that is, from our ordering of created goods, distinct from the realm of our own attenuated capacities. We order our lives well according to the limits of their createdness, and that is "good enough." Furthermore, this goodness of our present life is not diminished by the fact that it does not constitute heaven. It is not so much that the beatific vision—heavenly existence, our full possession of God, as the Christian tradition has had it—is discontinuous with the Good Life; rather, such a vision is a gift whose "possession" we cannot, by definition, orchestrate for ourselves.

In the great theological debate about the distinction between and the priorities of nature and supernature, natural desire for God and divine grace[25]—a debate that has raged from early modernity to the present—I would suggest a place to the side of these options: *all* is grace, even all created limitations, for it is all God's to do with as he mysteriously chooses. Our apprehension of this "fact" simply renders "nature" graciously sufficient in its creaturely forms. Thus, the beatific vision's continuity with the Good Life is precisely its giftedness—a characteristic that encompasses all things. This giftedness of all things is lightly held on our part, though it will be apprehended and enjoyed in a transcendent mode in heaven, by God's grace. Heaven cannot be other than earth transfigured; it cannot be earth left behind (as Christian discussion of the millennium has rightly tended to recognize until the twentieth century). By contrast, if we tie our final end to the Good Life in a way that links them in some common nature outside of their shared giftedness—in some shared angelic mode of existence, for instance, that is meant to permeate our present lives—we in fact render that end hostage to the very limitations of such a life. We are not angels; and that is to the good. Making earth and heaven ethically or experientially continuous is something that the Evil One seeks to enact, constantly asking us why our present days, with all their ills, seem so unlike the blessings we hope for, and sowing seeds of fruitless striving, subsequent resentment, and finally despair along the way.

Distraction

Betterment and beatitude are but two responses to the evil days that mark our lives. There are others, and I will mention only one more, though it is perhaps the most common response of all: distraction. To avoid all thinking or pondering of our days will, of course, banish their character from our psyches and decisions altogether, a kind of superficial boon given that a focused attentiveness to the nature of our times can wear us down. Distraction bears some overlap with betterment and beatitude, because a person can believe in one or the other but in fact pay only occasional heed—"from time to time," as we say. Today, we might think of the here and now in passing; tomorrow, the beyond may intrude for some minutes of distant and perhaps uneasy meditation. In the rush from one moment to the next, we may catch a glimpse of modest hope for the future. Life is busy—indeed, consuming—for many, even for the rich. We have deliberately, it sometimes seems, made it this way. In the midst of our busy lives, thoughts about the value of making things better now, or for a bit, or for eternity are difficult to come by, and in fact that difficulty can seem a balm as we instead and naturally glide across their surfaces.

The most incisive commentator on the distractive approach to evil days is Pascal. His reflections on *divertissement*—"diversion," in the sense of activity as well as of direction—are celebrated and remain utterly apt.

> Death is easier to bear without thinking of it, than is the thought of death without peril. The miseries of human life have established all this: as men have seen this, they have taken up diversion. As men are not able to fight against death, misery, ignorance, they have taken it into their heads, in order to be happy, not to think of them at all. Despite these miseries, man wishes to be happy, and only wishes to be happy, and cannot wish not to be so. But how will he set about it? To be happy he would have to make himself immortal; but, not being able to do so, it has occurred to him to prevent himself from thinking of death.[26]

Pascal doesn't blame people for this, really: life is difficult, true happiness is not really possible here, and we confuse our natural instinct for quietness (permanence, as it were) with the steadiness of activity and pleasure, which then leads us, like an addiction, into a circle of dissatisfied seeking and failing ever to find enough.

> Weariness.—Nothing is so insufferable to man as to be completely at rest, without passions, without business, without diversion, without study. He then feels his nothingness, his forlornness, his insufficiency, his dependence, his weakness, his emptiness. There will immediately arise from the depth of his heart weariness, gloom, sadness, fretfulness, vexation, despair.[27]

So we busy ourselves, and this busyness becomes its own scaffolding: work (even intellectual work) and play as a means of pretending that life isn't so bad and that mortality is not the container of our hopes.

Whence comes it that this man, who lost his only son a few months ago, or who this morning was in such trouble through being distressed by lawsuits and quarrels, now no longer thinks of them? Do not wonder; he is quite taken up in looking out for the boar which his dogs have been hunting so hotly for the last six hours. He requires nothing more. . . . However full of sadness a man may be, he is happy for the time, if you can prevail upon him to enter into some amusement; and however happy a man may be, he will soon be discontented and wretched, if he be not diverted and occupied by some passion or pursuit which prevents weariness from overcoming him. Without amusement there is no joy; with amusement there is no sadness.[28]

There is no real answer to the mindless *carpe diem* of work or pleasure that simply consumes our days, the acknowledgment of which can indeed be a justification for life as long as it lasts. Except that *carpe diem* in this sense is rarely effective for most people. It is not just, as Pascal writes, that "we run carelessly to the precipice, after we have put something before us to prevent us seeing it," and so end up hopelessly surprised by our deaths.[29] That happens, of course. But more commonly, because the days are evil, they inevitably end up twisting our patterns of distraction suddenly or gradually but nonetheless horribly. Pain and loss, of whatever kind, do not just occasionally intrude; for many (though perhaps not all), the intrusions are continual and unrelenting and often render distraction not only superficial but distasteful, repugnant to the soul and body both. The phenomenon of the lottery winner who is immediately and suddenly "bettered," but then discovers that life falls apart through greed, betrayal, and foolishness, is well known. The distracted are but a more quotidian version of this: "We have enough to keep us busy and happy, sort of." The problem is that family and friends and the taxman and wars—which pull down the burnished walls of even the lottery winner's material windfall—are exactly the same for the modestly amused.

Pascal is clear that, however understandable, distraction is ultimately counterproductive to happiness, meaning, reality, truth, and yes, faith, hope, and love. It is important, though, to realize how distraction informs even most morally pure seekers after betterment or divine beatitude. The activity itself becomes the distracting instrument that leads us away from attention to the actual gifts, active in their own demands, that God has given us as the vital ingredients of our creaturely moments: feeding ourselves and those we love—"feeding" in a host of ways, though often ways that are earthbound, hemmed in, certainly brief. Here the desperately distracted and the vigorous promoters of betterment often coincide, through their self-absorption, in a common imperviousness to earthly destruction; the sorry experience of families of political activists and religious devotees, or assiduous scholars, scientists, politicians, and writers, is well known.[30]

Mortal Generation

Paying attention to what God has in fact given us seems to mark the limit of our ethical range within our days, evil as they often seem. Even atheist thinkers have sometimes realized the intractability of our circumstances and wondered why we cannot better commend more modest efforts and time lines. These, after all, are probably the most "effective" channels of betterment. Why always press for the long-term, as if temporal extension is an ethical value? Why not pursue and embrace, as it were, what is good for now and at least for a little longer?[31] This kind of "pragmatic" attitude has its salutary insights but also refuses to acknowledge the very nature of God's creating grace, which, while it places immovable limits on creation's gifts, injects the loves that inhabit them with an aching thirst for the Giver himself. "The long-term" may be out of our reach; but its grace colors the short-term and, most importantly, dissolves the distinction of value between short and long altogether. Maximizing short-term betterment is itself probably a perverting motive in terms of how it shapes human expectations, relationships, and self-awareness: *everything* becomes a tool whose imminent goals are all the more tyrannical and depleting for their purported proximity.

Yet because everything belongs to God, our entwinement with all of creation cannot be humanly manipulated. We can only sense, not appropriate, what Another alone can do. In this sense, little that I am suggesting has any relationship to older "theologies of immanence," whether in the hands of those who have extolled Dietrich Bonhoeffer's purported turn to the secular or of those who would collapse God into matter. Human beings are creatures; God is creator. But in the words of the Second Vatican Council (*Gaudium et Spes* 18), man "rebels against death because he bears in himself an eternal seed which cannot be reduced to sheer matter." This notion that some inherent human orientation toward God somehow reconfigures our expectations from the ground up is central to Christian understanding, though it is also elusive to explication. Some have taken Ecclesiastes 3:11 as an indicator of this, though its translation has proved contentious. The Authorized Version, following one interpretive line suggested by the Hebrew, renders it as "He hath made every thing beautiful in his time: also he hath set the world in their heart, so that no man can find out the work that God maketh from the beginning to the end." The Revised Standard Version, perhaps closer to the Septuagint's understanding, has God setting "eternity" in the human heart. But whether "eternity" or "the world" dwells in the human heart (the "whole" of creation or reality—in the Hebrew, 'olam), the verse points out that human creatures both know something true and fail to know it at the same time, the "everything" that God has made, offered to an uncomprehending finitude—a rather Pascalian outlook itself. In this tension we are always thrust back into the midst of our world with a desire to see it whole and to find its beauty somewhere else, as lying mysteriously in God's purposes.

Yet this tension is also what subverts, experientially, our pursuits of betterment, beatitude, and distraction within the evil days of our lives. For Christians, in theory, the transcendent value of the modest, everyday realities of mortal life is assumed, however difficult it is to gauge. Each moment's value, in this respect, fills in the character of the future—any future of any length—only through the connective tissue of its mortal links that somehow are able to span the uncertainty of the "whole" truth as it threads together the obscure beauty of each moment. Scripture expresses this spanning in a very restricted but embodied fashion—that is, in terms of generations, of the mortal but extended movement of life from one time to the next through procreative struggle and fidelity. We are but dust that disappears in a moment, the psalmist writes, but that which endures is given through this generative reach across time: "As for man, his days are as grass: as a flower of the field, so he flourisheth. For the wind passeth over it, and it is gone; and the place thereof shall know it no more. But the mercy of the LORD is from everlasting to everlasting upon them that fear him, and his righteousness unto children's children" (Ps. 103:15–17).

This generational reach, whereby the eternal touches us through the basic order of our offspring and then of theirs, is granted to those who "keep [God's] covenant" and obey his commandments (v. 18). The character of transcendent value is thus lodged in the mortal concern for and of children, and of our teaching, tradition, and faithfulness in their regard. What is "good," even for today, is located there, even while the context that surrounds it is unsteady, uncertain, a kind of wilderness in which one wanders on the way to a "whole" that God alone possesses.

The real issue, then, is not how long the "evil days" of this world may last, so that a good life might get us beyond them or be found across the frontier of mortality—hence pitting "this world" against "the next world" (or its failed embrace). Rather, we are asked to decide whether this world is good in itself, good enough for any life that is good. The choice is hard because, in itself, short and long, the life of this world is colored by qualities that are not only contingent but seem often, and for many, to be imposed, either randomly by "chance" or "fate" or, for the Christian, by God's grace. For by grace God "shortens" the evil days in their various configurations, just as by grace, as well, he lengthens their reach (see Mark 13:12; Ps. 91:16). "Evil days," it turns out, refers to the gifts of God, not to our own wilting within a world from which God's life is absent.

Distraction has always been one way to avoid the God of "evil days," despair a way of judging distraction's incapacity. The Christian tendency, in recent centuries, has been to plow through evil days wielding the tools of betterment. This has been the case even among admirers of Augustine, from the Reformation to the Puritans to contemporary political theology, who seek to transpose the eternal into the motor of this-worldly effort. This all seems so unrealistic, and Augustine himself was deeply skeptical of such efforts. Yet the alternative neither was nor is to await our arrival "home." The Good Life is possible, surely, in the midst of any "day," good or evil. For God offers goods, and hence the Good itself somehow, in the midst of all days, since every day is his. He calls us into the good of living "in and through." And for this, God gives grace that is joined to the very limitations that shape our burdens.

Within the desert of our world, Christ Jesus was tested by the Evil One, who goes "to and fro" within the world. The days are evil. Yet "no temptation has overtaken you that is not common to man. God is faithful, and he will not let you be tempted beyond your strength, but with the temptation will also provide the way of escape, that you may be able to endure it" (1 Cor. 10:13 RSV).

Three

Days of Sojourning

I am a stranger in the earth.

Psalm 119:19

Where shall we escape the evil that turns each day into a test? How do we locate in time the way that the Good Life, however much entwined with "today" and thus with today's evils, also engages something beyond such contemporary burdens? Another way of putting the question is, "Are we heading somewhere?" The question arises importantely *just because* betterment, beatitude, and distraction derive from hopes that we cannot seem to suppress. Even if they cannot actually, honestly respond to evil days, surely they indicate, however imperfectly, some more adequate way of holding on to hope. This chapter tarries with the question of hope's location within a world that we cannot improve significantly, escape morally, or ignore successfully. It is not so much that we are stuck with this world—and we are—as that we are given the world to *live* within. And since the world is as it is, such living will always be insecure and unstable. The Christian tradition has described such a life in this kind of world not in negative terms but in terms of a relative movement: sojourning. Sojourning, besides its temporal and spatial contours, has a content. It describes a "way" in both direction and posture, both of which are determined by a director and a form, a determination that has generally been spoken about in terms of God's commandments. Hence, I raise here the rather uncontroversial notion, at least in Jewish and Christian tradition, that the Good Life to which all Christian politics is ordered is constituted in some essential manner by following the commandments of God (Matt. 19:17).

This conjunction of an unrooted life and the ordering of God's commands is at the center of Psalm 119, whose startling length, and only undulating variations in content and tone, seems to mirror the ever-reiterating rhythms of human existence in its limited receipt of the eternal. If the "world" or "eternity" is given within our heart, we grasp it only through the modest means of the divine statutes we embrace, in their repetitions of meditation and obedience. "I am a stranger in the earth" (Ps. 119:19). This verse stands behind a long Christian tradition about what it means to be a human being, in a psalm that is the Bible's longest and most concentrated discussion of God's commandments. The discussion does not proceed as a code or list of laws themselves—we get that in Exodus, Leviticus, Numbers, and Deuteronomy. Rather, the divine commandments are lifted up, with an almost numbing insistence, as themselves (in their being given at all) constituting the framework for a life lived across time—the life of a stranger or sojourner upon earth. *Where* we live, during evil days, is not *in* that evil itself but in the divine commandment that is enacted upon the earth, across the earth's time, in any place and on any day.

While there is debate about the technical status of a sojourner in Israel—the *ger* who in fact has a special place in Israel's law (cf. Exod. 12:49)—there is little disagreement on what is meant by the term more generally: someone who is far from their home. Thus, the people of Israel will become strangers in Egypt (Gen. 15:13; Acts 7:6), just as Abraham himself lived his founding vocation as a stranger (Gen. 23:4–7). This aspect of Israel's life was to be perpetually remembered, etched into its own sense of identity (Deut. 10:19). To be a "stranger in the earth" is thus to see Israel's history as intrinsic to human life itself. And the Christian life, from one vantage, is one that recognizes human existence as stranger-like, especially if one lives faithfully (1 Pet. 2:11).

At the same time, God's gift of new life in Christ is seen as addressing and resolving just this alien aspect of life: "You are no longer strangers and sojourners, but you are fellow citizens with the saints and members of the household of God" (Eph. 2:19 RSV). This household, in turn, somehow stands outside the contours of earthly experience and is located in "heaven," whatever exactly that might mean (cf. Heb. 11:13–16).

"I am a stranger in the earth," then, is a claim about life that reflects a deep understanding of faith. And when the psalmist goes on to say, therefore, "Hide not thy commandments from me," it is faith that seeks God's laws in the midst of just this life, that spreads itself across any number of places without yet being fixed in one. The law of God, in other words, is the gift of God for the life of a stranger in the earth. It is the manifestation of God's life in the midst of a human existence that is otherwise "far" from what it most deeply feels to be truly its own, but that is also wrapped up in the One New Man whose own life, as one driven "outside the camp" (Heb. 13:13), encloses his own household in this movement.

Psalm 119, in this perspective, is about how to live, with eternity in mind, the life that is *not* what one wants most of all: the difficult life, the life that wears one down and finally disappears from one's grasp. Thus, the psalm lays out a "way" (v. 9 RSV)—"How can a young man keep his way pure?" the psalmist asks—one that is clear and clean, that can lead from one place to another. This is not only a way of virtue. It is that too, of course; but it is even more so the quite physical way between hills and valleys, the way the body travels between places and times, in its form of beauty or ugliness, goodness and evil—the way from birth to death. And that way is the path of God's commandments, the following of which, with others (vv. 63–64), marks the simple shape by which one faithfully navigates the earth as God's own, in a way that embodies the household of faith.

In the midst of this traversal, ordering its contours and forms, is "affliction" (Ps. 119:50, 71, 75), pleading and crying out in tears (vv. 84, 145, 169), finding a way through the midst of wicked people and harsh treatment (vv. 113–29). Evil days are presupposed as the time of the psalmist's life. The psalmist tells us, and God, that life is short (v. 84). Hence, the whole traversal itself is fragile; missteps can easily derail a person appallingly. How can a young person make his or her way? By means of God's commandments: just these, yearning for them, studying them, following them as far and as well as one might, holding to them in the face of opposition and weakness. The claim is straightforward here: in his commandments, God comes "near" us (v. 151). Indeed, God's nearness in his law is like the nearness of kinsmen and neighbors, the very ones we love and whose loss or failures in large part mark our afflictions (cf. Ps. 34:18). "Like," but far better; *like* theirs, in the midst of our lives, yet it is *God* who is present, not someone else.

The strange means God has provided, by which what is hardest to bear becomes the door of grace, is central to Psalm 119's proclamation. "I am small and despised," cries out the psalmist (v. 141); yet this is exactly how God took on flesh in Christ, coming among us in Bethlehem, the "smallest" in Judah, and in the form that was most "despised" (Mic. 5:2; Isa. 53:3). This is a door of grace, the very substance of grace, because this small and despised place of our lives, now bound to the commandments of God, also binds us to heaven itself, the place from which our sojourning seems to keep us distant: "For ever, O LORD, thy word is settled in heaven" (Ps. 119:89). The stranger's life, short and hard and in so many ways bereft of God, yet "stands" with God in acts of obedience to God's commands. The link with immortality, with God, with the lasting is given in this small, constricted space of a short life that longingly reaches after God's commandments.

This whole outlook, as I said, stands behind a long Christian tradition most famously associated with Augustine, who created a powerfully influential imagistic universe colored by the theme of sojourning or pilgrimage.[1] Augustine saw our human life in the world as an extended (or, for most people, not so extended) journey through fallen creation and its evil days to our true heavenly home. Homeless now, we live lightly with the things of this world—our bodies, our families, our possessions, our careers and reputations. And, as we saw in the last chapter, while existence here is (in Augustine's view) nothing but misery in most ways, we are offered a taste of what is to come through God's Word itself.

> This heavenly city, then, while it sojourns on earth, calls citizens out of all nations, and gathers together a society of pilgrims of all languages, not scrupling about diversities in the manners, laws, and institutions whereby earthly peace is secured and maintained, but recognizing that, however various these are, they all tend to one and the same end of earthly peace. . . . Even the heavenly city, therefore, while in its state of pilgrimage, avails itself of the peace of earth, and, so far as it can without injuring faith and godliness, desires and maintains a common agreement among men regarding the acquisition of the necessaries of life, and makes this earthly peace bear upon the peace of heaven. . . . [The City of God] believes also the Holy Scriptures, old and new, which we call canonical, and which are the source of the faith by which the just lives [Hab. 2:4] and by which we walk without doubting while we are absent from the Lord.[2]

Thus Augustine holds on to one of the key elements of Psalm 119—that is, that something of God's own life is granted us in what he offers in the Scriptures, in his commands.

Yet there is much that Augustine does not say in his application of the psalm, and his reticence in this regard has had its own troubling effects on our Christian expectations. The whole struggle of political life for the Christian is bound up with this image of sojourning·in the world, after all. So much of what we call "the Good Life" is seemingly wrecked by the limitations intrinsic to its forms. One seeks what one is forced back into repeatedly seeking without resolution by that goal's constant contradictions.

That is, the goods of human coupling, children, fruitful labor, communal support, and common prayer—and joy in all of this—are over and over again opposed, subverted, dismantled, and torn apart by circumstance and assault, by illness and time. The goods of the Good Life are good because, on one level, they are the bulwark and balm against mortality, as Augustine indicates; yet each good itself is nothing *but* mortality's form in the flesh. Hence, mortality's specifically *political* force—what it asks of us in political terms—seems to lie in apprehending, holding, cherishing, and finally properly relating to that which is intrinsically bound to being taken from us: our earthly loves. What we love is defined in its loveliness by its transitory nature. Augustine solves this by subordinating earthly loves, which are at best penultimate and more often distracting, to the only true love one could have, which is God. But his solution is belied, at least experientially, by his own account of sorrow over the death of those whom he loves, a sorrow that in itself colors the world's days as evil.[3] In any case, the politics of mortality will always be framed by the character of time, of generation, of the unknown, of the open-endedness of love and loss, however relative we (unsuccessfully) insist they are.

While there is nothing novel in putting matters this way, in practice this framing is admitted mostly in order to overcome its demand. So Augustine attempts to do, with his early promotion of the *vita beata* and its granting of permanence and possession versus transience and dispossession. While the notion that life is hard and that the achievement of "the good" lies in navigating this hardness well is the basis of most social philosophies, the content of this "well" has often been defined in terms of what *escapes* mortality. Aristotle's general take here is, in broad strokes, common and stands as a nontheistic model for Augustine. The frame of human existence is, to be sure, burdensome and, in many ways, subject to misery. But a virtuous life can in fact, says Aristotle, render a person "happy" in the midst of existence; indeed, a virtuous life *is* the only truly happy life a person might have. It is not so much that virtue is independent of mortality for someone like Aristotle. After all, courage or patience and the like take their particular form just in and through the pressures of mortal life: one is courageous in the face of danger, patient in the face of suffering. Still, the idea here is that a virtuous life somehow transcends the limits of mortality, and just this transcendence is what provides its practitioner "happiness." In this general outlook's Christian versions, spiritual fruits or pneumatic gifts—faith, for instance—or perhaps religious virtues themselves perform the same function of overleaping the limited goods of this life for the sake of something permanent. On this view, sojourning provides an arena for the formation of character, but the arena's value is only as a necessary context. No one, offered the choice, would wish to make the Colosseum their home.

Yet even the claim to virtue formation as a gateway to heaven is subject to the critique of existential logic. Recently, readers of Aristotle such as Martha Nussbaum and Bernard Yack have paused over some of the philosopher's own uncertainties about his general outlook in regard to transcendental happiness.[4] A key text can be found at the beginning of the *Nicomachean Ethics*, where Aristotle is laying out the general principles of his discussion of the happy life of virtue. Honesty, he admits, forces one to face the fact that there *are* limits on happiness that virtue cannot eliminate or get beyond. This was, it appears, a rather obvious fact accepted by many popular Greek views of life.[5] Aristotle mentions in passing the experience of King Priam of Troy, who loses family, people, and position—all that he cherishes most deeply. It would be "nonsense," Aristotle notes, to say that Priam, for all his virtues, was "happy."[6] Happiness, in fact, depends in many key respects on circumstance and chance, not on an individual's well-honed virtues. One's span of life, we remember, makes a difference for Aristotle. There are kinds and extents of misery that are immune to the softening powers of a well-ordered moral or spiritual character. Aristotle, however, is clearly uncomfortable with this troubling line of consideration. (Interestingly, once he comes to his *Politics*, he avoids the topic altogether.)[7] Somewhat peremptorily he stops short of subjecting happiness, *eudaimonia*, to the limitations of mortal constraint—that is, to the suffering of loss: the virtuous person, buffeted by suffering, can still be happy, he insists. But probably he cannot be truly "blessed" (*makarios*), like the gods.

It is by no means clear what this distinction is meant to accomplish. It is certainly not ordered to a vision of an afterlife in which the virtuous participate in divine beatitude. For Aristotle then raises the difficult question of whether the dead themselves, however happy they once may have been on earth, can be negatively affected by the suffering and misery of those they have left behind, whether their children or their later descendants. Can we claim, to put it in more recent terms, that the European Jewish parents who died in 1925 after a "happy life," but whose children and grandchildren were then tortured and butchered only fifteen or so years later, are truly happy? It all depends on what we think about the state of the dead, Aristotle notes; and that is a subject too obscure to worry much over. He moves on.[8]

The worry and the hesitation both can be seen in a book like Ecclesiastes: *I have seen much misery; who knows what will happen to us?* The conclusions Solomon offers are difficult to synthesize: on the one hand, take joy in the things of this life (2:24; 3:12–13); on the other, fear God and keep his commandments (12:13). There is a kind of press back into the somewhat starker world of Psalm 119 here, but it is more openly colored by the tangible goods of this life that one is blessed to enjoy, when that is possible—something other psalms, if not 119 itself, can frequently emphasize (e.g., Ps. 128). The good is fragile because it is mortal; yet just such mortal goods are gifts whose source opens up the determinative reality of God and God's commands, that which is established in heaven, permanent, invulnerable. One can call this recognition of the divine embedded in a faithfully navigated creation "wisdom," though "wisdom" here is not the same thing as beatitude in its developed Christian version. In Ecclesiastes, worries over the vulnerability of life (like Augustine's) and the long journey through its terrain are less impelled by a desire to get beyond such fragility altogether than they are embraced with a kind of worldly hope: hope in God, yet a hope in what God gives even here, a present donation that is crystallized in his law. But "here" is no less uncertain for Ecclesiastes than it is for Aristotle and Augustine. It is just that the goods of "here" are not to be jettisoned until they are in fact taken away; and "here" is what it is, in all its goodness and sorrow, because it *is* one day given and taken by the Giver of both conditions.

Does the sojourning life, then, "go" anywhere in the sense of getting us closer and closer to our goal, our greatest good? This question is important for human planning and expected outcomes, and thus for politics, and we will repeatedly raise it in what follows as we continue to ponder the character of "progress." For now, I will simply give my general response: Do our lives, or can our lives, close the gap between us and the fulfillment of our longing for God? Probably not. The equation of sojourning with a pilgrimage in its ecclesiastical context, in the sense of aiming at a destination of holiness toward which one can mark a gradually closing distance, is perhaps misleading. Even with all his language of running and being "before" and "behind," Paul himself does not seem to trade much in the idea of life as a process of "getting closer" to God. In an important text like Philippians 3:12–21, the key element in life is, as with Psalm 119, holding to a given measure in a world separated from one's true heavenly polity. The measure or canon in this case is the cross, and the transposition to Paul's goal is a gracious (that is, unsecurable in human terms) resurrection, not a process of approach and arrival. "Pilgrimage" comes from the Latin *peregrinatio* (Augustine's term), whose root seems to mean, as with the Hebrew *ger* of Psalm 119:19, "foreigner" or "stranger." In this light, pilgrimage is as much a wandering and unstable identity as it is a determined journey by a particular citizen. Once there came to be official sites to be visited—Jerusalem, Santiago de

Compostela—"pilgrimage" lost its deliberately open-ended vagueness. But vagueness is intrinsic to the sojourner's existence: if a pilgrim is ever happy, it is a happiness hemmed in irregularly by who knows what or when or where. To be a pilgrim is a life itself, not the end of a life.

Paul, of course, does not see the Christian life as desultory. At times he compares it to a race with a goal and a prize (cf. Phil. 3:8–21). Yet even in this context the actual form of this goal-oriented movement, given in the letter as a whole, is one of uncertain suffering, puzzling choices between life and death, and a hope that is bound by still-hidden divine determinations. Thus, the focused prize takes on the shape of the world's limitations, just as they are. The Christians Peter calls "strangers" (1 Pet. 2:11) are not "on their way to Zion"; they *are* Zion in *this* place. What they are close to is Jesus, whose own life is manifested in suffering, resurrection, vindication, and glory, the Word made flesh. While there is a concrete connection between the trials of this life and any future glory, it seems to lie not in a measured and traversed distance between two points but, more directly, in a life that is bound to the experienced forms of Jesus's own life. These forms, in word and deed, become the "commandments" that establish the mortal life of his followers as near to God here and now, much in the pattern of Psalm 119 (cf. John 14:23). The life of Jesus is that supreme life, given in mortal form, that is born, grows, lives, suffers, and dies "committed . . . to him that judgeth righteously" (1 Pet. 2:23). This form, in all its details, constitutes the "commandments of God" that define the sojourner's happiness just here, in whatever days these may be.

All this may seem very *un*political. It is so, at least insofar as politics is viewed as the definitive acts or goals of the citizen of this or that polity ordered to a clear end. It is important to see how unsystematic the sojourner's life—the *human creature's* life—must be, at least in terms of its analytic details, because such a life simply is not amenable to the definitive acts and goals of much political self-understanding. If there are better and worse moments that the sojourner encounters, they are not arranged in some incremental fashion. Even if one would wish to value the way that the virtues are nurtured and deployed only gradually over time—and one should value this—there is no predictable shape to the contexts and means by which such virtuous habituation takes place. Great political commonwealths of virtue are fantasies because the ordering of a commonwealth for the sake of virtue must always be stymied by the vagaries of mortal life; they cannot be consistently or sustainably organized. Nor can one predict the resiliency—let alone permanence—of such habits in the face of the utterly unpredictable depredations of circumstance and chance, as Aristotle notes (and just as Augustine himself will later say, as he reflects on the need for the grace of "perseverance").[9] The fact that sojourning is the posture of a mortal human being simply means that the human creature is constantly being thrust back into a world of things, of created gifts and limitations, of swimming within them, of finding them ever anew and losing them ever anew, such that "newness" is both real and not capable of being tamed or manipulated—as much a source of fear, therefore, as of promise or hope. The "new" is certainly not a thing to be grasped but something to be borne, with regret or welcome, as it may be.

Where is the Good Life to be lived? In the nondeveloping world of the sojourner. This is a world in which politics will take on a vastly different character than it has assumed within modernity. While the explicit categories of "developed" and "undeveloped" have gone out of fashion in economic and political analysis, their connotations remain embedded in the social expectations of our era. Measures of well-being, tied to ever more intricate statistical data, are deployed to evaluate the condition of this or that nation or segment of society, always according to "better" and "worse": income, education, health care, rates of incarceration or drug usage or divorce or suicide. Applied on a global scale, these measures become benchmarks of "progress," and political activity is itself evaluated in terms of meeting these benchmarks. (We shall look at some of these later.) Ours is a world in which nothing really develops in a fundamental way because nothing lasts long and everything is quickly and unpredictably taken away. Ours is a world in which obedience to divine commands is the only door to permanence and in which human beings are born and live variously for a short time, engaging the goods they are offered for such a moment and place. It is not so much that such measures of progress have no meaning or interest— after all, they intersect with and point to influences upon the mortal goods of common creaturely existence. Rather, a politics that is driven by these measures must appear impotent and finally distracting or even intrusively destructive, just insofar as the judgments and means that inform "progressive" politics finally bulldoze the divine commands that constitute the only hope and source of joy that mortal goods reflect. Any politics that cannot value the fragile and limited nature of the goods of the Good Life, and value them precisely in their limitations as shaped by God's Word, is a politics irrelevant to and unworthy of the human sojourner.

It has long been noted, in fact, how "undeveloped" societies have weighed upon the "progress" of nations, acting as a drag to the implementation of policies and practices aimed at advancing human well-being. Age-old ways of agriculture, "oppressive" familial structures, wasteful religious duties, and hierarchies all stand in the way of progressive well-being. References to the "moral economy" of "peasant societies"—phrases made famous by the work of social historians whom we shall touch on in the next chapter, such as E. P. Thompson, James Scott, and Edward Banfield—were meant to draw attention to the manner in which shared values shape economic and political thinking and action. Those who deployed these categories were critical either of emergent capitalist value systems or of the "fatalistic" and "oppressive" family orientation of agrarian noncapitalistic peoples, for whom some kind of liberative politics was desirable. Marxists and anti-Marxists both, in these discussions, have had little good to say about the peasantry themselves: they are always somehow "backward."

Yet one might wonder whether the moral economy of the peasantry—not much different across societies and epochs—is not a better foundation for Christian politics than are most other theories on offer.[10] The question has been raised by Ivan Illich's reflections on the virtues associated with "subsistence," a term that is less about mere survival and its modes than it is about the integrity of a human life that depends not on manufactured values but rather on what it is given. Almost everything about the peasant existence is aimed at ordering the goods of birth, family, toil, neighbors, suffering, friendship and joy, and finally death, goods that are understood to be exhaustive of life in this world. There is nothing romantic about such an existence, of course (and Illich himself would find my own observations here crudely sentimental—wrongly, I think). And the degree to which the commands of God inform this ordering has determined a vast, varied range of, in Christian terms, "happiness" that can be ascribed to such societies. The happiness involved here is rightly vague in the sense of systemically uncentered "peregrinating." But, in these contexts, the goods have remained steady, and the religious value of these goods has directed the kind of politics that must, in this light, be valued in its turn.

But whatever politics applies to peasant societies, these societies them-selves are probably rightly examined for the way they historically figure an *undeveloping* world, a world of wandering and strangeness, where home, in all its vulnerable forms, is "just here," though with "here" always standing as an image of another home, the establishing of which is given nonetheless *just now* in faithfulness to God's commands. "I am a stranger in the earth: hide not thy commandments from me" (Ps. 119:19). Time—and political time, especially—in such a world is given in certain activities as they come and go, not as a strategic chronology. The activities themselves are ones of sifting the stuff of today for its shapeliness with respect to God's com-mands, engaging such conformities, being taught within them, following their demands, failing, repenting, again and again, or at least until time is no more. *Whom shall I marry? How shall I feed my family? What tool shall I use? Whom shall I comfort and with what words? Whom must I evade? How will I rebuild? Where will I bury him? Where will I be buried? What prayer shall I say? What song will I sing?* The tasks are repeated over and over until strength and breath are gone; but the form of their repetition is ever measured by the Word of God. "O that today you would hearken to his voice!" (Ps. 95:7 RSV; cf. Heb. 3:15).

It is true that politics of such immediacy may seem incapable of meeting the challenges precisely of the greatest threats to common existence, especially in our era of climate change, but also in all eras where planning is demanded in the face of scarcity, war, and winter—not to mention the smaller needs of taxation, savings, and systems of care. But the conjunction of goods and their formation through divine commandments within the limited scope of mortal life neither rules out planning nor requires it. Ruled out is only the principle of absoluteness in either regard.

Peasants have their own way of planning, in any case, and it follows the immovable values of a faith tied to the impermanence of life itself. The commandments, after all, are transcendent, given in the midst of time, composed for temporal existence and thus clothed in the shadow of death, yet ever the gifts of God. God's commandments infuse our limited times with light, proclaiming such times to be, finally, in a teleological sense, God's. Planning is thus circumscribed by the values of the immediate, and it is the peculiar Christian political vocation to make that clear.

It seems obvious now that the debates and struggles over COVID-19 public policy and its social restrictions and reorderings would have been clarified by such political sensibilities. Calibrating risks according to the values of divine command within an impermanent world would have made Christian political sense, even though the debates themselves, by Christians as much as anyone, rarely attempted such reflection. "Here we have no continuing city" (Heb. 13:14), yet everything we have here, whether the days be evil or good, is a divine gift. Every political decision the Christian makes must reflect the power of this paradox, which is simply that of our being created at all. As a creaturely activity, time is always pressured, not as a directioned history, but by all the limits of creaturely life, from all sides at once: beginnings and endings, ups and downs, enclosed in the grip of createdness, which is itself but the quivering trace of God's own hand.

Everything the creature is, is given exhaustively by God. Without such givenness, the creature is nothing. That is why mortality is constituted by goods. That is why our life's vocation is the ordering of such goods. And that is why, finally, these goods, as mortal, are subject not to our strategies of temporal purpose—a utilitarian fantasy—but to the commands of the one who has given them, commands that simply lay out the shape within which our mortal goods are attended to. How do men and women interact? How do they become parents? What do they do with their children? How do children relate to their mothers and fathers? What governs our speech with one another? Our eating? Our labor, our wealth, our prayers, our fears, our songs, and our deaths? Mortal life "goes nowhere," at least on its own; it is, rather, a divine design, whose beauty we offer up in thanksgiving. Our next four chapters now turn to this offering of what is beautiful and to some of the political dimensions of this ordering of our mortal goods.

Four

The Service of God

And Moses said, Thou must give us also sacrifices and burnt offerings, that we may sacrifice unto the LORD our God. Our cattle also shall go with us; there shall not an hoof be left behind; for thereof must we take to serve the LORD our God; and we know not with what we must serve the LORD, until we come thither.

Exodus 10:25–26

With this initial request by Moses to Pharaoh, the whole direction of Israel's popular life is set in motion, with all its purpose and with the implications of that purpose's frequent frustrations. Sojourning's shape is here presented, whose purpose is, quite simply and basically, the "service of God," *avodat Hashem*. This chapter aims at bringing into relief the fundamental good of mortal survival as an offering to God, and thus at indicating survival's central place in how Christians should conceive of their political calling.

Service and Survival

Moses explains to Pharaoh how the service of God involves everything of the Hebrews' created existence—the people and their "things," as provided by the Egyptians. We shall see that this will encompass material goods (Exod. 3:21; 12:36) in the famous "spoiling" of the Egyptians that is also wrapped up in divine "deliverance" (the more common meaning of the word—e.g.,

3:8). Taking hold of the things of this world, of all its goods (cattle included), for the sake of offering is itself a form of freedom and deliverance. In this case, Moses explains that the Israelites need these goods in order to offer to God a "service" that is comparable to God's open-ended requests: "We know not with what we must serve the LORD," and so we offer it all.

Thus, this open-ended offering is bound to and takes the form of a kind of sojourning of its own. Israel's deliverance from Egypt, from the slavery and toil of Pharaoh's rule to the service of God, lies in the desert. A journey must be taken, indeed, a journey finally of four decades in the wilderness, with a goal but without a straight path—a wandering. The fourth book of the Torah is called by Christians "Numbers" after the early Greek translation, which identified the book in terms of the census mentioned in 1:2. But the Hebrew name, *midbar* (wilderness), taken from 1:1 ("The LORD spake unto Moses in the *wilderness* of Sinai"), is more telling. A *midbar* is an open tract of land, not always a desert in a modern sense, but land without roads or settlements. And the book of Numbers is properly read as a vision of sojourning, of life in the trackless world, where Adam—that is, all the people—in his joys and frustrated needs receives life and death from God.

In this sense, the service that Moses lays out for Israel is itself a service of survival. If read in these terms, the traversal of the wilderness inevitably takes in forms of toil (Gen. 2:5–15; 3:23) and its previous history: tilling in Eden; tilling in the fallen world after the curse, sacrifice, violence, and wandering again (cf. Cain, 4:2, 12). To be sure, the *avodah* of service that begins with toil turns, over time, into the service of the forced laborer, the servant, the vassal, the slave as individual or people (Gen. 15:13), a slavery that becomes the setting for Exodus itself (Exod. 1:14). Only in Exodus 3:12 does this service turn deliberately toward God, now laying out the character of Israel's life: survival, obedience, offering. Israel takes up all of this in her vocation, and the laws that follow from this open-ended journey do not foreclose its uncertainty, but only structure it in a way that focuses its meaning as a "pure" offering. Thus, the service of God takes over all other services as well as taking them in. By the time of Numbers, the meaning of Exodus 10:26 will include the "service" of priests and Levites in the tabernacle; in Deuteronomy, *avodah* is now tied intimately not only to the articulated commands of God but also, in contrast, to the corrupted service of other gods (Deut. 5:9). Thereby, *avodah* becomes the subsuming vocation of Israel: "And now, Israel, what doth the LORD thy God require of thee, but to fear the LORD thy God, to walk in all his ways, and to love him, and to serve the LORD thy God with all thy heart and with all thy soul" (Deut. 10:12). And so Israel's service, and its obstacles and failures, unfolds through Joshua, Kings, Job, Psalms, and the Prophets.

Let us return to the question of service and its form. As it emerges in Exodus, *avodah* draws together the sense of labor on the land, of the raising of cattle, of the production of goods, of difficult survival, of journeying, and suddenly of the offering and sacrifice of all this back to God, now in a posture of obedience. Like that of the sojourner, the "way" through the wilderness, which is less a clear path than a wandering, is bound to the "way" of God's commandments—a "walking" that both takes us through trackless desert and brings us close to God. Once they are no longer slaves to the world, Israel's embeddedness in this world becomes the stuff of praise and faithfulness. One cannot be a slave to what one offers up. This, then, is expressed as the law of Leviticus, which covers every element of daily life, from beasts and plants, to food, clothing, sex, and family, to birth, illness, and death, to housing, money, and land, to the years that pass by, one by one, and often one just like the other. All of this is God's, and its ordering by God and its offering to God constitute the service of God. Yet in such a service we do not know what God will ask of us with specificity, for in asking for *all* of this, God leaves us where we are, though turning this "where"—the here and now, in all its permutations but also all its limitations, its mortal shape and force—to himself.

Put another way, Israel's service is the offering of survival and obedience both. "Going" or "walking" in Exodus 10:26 sums up the "way" through the wilderness (Deut. 1:19), as well as the "way" of God's commandments (Deut. 5:33). That Israel survives the wilderness, in the form of a remnant who have somehow held on to life—they are, literally, "alive"—all through the journey into Canaan (Deut. 4:4), is due to those who have "cleaved" to God (an unusual word), those who have found themselves intimately near to him through their adherence to the Lord's commands (4:1). Here is where life is found. From one perspective, "being alive" is simply life, the breath of created being granted by God in this world, which is still at work in this or that person. But in Moses's description of Israel having lived through the wilderness (Deut. 4:1, 4), "life" is also the will of God. Hence, just in the forms of its survival, a life offered to God in the service of his will is manifest as true life, life as it really is.

The notion that the service of God is bound up with the hard work of survival—with the affliction of enforced labor, with a kind of slavery and offering up of one's goods and life—and that this is "real life," in the sense of God's own gift of life in its purpose, is perhaps unsettling. We would prefer that our service engage the principles that transcend existence or that they somehow be capable of transforming its hard and final edges into something that permits us to leave existence unscathed with respect to what is most valuable. Art, knowledge, effulgent goodness, and justice—these we can offer, in the sense of creating them and thus honoring God perhaps. In so creating them, we hope that we are somehow embellishing the world and our lives within it, granting our existence a more lasting character. The transcendent aspects of our lives, however, are already given in their being created; and the commandments of God, which touch no more than the forms of this given, created life, establish that transcendent aspect not elsewhere but in the life that we have right here. The very notion of a "mortal good" is founded on this reality: there is nothing added to God's gifts that makes them *more* divine.

So, Abel and Cain begin human history in this world—just here—with a set of offerings that establish the dynamic of the service of God and its forms for the future. They work, they seek their food, they offer it well and poorly, and their lives are upended by their weaknesses and sin. Their generations come to an end, although Seth then takes their place. Through him it seems that the long tremors of their service rumble through the ages, with all of that service's difficult fulfillment now given greater clarity in Israel's history. But the history of *avodat Hashem* continues in Christ, who like, with, and in Israel leaves Egypt to serve God in ways that refocus the offering of mortal goods to his Father. The whole nexus of work, labor, slavery, and obedient service becomes Jesus's own—along with its detailed elements of birth, blood, family, toil, friendship, betrayal, and loss in the service of God's law, which he fulfills "in the days of his flesh" (Heb. 5:7). In all this, Jesus offers not only "prayers and supplications" but "new commandments" (John 13:34) that accompany and uphold the wanderers that constitute his body, the church. In this—not in something else—the obedient "slave" is "exalted" (Phil. 2:7, 9).

We can see that, despite the clarity of Jesus's revelatory teaching (or is it so clear?), the nature of *avodat Hashem* does not change for the Christian as compared to the Israelite Jew. Greek words already used to translate Old Testament texts are now deployed in Christian phrases that describe "service": *diakoneō*, but also (in the Septuagint) *latreuō*, the latter of which we often translate in English as "worship," but which is no more than a straightforward rendering of *avodah*. The aged Zacharias uses *latreuō* in Luke 1:74; Satan elicits the word in his temptation of Jesus, who answers him with the same (Matt. 4:10); *latreuō* appears throughout Acts in connection with Old Testament prophecies (Acts 7:7; 24:14); Paul takes it up repeatedly (Rom. 1:25; Phil. 3:3; 2 Tim. 1:3 [where the term is tied to serving God in Christ]);

Hebrews is fond of the term in connection with the temple (Heb. 13:10); and Revelation summarizes the consummation of heaven in terms of such "service" rendered at the throne of God (Rev. 7:15; 22:3).

Political Regimes of Service

The people of Israel, ordered by the law of God in the midst of an experientially aimless geographical existence, seek to serve God in this comprehensive form of offering. Surely, if anything has a political bite, it is such a service! Yet modern political activity, as it has developed in the wake of a civic existence that guards its purview and interests from the encroachments of religion, has little to do with such service any longer, though it was Israel's purpose to organize its common life according to this calling. Elected officials may today be described as "public servants," mostly in an aspirational sense. The notion of "public service," however, is deliberately restrained in comparison with the breadth of mortal life's self-sacrifice. And perhaps well it should be, as attempts to rein in the power of magistracy and crown long before the advent of modern liberalism seem to indicate. But Christians themselves now seem to have accepted this modern distinction as definitive of their own existence more broadly and have taken up notions of politics that adhere to this restraint. While they may insist that their religious faith informs this political realm, in doing so they actually respect that realm's boundaries in a way that inevitably circumscribes political accountabilities. For the Christian's political question ought to be "How can I live with others such that I may offer the mortal gifts of God to my Maker?"

Instead, the kind of service of God that comprehends our life on earth and all its components is a notion that has been sequestered into often pietistic corners of theological ethics or the perceived spiritual extremes of vowed religious orders. What has politics to do with the analogous claims made in marriage (according to the Book of Common Prayer) that "with my body I thee worship; and with all my worldly goods I thee endow"? The very thought that I should make a vow like this within the mortal world of my biological appearing—a vow, then, that touches my body, my family, my work, my bonds to each of these in their joy and loss—and that I should order my political will to the securing of such a space of offering just such things smacks of tyrannical theocracy in our day. Even pietism has come to be viewed as oppressive.

If organized according to a structural calculus, that is in fact what it would be. But Moses's assertion that "we know not" what to offer until we arrive at the place God has led us—only that we must bring all and go where we are led—seems to unsettle strategic reflections here. Laws are given, of course. But as time goes on, Israel's organized common life unravels in many ways (if ever it was well woven), and the people's service is subsumed into a narrative that is both broader, taking in the ages unto the consummation of creation, and more spare, described in the limited bodily terms of individual lives. There is absolutely nothing in the grand biblical story about the emergence over time of either a just society or a righteous Israel. We hear about small struggles, all too familiar to us, and about a great promise that lies beyond these struggles but that cannot itself alter the terrain of the moment.

Thus, modern politics has drifted away from the immediacies of the sojourner's obedient and circumscribed life in its open extent and its personal limits. More and more, politics has turned its attention to a social cosmos of unrealistic abstraction and has transformed limited creaturely lives into the aggregate measures of pursued principles. While the theocratic path is not without its travelers, most contemporary Christian resisters to this drift have attempted to reappropriate aspects of earlier political self-reflection and description—of the happy life or the "good life" of the smaller *polis*: virtues, activities, communal engagements.[1] Communitarian, localized grassroots organizations—even attempts at implementing, within schools forming the young, curricula of civic values—are the fruit of this modest resistance. Although these kinds of efforts and programs are driven by rightly perceived needs, they have nonetheless approached much of their purpose still in terms of a constrained instrumentality, even in their goal of furthering virtue. Even self-conscious Christian politics tends, in our day, to be driven by the question of how to "better" the political outcomes. That might include the shape of a society that inculcates the right virtues according to various measures of progress in our common life. But rarely is even such virtue orientation aimed at formation for how to live well for a few short years, let alone how to offer our short years to God.

The demand for betterment, which I will frequently judge negatively in this book, seems to fuel every political effort these days, genuinely or disingenuously. But the demand itself is misplaced as a central motive for our common life, for a major and a minor reason. The major reason is that the demand does not cohere with *avodat Hashem*, the service of God, as we have outlined it. The minor reason is that the demand is, in any case, unworkable and unrealizable. The minor reason derives from the major one: to offer our limited lives to God in thanks involves a valuing of mortal goods even in their divinely oriented relinquishment—sojourning. It is not so much paradoxical that the value of survival is defined by its inherent limits as it is axiomatic. Such relinquishment is inimical to the organized pretensions of human political evolution, pretentions that rely on possessing, holding on to, accumulating, establishing and demonstrating, and furthering something that the "mortal" aspect of our deepest mortal goods cannot sustain. That everything is but a "breath"—"vanity," in Solomon's words (Eccles. 1:2)—does not render our lives empty or pointless; it only states the fact, infinitely marvelous, that our lives belong to God and not to us.

Every virtuous act and habit, when ordered to or by some organized instrumentality, is swallowed up by the multiplied forces set in motion by humanly—individually and relationally—disarticulated decision-making and pressures, each of which by definition must end in irresolution and even disappearance. We can make neither ourselves nor others good. *Avodat Hashem* is not such a making, certainly. For just such "making" is fundamentally antithetical to the character of our creatureliness. I shall say something later about the "artistry" of our lives, the making that is in fact ours to accomplish. But whatever that beautiful thing our lives may become, our service of God is itself not an achievement but a giving back. Things do not get better much, nor are the people who try to make things better themselves better people for all their efforts. The parable of the talents has been read in a kind of bettering fashion: "make something of your gifts/ self," take advantage of what God gives you, and so on. But perhaps the problem for the fearful servant given a sum of money was simply the fact that he did not treat the gift as just that, something to be received with joy, tended and engaged. Instead the gift is, in the Gospel tellings, either buried in the ground or wrapped up in the dirtiest rag, covered either way in an obscuring filth. The general term "corruption" seems to apply fairly broadly in the political realm, not just with respect to the corruption of processes distorted at the hands of participants, but with respect to the spirits of the participants themselves.

Politics, and certainly in the modern version of political activity, is often seen in terms of the service not of God but of making people better. Let us pause on this question for a moment (one we shall be returning to on more than one occasion). The question of political virtue or of politics for the sake of virtue can be approached in terms of virtue's encouraging regimes: What works best either to embody better people or to make people better? The great typologies of political order were originally laid out, according to Aristotle's influential template, in order to indicate the moderate forms of each rather than to identify the best of the lot. Each type of government— democracy, aristocracy, monarchy—might in fact be more suitable than others for a given context.[2] And each can be perverted to different degrees, such that a monarchy becomes a tyranny and so on. The "best" constitution, for Aristotle, is the one that is able to maintain, given its context, a balance of class interests (rich, middling, poor).[3] Aristotle had his own views (he favored a certain kind of democratically tempered aristocracy), and there came to be favorite types for different theoreticians, in part based on the scope of moral and practical efficacy that each type was viewed as offering. While Aquinas wrote in favor of monarchy, notions of "mixed" constitutions gained traction in early modern Europe, and "republicanism"—a vague term that took in many types of mixed constitutions—gradually became more virulently anti-monarchical and more democratically tinged.[4] The question of how a virtuous person and a virtuous state can be sustained in these various regime types was originally an important one, but has since mostly disappeared except among scholars.

The monarchist/tyranny type has obviously gone out of fashion as a suitable option for our era, although, at various points in the past one hundred years, it has been embraced quite explicitly in times and moments of increasingly overwhelming social pressures, whose complexity has rendered them impermeable to resolution. The populist "strong man" model, then, is not without its supporters even today. One attraction has been its claim to efficient virtue formation, either through the imposition of some comprehensive national pedagogy or through the comprehensive elimination of vice. Both fascism and Communism, in our era, have played on this attraction. More generally, however, the justification for the "strong man" (even, rarely, strong woman) has been a desire for efficiency, period: breaking legislative and economic logjams and intractable political conflict. Thus, even implicit individual or oligarchic authoritarianism has been a common alternative to the generally public valorization of democracy or republicanism. The Democracy Index, put together by the Economist Intelligence Unit, identifies 59 out of 167 nations in 2021 as "authoritarian" (with Afghanistan, Myanmar, and North Korea at the bottom of the list)[5] and includes countries like Egypt, Rwanda, Russia, and China as part of this category. The Index comes up with its rankings on the basis of assessments of a range of categories, such as free electoral process, civil liberties, participation, and political culture (on the latter two of which the United States has stumbled of late).

Whether or not politically ordered virtue formation is really what people want, it is fair to say that only authoritarian and exclusivist (elite-centered) government can in fact exercise political virtue in a traditional sense. Oligarchies, monarchies, and so on, in which decision-making is done by the few, provide the only amenable class in which virtue has functional and deliberative purchase. This is, of course, just in theory. For, as we know well from experience, such authoritarian regimes in our era—Russia, China, and scores of other polities around the world—constitute the *constriction*, even elimination, of classical understandings of virtue politics altogether, as this was understood in ancient and early modern times.[6] Things are no better among the democracies, where virtue formation works, by contrast, only in small bites and within a straitened compass, and where the sheer breadth and complexity of decision-making and executive implementation is riddled with corruptive infections. In fact, so-called democracy in our era, as in the United States (however "flawed," according to the Index) and many other Western polities, is the worst of both "the few" and "the many": for lack of a realm in which political virtue has actual purchase, we press for "voice" and franchise without true knowledge, in a context without virtuous restraint. The result is indeed an oligarchy by default, but one without virtue and with only passion and power: mobs and tyrannies abound. The consequence, in this case, belies the basic principle of service as betterment.

Whatever the regime type, the history of political service, in the sense of shaping mortal lives that are properly offered to God, has proved at best desultory and at worst a contradiction in terms. This does not mean that such lives have not in fact been offered, and offered within and at times even informed by the particularities of this or that political system or structure. But, more often, *avodat Hashem* has been embodied in forms of distance from, sometimes even resistance to, the self-conscious orders of political systems. There are good reasons for this.

The Holy Peasant

The Christian is called out from Egypt to wander in the service of God. We must, therefore, retreat from the mob and disengage from the tyrant, exercising virtue where its forms are tangibly emergent and flourishing. Is there more? As it turns out, *this landscape of wandering and fleeting virtue has been the realm of most of human history for most people.* This common sojourning experience, framed politically, is something we perhaps fail to identify because political history, theory, and policy, of whatever sort and stripe, are by definition predominantly articulated by an elite, the materially and authoritatively chosen of an era, whose goals are aimed at freeing people from aimlessness and getting them on track with a well-ordered social good. Even popular histories of the "voiceless" cannot be anything but the arguments of a metamorphosed aristocracy who have, through some applied intellectual apparatus of their own, supplied a sound and called it a shared reality. As in quantum mechanics, once the "normal" is identified, it becomes fixed in its own elitist state of being. Does Augustine really represent the people for whom he speaks? Yes and no. Only when we do not pin him down theoretically, but simply pray with him, is he a part of the Great Church, politically conceived. And Aristotle, with whom we cannot ever pray (for what are his prayers? we do not know them), lives in another universe altogether.

Yet Israel's and the church's wandering is their normal mode of life. Jews celebrate Sukkoth, the Feast of Tabernacles, to remind themselves of this fact. The forms of this feast witness not to a privileged way of life but simply to life with God—in the end, anybody's life if they care to admit it, let alone give thanks for it with Israel. Despite the fact that "voicing the voiceless" is intrinsically distorting, it is nonetheless worth making quantum determinations of what "normal" people think and do because this ought, to some degree, to clarify the proper parameters of a political life aimed at securing the offering of a people to God. Once this is done, and even if we take the result with a grain of salt, certain otherwise obscure things come into view that in fact subvert much political principle in our day. We can take as one example of the search for the "normal" the category "moral economy" and see what it might say about the "normal service of God."

In the mid-twentieth century, social scientists such as E. P. Thompson applied the concept of a "moral economy" to a class they identified as the "peasantry." Thompson was interested in delineating the ways in which the developing capitalist economy of Europe, and the decisions made to further it, tore apart the deeper values and moral commitments of the common people. Tracing the interplay of these forces, one could explain more clearly the dynamics of unfolding class conflict. Other scholars, such as James C. Scott, applied the concept of the "moral economy of the peasantry" to an analysis of political and economic change in Southeast Asia, examining how the threat to subsistence agriculture ordered popular reactions and events.[7] The category "moral economy" can be used descriptively (how, in fact, social morals and economic life intersect and shape each other). But it can also be used evaluatively, as Thompson does to a degree, in order implicitly to commend the English peasants' anti-market sentiments in favor of more basic concerns with food production, costs, and access to the basic goods of survival. Having identified these values, one can apply them as benchmarks for political judgments and action.

The category of a "moral economy" is one worth taking up, but perhaps only in a definitionally limited way—applying to it, that is, the "grain of salt." Any "moral economy" seems to be precisely that which describes the values that undergird the life of the household (writ large, that is, in an Aristotelian sense): what happens and why and according to what commitments within the basic frame of human life in which individuals are born, are raised, are fed, work, and do the same until they die. Moral economies come in many forms, as the household changes shape or as the household itself is unraveled, attacked, or dispersed, as in war and disaster. But there is a sense in which all moral economies have as their comparative base the moral economy of "the peasant."

On this score, the political virtues of the peasant are, as it were, almost wholly subsumed in their "moral economy." That is the only space in which they live. As these small virtues (one can think of the virtues that sustain parenthood, toil, learning and tending, and care in illness and dying) are extended into further and further reaches of relationship—for example, within and between nations themselves—they inevitably move out of the realm of a truly shared moral economy and become the purview of elites (e.g., controlling merchants, bureaucrats, technical experts, political functionaries, and thus oligarchies and tyrants). Indeed, there are no really formative and effective human virtues at all in this extended context, only policy goals. If there is a moral economy in modern Western nations, it is thinned out in a way that mirrors the dissipated character of the Western household itself. One gets a sense of some of the dynamics in play through the sweeping economic argument of Karl Polanyi's *The Great Transformation*, the title of which refers not just to the rise of the capitalist market economy in modern Europe but to the profound ways this development involved a remaking of the dominant household value system that predated it, values that were not at root economic but relational and more or less family- and community-centered.[8]

Whatever the grip that economic change had on moral economies, the Great Transformation was only one—and perhaps only a limited—element in the obscuring of the sojourning shape of human life within which the virtues of common relationship arise. The Great Health Transition of circa 1900 has been just as important, if not more so, in hollowing out our perception of human existence's created character. When, around 1900, average life spans began their rapid extension to the point of, in many and now most parts of the world, actually doubling—from forty to eighty years—a complex stream of social changes followed, in sexual practice, fertility, social configurations, and self-awareness. These in turn tended to relegate the households in which moral economies (fundamentally "peasant" moral economies) flourished to either obsolete or even oppressive arrangements.[9]

I would argue, in fact, that the occlusion of mortality's driving power in human existence has done far more to destroy the perceived possibility of a life of service to God than the advent of "the market."

The moral economy of the "peasant," as some have pointed out, is riddled by fatalism in the face of obstacles to change. Edward Banfield's influential study of a southern Italian village (*The Moral Basis of a Backward Society*) traced the inhabitants' hemmed-in vision, which was, according to him, perversely bound to the family (Banfield coined the phrase "amoral familism" here), suspicious of larger groups, unresponsive to larger political and ethical concerns, and incapable of grasping the gifts of social development. This, as the title to his book asserted, is a "backward" way of life, one he attributed in part to high rates of mortality and the grinding struggle to survive. Other, less judgmental reflections on peasant society have noted a similarly constrained vision.[10] But mortality *is* a "fate," insofar as it is an immovable limit. Banfield's point is important, however, because it (inadvertently) underlines the reality that there is a specifically Christian character that must undergird a "peasant" morality if it is to be truly an *avodat Hashem*, one that involves the calling of a people. Without the recognition of this calling and its purposeful pursuit, peasantry is, as the word's etymology suggests (see below), a form of paganism, what is left when we are left to ourselves, "without God in the world" (Eph. 2:12).

Yet the "pagan" (the root seems to mean "rustic," just as "heathen" referred to heath-dwellers) *did* become the "peasant"—a complex linguistic transformation—the *paysan*, the land-dweller outside the city walls, cultivating and toiling, herding, making do with a few others while the days ticked by. And the peasant—rural, reticent, and recalcitrant—became the core of the church's *populus*, scattered widely across the terrain, from one sea to another. With each of the Christian peasant's days came a prayer, and the prayers were wrapped around the content of the days—children, animals, gardens, feast days, marriages, bedsides, burials. All this was good, however hard and however brief. All this was good, not on its own, but because this is what God gives.

In this sense we are all of us peasants or "children of Adam," the man of the earth. Many of us are now highly paid peasants, to be sure, but of such a class, the class of the human creature, that our main focus is ever—or at least must in the end only be—upon the limited realm of mortal goods. This is the only realm in which political virtue can be exercised, a proximate and impinging realm because it is the actual field of the Good Life. Politically, all that is important is that individuals and their progeny in their filiated relations can exercise agency over these mortal goods such that they can be used in the service of God. The last point is the most important for the Christian: agency itself is less critical than is the *matter* of life—the soil from which God forms life—that is taken up and that is the object of such agency. This "matter" is nothing less than the mortal goods granted by our creator to be used in the service of the Lord God, King of the Universe.

Five

The Good Life as Offering

Give unto the LORD the glory due unto his name: bring an offering, and come into his courts.

Psalm 96:8

Let us further explore this claim that our politics is aimed at permitting and preserving our offering of life's matter to its Maker, in the form of what I have dubbed a sanctified peasantry. Over and over, in any case, Scripture seems to press this point.

The world in which we serve God is nothing other than the stage of our self-offering of just this world and its goods back to him. So we come into the world—"Then said I, Lo, I come" (Ps. 40:7)—to do God's will in obedience. This offering of obedience, according to Hebrews' description of Jesus fulfilling David's psalm, is represented by his body given over (Heb. 10:5–10). In both his and our coming into the world, therein is the offering made. While John 1:9 is clearly indicative of the incarnation of the Word, it is also true for us: the verse can be read as referring to both the Son and human beings, the "light that enlightens" and "every man," each "coming into the world." Offering is what we do insofar as we are created, as we are born, as we "come."

We come into the world with and as our offerings. Psalm 96 speaks of coming into the courts of the Lord. These two destinations coincide. The "courts" (*hatser*) of the temple were the areas, especially the outer court,

61

where the people were allowed to come and gather as closely as possible to the inner sanctuary, which was reserved for the priests. The relation of "court" to people is strong, and in fact the word is used more generally of communities where peoples gather and live together—that is, villages and towns. The "peoples" and "kindreds" of the earth (96:7), then, are those called into the courts of the temple to join with Israel in its service. This service is one of "offering" (*minhah* here).

But the courts of God—this convergence of peoples' lives in village and town and of the people's service in the temple—are therefore also places where the whole of life is intermingled. In fact, the cosmic symbolism of the temple and the earlier tabernacle's form and decoration was a long-standing subject of interpretation.[1] When Ezekiel, in 9:7, sees the punishment of God at work on Israel, it reaches its summit of horrific destruction in the piling up of bodies in the courts of the temple, murder and death both constricting the proclamation of Psalm 96 even as they perversely fulfill it corporeally, as if the service of God that is called for and withheld is now squeezed out of created flesh by violence.

This place of bodies gathered and given over, in song or in gasping for breath, marks out the "courts" of the Lord as the wide space of human life, such that just this space is laid out as the altar of sacrifice. The book of Leviticus displays this vision as a symbolic icon, whereby the ordering of Israel's cult functions as the mapping out of this world-offering in terms of the range of elements that make up a human life. Leviticus's "icon" also locates these elements within the broader context of the created world, through which, spatially and temporally, our lives take their form. If "any man," *'adam*, brings an offering to God, Moses is told to instruct the Israelites, he shall bring it to the door of the tabernacle (Lev. 1:2). This "bringing" is literally a "coming," a "coming near" in the way that God draws near to our fearful souls (Ps. 69:18) and in the way that our tears themselves draw near to God (119:169). *'Adam* comes into the world and offers; and as Leviticus presents this wider movement, the offerings are detailed in their breadth: flocks, harvests, food, clothing, plantings, songs, money, families, neighbors—all brought near to the Lord's presence in his courts.

It is also the case that these courts into which these offerings are brought are themselves the movable precincts of a wandering people. Leviticus is placed between the journeys of Israel in the desert (Exod. 40:38) and the unwinding paths of these journeys (the entire book of Numbers). *Lo, I come as a sojourner, and I offer all that this often aimless movement through the wilderness gathers to it.* The notion that the cult of offering in Leviticus constitutes a static code of formal rituals could not be further from the truth. The later chapters show us this clearly with their discussion of the feast days, defined by the geographical and calendrical details of their referents, exposing the sweep of creation, wandering, provision, and difficult obedience across the miles and years of a people's struggling existence.[2] *Lo, I come into the world, and I traverse it, says the Son of Adam, and as I go, the miles and minutes of my life are offered up. In this I do Thy will.*

When Paul speaks of offering up our bodies as a "living sacrifice" (Rom. 12:1), it is this whole life with its gathered but loosely held belongings—the stuff of a life—that is offered. But the stuff of a life that is literally transient, moving insofar as it comes and goes in the midst of a time and space, is not its own but is always God's to have given, to have offered first of all. I come to do your will, but with my *body* (Heb. 10:5, 10), whose offering is my death and the gathering of my life's contents as now divested, dispossessed by the one who is their Giver. The Levitical cult—continually misunderstood by Christians to this day—is fundamentally about this stuff of life, the stuff of a person's created being, the offering of which honors God's Name. The offering itself is always a "sacrifice" insofar as it is the giving up in thanks to God for that which is, in any case, always taken away by its fashioner.

Whatever is good in offering, in sacrifice, is by definition a mortal good. It is mortal because it too must disappear; it is mortal because its disappearance is bound to the blessing that is human life itself, the mortal createdness that constitutes being the object of God's love. It is important to grasp this fundamental aspect of offering, if indeed, for the Christian, being "delivered to serve God," to "worship God without fear" (Luke 1:74), the *avodat Hashem*, is what motivates and frames political life. For this implies that the political "good" of a people is concentrated on their mortal goods and on the offering up of these goods to God, the capacity for which is the goal of human ordering.

There is certainly a deeply intuited sense of this goal across history and cultures. Perhaps, in some "natural law" manner, this offering of our goods to God is a universal aspect of religion, and although religion has often served personal political power as much as God, the linkage of our material sacrifices to the peace of our common life has been steady.[3] This deep sense of politics as ordering the offering of mortal goods has, however, been steadily eroded, denigrated, and marginalized in modern times, and political theory as it has developed in the West, especially, has buttressed this marginalization by providing an alternative set of definitions for "the good" that politics is meant to serve. In short, "mortal goods" have been demoted, even rejected, as truly "good." Why, then, might we offer them at all to God?

The historical logic of these changes in conceptualizing the good is not always clear. One line lies in the distinction of "the good" from happiness. Aristotle most influentially pressed this point, injecting into the category of happiness (*eudaimonia*) a quality that could transcend this or that particular good. "The good" (*kalon* or *agathon*) might apply, after all, to transient and physical realities, including sensual pleasures, that could only falsely be attached to happiness, in large measure because they are limited. The goal of human life, in this perspective, lies in possessing—a concept that connotes a kind of participatory identity—the permanent, the stable, the transcendent. This can be achieved by a life shaped by virtues that engages the realities of the world in right proportion—for example, with patience and courage, generosity and justice. If we wish to call this kind of happiness the possession of "the Good" in some larger sense, then we must distinguish that capitalized "Good" from the "goods" that litter our mortal lives and often cause us to stumble in our quest for happiness, either because they are deceptive in their qualities or are simply weak and transient in their positive gifts. As we have seen, even happiness in this sense, according to Aristotle, is vulnerable to the limited character of mortal goods—*fortuna*, chance, circumstance, which may cause pain and sorrow—and so must be distinguished in turn from the utterly invulnerable condition of "blessedness" (the life of the *makarioi*).

The Christian tradition held on to these somewhat shifting definitions, transposing them into robust theistic terms: there are "goods" in a kind of general and loose sense, there are "mortal goods" in a more specific sense of limitation and transitory value, and there is the blessedness of the eternal Good who is God; but none of these different senses of "good" are connected in any essential or stable way. One can turn to the famous discussion by Augustine in his *City of God*, book 19, where he details the elements that ought properly to give value to the sojourner's life.[4]

Augustine here takes his cue from the categories of the Roman philosopher Varro, who outlined the good life as a "composite" reality, one that makes use of both bodily and spiritual goods through the exercise and ordering of virtue, in a way derived from Aristotle's framework but with a greater emphasis upon the necessary value of this-worldly realities. Augustine rejects this by underlining all the ills of bodily life that subvert the essential connection between mortal goods and the Good. The wedge he places between the two is enormous. The fundamental distinction he makes between lasting and nonlasting, transitoriness and permanence, he ties to the causative restrictions engendered by sin against God, which brought death into the world. Given sin and its poisoning of all things with limitation, we are driven to get away from sin's limiting handiwork and to seek God's eternal and unchanging goodness if we want any real happiness.

Augustine is not always consistent here, however, and he allows that mortal goods can be used for the sake of the Good in this fallen world, and hence that they have a historically essential role to play for the Good. Mortal goods, in this respect, can even reflect the Good as an embodied figure (the love of parents, for instance, might figure our love for God as a kind of shadow). But Augustine's general aim is to drastically thin out the realm of mortal goods. He enumerates these goods explicitly—household (which includes friendship), city, and world—but then works hard to show their corruption, instability, and lack of trustworthiness, contrasting them with corresponding "heavenly" realities (e.g., the saints). The fundamental figural move here is moral, and it moves in one direction only: the first term (the realm of earthly goods) seems to exist for the express purpose of manifesting its devalued status in comparison with its heavenly antitype. Hence, he argues, we rightly rejoice in the death of our friends, however much sorrow we may also feel, because they are "going to a better place."

In a way, Augustine in all this seems too bound by his pagan philosophical background. We have already mentioned his early work *De beata vita*, but it is worth returning to it for a moment. Written when he was a new Christian, this small treatise on the blessed life (or the life of beatitude) follows a general antique philosophical notion that happiness (*beatitudo*) lies in "possessing" the greatest good. But possession—Augustine, as we saw earlier, uses the basic verb for "to hold," *habere*—is dependent on enduring goodness, on nontransitoriness. Hence, no one can be truly happy with mortal realities, no matter how relatively good they seem. Happiness lies only with God, and hence true human happiness lies in *habere Deum*, "possessing God."[5] The contrast between types of "possession" maps onto the nature of the goods possessed. For Aristotle, by contrast with Augustine, we seek to possess virtues that reflect what is most permanent about *our selves*—our rationality, in practical and contemplative reasoning, and thus the habits that sustain such reasoning—because somehow they describe the intrinsic nature of the human being. Each thing has a nature that determines that thing's good, and natures are therefore, in some sense, more important than particulars. Human nature, then, shows us the overriding value of rationality and contemplation. Yet for Augustine and Aristotle both, "possession" is a key to discerning the nature of the Good.

The whole paradox of created existence as a good in and of itself, just in its unpossessed transitoriness as a gift, is ruined in this vision. For a key claim for Jews and Christians is that what is good is what is given us, not what we seek or what we possess, measured by some criterion of permanence. Thus, creation itself is a good, and the things of creation are goods, though they are but "dust." So too, of course, are our (not always fulfilled) capacities, such as rational reflection and practical reasoning. In a world that exists only through divine creation *ex nihilo*, however, our "nature," defined in terms of rationality, can mark secondary elements only with respect to the human "good" that is more properly viewed in terms of its composite character as a welter of various goods. I am coming out more on Varro's side than on Augustine's here.

Is politics about attaining heaven and the permanent? To think so is to sell one's soul to the engulfing corruptions involved with "bringing heaven to earth," the riptide of betterment. Politics can only be about the earth, if only because this is where practical reasoning is confined. But more importantly, as I will argue, politics is about the earth because this confinement—or, rather, "gifted identity"—is what it means to be a creature made by God.

For human beings, "the Good" of "the Good Life" is not the possession of God or the attainment of some end—the beatific vision, say—but the right ordering of God's goods offered to us. This is not to marginalize the beatific vision as an end to human life; it is, rather, to locate its "attainment" in a sphere that is distinct from the Good Life—distinct, that is, from our ordering of goods, distinct from the realm of our own attenuated capacities. It is not so much that the beatific vision is discontinuous with the Good Life; rather, it is a gift whose possession we cannot by the nature of the case orchestrate for ourselves. The beatific vision's continuity with the Good Life is precisely its giftedness—which encompasses all things—but now apprehended and enjoyed in a transcendent mode: earth transfigured rather than earth left behind. (Traditional discussions of the millennium or even a "new earth" speak to this.) Otherwise, if we tie the beatific vision to the Good Life in some continuous fashion, we in fact render it hostage to the very limitations that such a life within our mortal world necessitates.

Obviously, as Augustine rightly insists, the Creator God himself *is* the summum bonum, the "greatest good," on this view. But, versus Augustine and his contemporaries, I would insist that God is such a good, not as a possession to be grasped by employing our rational nature, but rather, in relation to human creatures, as a creator, a giver of gifts. To engage the Giver, the Good, is to engage his gifts, which are boundless but are also rooted in our created existence. Thus our lives, in their goodness, are not reducible to the functioning of our natural powers (or reason), with other realities standing as supports or obstacles to this; rather, the exercise of these powers determines, but only to some extent, our engagement with

God's gifting and gifts, which supervene upon our powers in an absolute way. All is grace (*Tout est grâce*), as Thérèse of Lisieux simply put it.[6] Happiness, if one can speak this way, is simply bound up with the exhaustive reality of this divine giving.

Augustine, to be fair, comes to insist on this as well, but not consistently when it comes to the shape of a human life. Still, he *does* see that "possessing" God in or through the course of a human life requires judgments and actions as well as, finally, habits of perception and understanding. Given his supreme valuing of permanence, he argues that we need to be able to recognize the penultimacy (at best) and transitory nature of earthly goods and thus know how to steer through their attractions and vulnerabilities in the search for the permanent. This need is properly guided by wisdom (*sapientia*). And this, in turn, is bound to the teachings of the Word or the Truth. The logic here is significant because, despite his theoretical demotion of earthly existence, Augustine ends up providing a vision—one he will develop over time—that sees happiness as bound up with the proper ordering of earthly life *in the service* of possessing God, and this proper ordering lies in fact with following the teachings of—being obedient to—Christ Jesus, whose coming to us lay in the form of the offering (not abandonment) of his mortal createdness.

Alas, the grounding categories of possession and permanence that are so central to Augustine's broader vision nonetheless lie behind the sweeping temporal-eternal framework of value that colors much Christian moral evaluation in a distorted way. The eternal, at least popularly, seems to mark values that stand outside creaturely reality and experience, values that are divine somehow yet are cleanly severed from that divine eternal reality that *in fact* created our mortal frames. Thus, the Christian tradition has in practice pressed for permanent possession over limited order and, indeed, has—when not simply succumbing to material greed and pleasure—adamantly discounted the eternally established good of limited mortal goods. Within this current, Christian politics has been either too grandly demanding—with possession practically expressed by coercion on behalf of the "truly" (eternally) good, in terms of habits and habit-forming symbols of the eternal—or too disdaining altogether of the world's undecipherable but inescapable constraints. Augustine insists that mortal goods—health, air to breathe, water, neighbors, social peace—are valuable to the degree that their good use leads us to immortality. They are otherwise not only useless but deceptive, leading those who enjoy them to hell.[7]

At least Augustine understood quite precisely the *mortal* character of the goods God gives us; and thus he understood the relativizing force they bring to bear on political regimes that are after larger claims. The mortal character of mortal goods—inescapable for both those who value and those who devalue them—relativizes both regimes and their programs because of the inbuilt failures that must characterize all political processes, especially those that strive for perfection of some kind. The "perfections" that are most frequently pursued by even the best political regimes or strategies, after all, tend to deny the "permanence," in experiential/moral terms, of mortality itself and of the goods within it. We cannot erase the fundamental vulnerability and limits of our lives and attachments (and of their perceived goods). To the degree that political life engages mortal goods as ordering goals, it will always fall short simply because any mortal order must crumble; and to the degree that political life seeks to escape such failure in pursuit of perfection, it will fail all the more miserably.[8] We cannot evade these failures because they define who we are as creatures. We can only offer them to God.

When Paul speaks in Romans 12:1 of offering our bodies to God as a "living sacrifice," he uses the exhortation as the opening to his discussion of what it means to be engaged in a common life within the One Body. This will mean taking in all the interactions and labors of that corporation, including its challenges, disgruntlements, and oppressions. He then notes that such a common life is rightly governed by the commands both of Jesus and of the Scriptures themselves (12:17–21), paraphrasing or echoing texts from Exodus, Deuteronomy, Proverbs, and the Sermon on the Mount. These texts speak, as we know, to matters of marriage, children, the life and material of food and livestock, damaged property (and people), conversations, testimony, slander, sexual norms and their transgressions, and the relations of all these things to neighbors.

These are all the mortal goods that Augustine wants to get away from, goods that, if worried over, drag us into the pit of transitory and shallow joys. It is true that, from an emotional vantage, Jesus himself sweeps away the material elements that inhabit our worries—"do not be anxious about," "take no thought of," food and clothing (cf. Matt. 6:25–34). Yet Jesus does not thereby sweep away their reality: God gives them to us as he chooses, one way or the other. Indeed, evil ("bad things," *kakia*) doesn't disappear in his promise; evil comes day by day, immediately, just enough for today (6:34). Jesus seems to think that God has it all properly proportioned. And if God does—God, the virtuous governor, in Aristotle's terms—then our calling is to let go of our own insistent proportionalizing, our calibrated functionalizing of these goods, in our attempts to achieve something "better." Mortal goods stand simply as goods from the Good, not as rungs in a ladder that, if properly climbed, will take us to heaven.

We can turn back now to the question of the "good" that we offer to God, the good of a "good offering" itself. Why speak of mortal *goods* at all, in a way that locates them in the context of "the Good"? Indeed, in English usage "goods" can refer simply to material property, especially things that are made, as in the phrase "worldly goods." So the early translators of the English Bible used the term "goods" in verses like 2 Chronicles 21:14, where God threatens the Israelites with an all-encompassing punishment that will touch their material livelihood—that is, their goods. Both the English "goods" and the more literal Hebrew "possessions" come at the summative end of a list that includes "your people, your children, your wives," which, along with all your "goods/possessions," God will wipe out with a plague. "Goods" in English thus gathers up the fullness of a human life, now in a broadly filiative context. "Property" would surely be too narrow a term in this sense. The same broad referent was in play when English translators applied the term "goods" to Jesus's words in Matthew 25:14, at the opening of his parable of the talents: "For the kingdom of heaven is as a man travel-ing into a far country, who called his own servants, and delivered unto them his goods." The Greek word here—*hyparchonta*—connotes "substance," that which makes up a life materially, but in an extended way.

The elision of goods and the Good is embedded in Scripture. As in En-glish, a single word in Hebrew, *tov*, covers it all. God pronounces creation itself "good" (Gen. 1:4). Goodness here is often of a kind of moral or spiritual order and finds its paradigmatic referent in the tree of the knowledge of good and evil (Gen. 2:17). Yet, just as often, *tov* is applied to the material order as well: to a valuable house or domestic animal, for instance (Lev. 27:10), or to business profit (Prov. 31:18). Goodness extends beyond an abstract moral realm. Old age is good (Gen. 15:15), as are many sons (30:20). In contrast to affliction, the good thus counts as a kind of "prosperous" existence (Jer. 42:6). And prosperity and its blessings are measured by possessions them-selves (Ps. 103:5; 1 Sam. 15:9).

"The Good" and "goods," then, merge into a certain equivalence. Evil, of course, will inhabit the places where our goods are threatened. Yet, if we gather up all of these elements, we encounter the same lexical difficulty of distinguishing the realm of "the Good" in the Old Testament as in English. When we offer God something, it is this "all" of our lives that comes up, not in their totality but in their breadth of particularity. The goods that we offer are rooted within the matter of our livelihoods: sheep, cattle, grain—money!—but also bodies, all of which involves also our relationships with others. These point to the ethical aspects of what is good, but never as a principle, never as some broad characteristic, but always as something given us by God, vibrant for a moment, then weakening or taken away and thus fundamentally limited.

The sojourner's goods, therefore, are no more than, but are also utterly inclusive of, the matters of mortal life. They are just these mortal goods that have been pushed to the edges of our concerns by our grand principles, in large part because they seem impertinent to the permanent and thus, at best, instrumental elements to be deployed—used—for the gaining of some greater good. But the paradoxical aspect of our createdness—that we are given everything that we are, and that just this is revealed in its miracle insofar as it is not ours and is always taken away—means that the limits that shape our existence are themselves elements of praise, just when we articulate them as the reflection of God's grace. Here the whole difficult aspect of "sacrifice" comes into view and touches our political lives.

We ascribe honor to God's Name, we serve God, as we come into the world of his presence and offer to him the mortal goods of our existence, the shape of our bodies as they are born, live, work, relate to other bodies, and die. This offering is our joining with God's claim that these mortal elements are good in themselves because they are the stuff, the matter, the goods of our createdness that is God's to have given. God announces that this creation is good, and his creatures reply in kind, but from the midst of and as defined by the moral limits that constitute their beings. "This is good," they say as they are born. "This is good," they say as they grow. "This is good," they acknowledge as they work. "This is good," they pray as they marry, bear and raise children, and build up and then lose in some way those they love and share their lives with. "This is good," they insist in their joys and even in their anguish. "This is good," they affirm as they and their goods disappear and die. "Naked came I out of my mother's womb, and naked shall I return thither: the LORD gave, and the LORD hath taken away; blessed be the name of the LORD" (Job 1:21). Job's utterance is the mortal fulfillment of the psalm's command, "Give unto the LORD the glory due unto his name: bring an offering, and come into his courts" (Ps. 96:8).

A true republic, Augustine argues, is one that sacrifices to the only true God. Rome could never have been a true republic since it sacrificed to demons and false deities, and in so doing so disordered its people's affections as to subvert justice and the right order of bodily self-control and reason. Augustine's difficult assessment of mortal life is on view in this discussion—it is miserable, imperfect, mired in temptation and failure, ever crying out for forgiveness, and longing for a future immortality. But his conviction that sacrifice forms the nexus of political life, for good or ill, seems right. As does his final claim in this discussion that, in Christ, the true sacrifice of the Christian to the true God, a sacrifice from which the blessings of political order flow, is the sacrifice of one's self with all its mortal limitations.[9] What might normally count as a political good—social peace, for instance—is only so within this Christian sacrifice, the offering of one's own mortal life.[10] "But who am I, and what is my people, that we should be able to offer so willingly after this sort? for all things come of thee, and of thine own have we given thee. For we are strangers before thee, and sojourners, as were all our fathers: our days on the earth are as a shadow, and there is none abiding" (1 Chron. 29:14–15).

The political bite of this service of offering, however, is real. As the aged Zacharias sings, we long for a divine deliverance that permits us to worship—to serve God—"without fear" (Luke 1:74); and this we pray for and work for, ourselves and with others. But this service is one of self-offering, which, as I have said, is by definition granted the largest scope possible in political terms: we are always in a position, in theory and within any political regime, to sacrifice our mortal goods. The theory, however, here meets a concrete political challenge. We can indeed offer our mortal goods to God anywhere, but *only insofar as we have learned to do so.* Just as God calls Moses at the opening of Leviticus and thereby lays out the framework of offering, someone must call us, as in Psalm 96, to "come into God's courts" and to bring our goods with us before our Maker. This is where Augustine rightly focused his concerns as his pastoral career unfolded, even as the social scaffolding of his world began to crumble about him: one must *teach* offering; one must learn it. If the church has a peculiar political vocation, one that is just hers alone, perhaps it is this teaching and learning.

For it is not the case that all suffering joins us to God; although it is the case that all suffering is capable of doing so—that is, capable of being offered to God in Christ. "Lo, I come," he says; and we say in response, "Look, we have given up everything that is ours and follow you!" (cf. Luke 18:28). This movement from the capacity to offer to the enactment of offering is probably the main political sphere of the Christian life, in which the question of how one teaches and how one learns rises to the summit of concern, something I will touch upon as we end this book. But before we can face this question more directly, we need still to reflect on what the ordering of our offering really amounts to. I turn to this in the next chapter, as I reflect on how we might consider what makes our offering good.

Six

The Beauty of Limits

But Jesus said, "Let her alone; why do you trouble her? She has done a beautiful thing to me. For you always have the poor with you, and whenever you will, you can do good to them; but you will not always have me. She has done what she could; she has anointed my body beforehand for burying. And truly, I say to you, wherever the gospel is preached in the whole world, what she has done will be told in memory of her."

Mark 14:6–9 (RSV)

Our service of God consists of the offerings we render to him. These offerings are the very goods of our mortal lives that mark our thanksgiving for the divine gift of our creation. The political implications of this fundamental reality are perhaps troubling in their anti-utilitarian tenor: to give to God what God has given to us seems to leave us where we have always been; the movement is a kind of circle rather than a progression, an addition, a new creation.

There is nothing wrong with considering our own works, viewed in terms of our human accomplishments, as an offering to God; baseball players, writers, and entrepreneurs have all done this in the past. Bach famously devoted his works to the glory of God alone. But there is a real tension here as well: Is it only what *we* actually achieve that can stand as a true gift to God? It may well be true, as Augustine wrote, that God crowns our merits as his own gifts, but what if we have no merits in any case?[1] Second-rate composers rarely have their unappreciated or even disdained productions granted such oblationary status. They simply toil away with little recognition. A politics without influential effect surely must seem pointless. In what follows I will take up this common intuition, which I suspect is deeply misleading when it comes to that which is most important: our very lives as themselves mortal gifts, "crowned" by the fact that they have been cherished for themselves and in terms of their mortal givenness—it is enough just to live and to die—and not for their usefulness.

The story of Jesus's anointing at Bethany is a striking example of the unsettling character of a Christian politics of mortality.

> While [Jesus] was at Bethany in the house of Simon the leper, as he sat at table, a woman came with an alabaster flask of ointment of pure nard, very costly, and she broke the flask and poured it over his head. But there were some who said to themselves indignantly, "Why was the ointment thus wasted? For this ointment might have been sold for more than three hundred denarii, and given to the poor." And they reproached her. But Jesus said, "Let her alone; why do you trouble her? She has done a beautiful thing to me. For you always have the poor with you, and whenever you will, you can do good to them; but you will not always have me. She has done what she could; she has anointed my body beforehand for burying. And truly, I say to you, wherever the gospel is preached in the whole world, what she has done will be told in memory of her." (Mark 14:3–9 RSV)

Verse 6 of this text from the RSV translation of Mark—"Let her alone. . . . She has done a beautiful thing to me"—epitomizes what one might call the opposition between political usefulness and the (mortal) good. The phrase was memorialized in recent cultural memory by the 1971 book of Malcolm Muggeridge that made Mother Teresa famous, *Something Beautiful for God*.[2] Muggeridge, a celebrated journalist of often acerbic irony and, for a long while, mostly anti-Christian sentiments, had nonetheless long been struggling with his professed agnosticism, and in the late 1960s he had formally embraced the faith (as a Protestant, and then in 1982 joining the Catholic Church). Shortly afterward he went to Calcutta (Kolkata) to see for himself what this purportedly saintly nun was up to. He came back and produced a film and accompanying book that launched Mother Teresa into the international spotlight. The book was more of an impressionistic essay than, certainly, a biography or theological study. He tagged along with her and the other sisters, talked to her, filmed her in this or that context.

Like many afterward—including many passionate critics of Mother Teresa's order, the Sisters of Charity, such as the merciless Christopher Hitchens[3]—Muggeridge was intrigued that Mother Teresa focused on simple hospitality to the poor and dying rather than on alleviating their condition (through, for example, developed hospital care) or dealing with the social causes of their suffering. Her mission was to make them feel "wanted" and "loved," she would say—no more than that. Mother Teresa seemed well aware that, like those who were offended by the money wasted on anointing Jesus, some took offense at her ministry. Muggeridge wrote that "Mother Teresa is fond of saying that welfare is for a purpose—an admirable and a necessary one—whereas Christian love is for a person. The one is about numbers, the other about a man who was also God." Muggeridge explained this in terms of Mark 14: "Doing something beautiful for God is, for Mother Teresa, what life is about. Everything, in that it is for God, becomes beautiful, whatever it may be; as does every human soul participating in this purpose, whoever he or she may be."[4]

"Why was the ointment thus wasted? For this ointment might have been sold for more than three hundred denarii, and given to the poor." The issue here, for the woman in Bethany who does a "beautiful thing" for Jesus, is not that she has somehow spiritualized the service of God, making love a "work," envisioning the heart and its affections as an artist. The issue, at least as Jesus tells it, is how bodies are treated, in this case his own: with care, certainly, but also with something ravishing—perfume—and, in the other Gospel accounts, tears and the hair of the woman's own head. The idea of "something beautiful"—*kalon ergon* in the Greek—has often been rendered as "good work" (so KJV). If that is so, such "good works" might, and surely should, include the tending of the sick and the dying and the welcoming of the poor, but also the building of hospitals and enabling the expansion and improvement of health care.

The use of the word *kalon* is significant. Jesus himself does "good works" (*kala erga*), in the sense of miracles or signs (cf. John 10:25, 41), acts that are so astonishing as to give rise to the praise of God (cf. Luke 5:26; 18:43). So too does Jesus commend "good works" in the Sermon on the Mount (Matt. 5:16 RSV): "Let your light so shine before men, that they may see your good works [*kala erga*] and give glory to your Father who is in heaven." Somehow bound to the "light" and to visibility, perceptible to others, these works blaze before the eyes of onlookers and cause amazement and praise. "Good works," as rendered in English, can also literally translate the more straightforward *erga agatha* (e.g., Acts 9:36). Is there a difference? Probably not: the literal good deeds (*erga agatha*) are surely also "beautiful" in one way or another, and there is no point in making too much of the lexical distinction. It is one that is equally blurred in the Hebrew of the Old Testament. Hebrew words translated as "beauty" in English—*yapheh, tipheret,* and so on—often engage the glory of God (or glittering royal splendor) in rolling together the senses of honor, sightly attraction, and dazzling light. This is true in the Psalms (e.g., 96:6) but also, from another angle, in the founding linguistic exemplars of Genesis. The "goodness" (*tov*) of creation itself—see Genesis 1:4, regarding the light—is, in the Greek of the Septuagint, described as *kalon*. In English terms, then, the creation of the light is—as much as any "good work," indeed, as the very foundation of any good work—"beautiful," just as is the fundamental distinction between good and evil (Gen. 2:9), which we could articulate, as does the Septuagint, in terms of "the beautiful and the miserable" (*kalon* and *ponēron*).

I am pausing on this linguistic issue because it has sometimes bedeviled philosophical discussion. The Good, the True, and the Beautiful—are they not distinct? Do we not need to parse their particularities, as we would with an intricate grammar, in order to get our actions sorted out properly? Aristotle seems to make some such distinctions, though there is debate as to what they amount to. But in fact these categories—the *verum*, *bonum*, and *pulchrum* ("the true, the good, the beautiful," along with other divine qualities that were seen as underlying the integrity of created being, such as "oneness" and "identity")—are mutually refracting. In God's absolutely simple being they are in fact identical, so that, in human terms, they refer to each other necessarily. Lexical distinctions are useful, however, insofar as they bring to our consciousness some particular aspect of, in this case, God's singular being that can clarify our existence in relation to God.[5]

To speak of "the beautiful," then, is to bring something specific into view regarding our lives, some aspect of the singular reality of God's exhaustive priority with respect to our existence. "The beautiful" speaks of a kind of created "light" that touches a person and "manifests" God in a way that elicits praise. In Mark 14 (and in the versions of the event in Matt. 26 and, without the phrase itself, John 12), the language of *kalon ergon* tells us that the anointing of Jesus's body beforehand is "beautiful," a kind of service—like that of a foot-washing slave, like Jesus himself, in fact, as in John 13. It is a service rendered to one who will die, born out of a love for and an honoring of the mortal body before whom one stands in the present. The body of the Messiah, in its comprehensive breadth of enfleshed human experience, receives this gift of honor and thanks in the form of something valuable and enticing but also something humiliatingly personal (tears, hair), elements that are themselves aspects of mortal giftedness. The gift is "beautiful," and because of this it thereby also manifests the True and the Good and all qualities of the divine being, just in this single "work."

If the Good Life is constituted by these kinds of good works—beautiful works—then the Good Life, in this case, is essentially defined by the nature of what a life *itself is*. This is a central Aristotelian premise, for what is good can be discerned only according to the character of the thing or act in question. In the Gospel story, what is good is tied to bodies and their destinies—Jesus's, the woman's, and their deaths—and to the forms of toil and production, with all their failures and exclusions ("the poor" who might have been helped here but are not) that generate and distribute limited luxuries. Not this but that is chosen as an expenditure—not there but here for a man who is about to die. This is how the woman chooses to order her goods.

Contrary to common conceptions, then, "the Good Life" does not refer to a good soul. Instead, "the Good Life" must refer to the shape of a life, to the ordering of its mortal works, and this, not in a purely Aristotelian sense, but as "a thing of beauty" in its order, parts, and form over time and as a whole. Such beauty presupposes and is built up of mortal elements: the whole given in its limits and their circumference. The good, in this sense, is given in the beautiful that is offered to God in the course of and through the ingredients of a life; but this is determined by and reflects "what is the case," the shape of mortality itself, and hence "the true."

Here is where "good works" fall, including the beautiful work of the woman in Simon's house. For her anointing of Jesus constitutes the concentration into one act of a whole range of mortal elements—bodies on their way to death, bodies offered in demeaned service, artifacts of sensible delight, a meal, the hospitality of a (former?) leper, the tension of moral focus (money for the poor or for something else). That any of this, especially in its assemblage, might create or embody "the beautiful" is an astonishing claim that deserves our attention. Finally, Jesus says, this densely packed but simple act is expressing in its own way "the gospel." That is, the gifts of mortal service show forth Christ Jesus himself; they are an opening to the Truth of all things. When the author of the early Christian *Epistle to Diognetus* describes the transcendent signs of Christian witness—that is, signs that might indicate to onlookers the presence of the true God—he lists activities such as marital fidelity, the cherishing of children, gracious speech, generosity, and patience.[6] These, in their ordering or shaping of a life, are beautiful.

It is important here to see how the matter of mortality—whether retrospectively and in light of the promised redemptive life of the Messiah, or simply on its own terms—cannot therefore be reduced to sin. While death, we are told, is bound to sin's entry into creation (e.g., Rom. 5:12), sin does not exhaust the character and experience of being mortal, for that is something expressive of our very being, which is composed of created earth and divinely granted breath (Pss. 39:5; 103:14–16; Eccles. 12:7; 1 Cor. 15:47).[7] More fundamentally, this dust and breath is a reflection simply of the fact *that* we are and of this being in its substance—that is, as creatures, we are therefore a gift from God. It is a reflection, that is, of goodness and truth in their outward expression, as a created form. Hence, mortality, understood as the collection of mortal forms—the wealth of creaturely being and relationship—is the divine artisan's achievement; and mortality embodied actively, subjectively by an offerer and objectively as an offering, is a matter of divine delight, of beauty. To bury a dead body; to anticipate such death and burial; to honor that body's coming and going with the material stuff that comes from human toil, and to do so in the midst of vying moral demands—all this is to make something beautiful for God, because it actually reflects who God is as Truth, Goodness, and Beauty.

Mortality, understood as the set of limited elements that make up a creature, is a good and is rendered a sacrificial offering of praise when just these elements are deployed and fashioned according to a form that can manifest God's being. The articulation of the elements of mortality as "mortal goods," then, depends upon their fashioned form within the limits of created existence. The seemingly aesthetic aspect of this kind of talk can be distracting, but it is still worth pressing because of its implication in almost all forms of politics (if only by deliberate negation). In the limited context of the Gospel story (Mark 14:3–9), for instance, the burial of the dead is a political matter, just as we know from the breadth of human culture and, for example, in the Western canon, from a play like Sophocles's *Antigone*.

Thus it has always been assumed and asserted that the cosmos itself is characterized by formliness of some kind. The term "chaos," which one might use in popular, secular physics, is in fact always belied by the search for and formulation of "laws" or predictable frameworks, whether mathematical or physical, that somehow express what encountered reality "is." Genesis and the long tradition of Christian reflection on creation have primordially informed this modern materialist outlook: God turns the "formless" (and thus imperceptible, as the Greek of the Septuagint has it)—the "trackless" wastes of the wilderness, as the Hebrew word was later used (cf. Job 12:24)—into "things": shapes, forms, and entities that can be encountered, followed, traced, and named (Gen. 1:2, 5; 2:19; 3:20). Creation is an ordered set of forms. This is the sense that Renaissance theorists had when they spoke of divine *disegno* as natural order—a network of forms and shadows—that artists then followed so as to engage their own inventive energies as a kind of shadow of God.[8] Secular philosophers, including social and political philosophers such as Jane Bennett, are tentatively re-discovering this, spurred in part by concerns over environmental policy: the world is made up of irreducibly wonderful "things," each of its definite kind.[9] If creation is good in the eyes and words of God, that goodness is bound to creation's formliness, its "thingness," which includes bodies in particular, whose ordering then becomes a matter of artistry of its own kind. Ordering things, the land and its forms, foodstuffs, and animals and human relations—Leviticus can be read as a book of mortal beauty. Limits themselves form the stuff of beauty and thus its coordination and choreography.

Following this out, as we will do in a small way, can make politics seem a subset of some larger metaphysical aesthetics in which the ordering of limits becomes a major criterion for justice and decision-making. In mod-ern terms, such a subordination of politics seems problematic in that it can arguably lead to valuing stasis—a given form of order—over change. To rattle the great "chain of being" is to invite chaos.[10] Such an imagined invitation may seem to support conservatism of a radical kind. Be that as it may, if any being is actually alive, it must have a form. And mortality itself can be described as the quite *particular* form of any creature that, because it is God-given, is always vulnerable to its own self-possession, an act that by definition cannot maintain itself and tends to dissolution. To be mortal—that is, to be created—is to have a shape. To offer to God what is mortal—to serve God—is to provide a form to this shape that, however beyond our grasp to hold in a steady fashion, discloses the praise that is inherent in the creature's very being before God's eyes.

What exactly constitutes a "form" is, however, hardly obvious. Still, all theories of form involve a reflection on limits. To take only one of many such theories, there is the widely influential claim by the early twentieth-century critic Clive Bell that art is characterized by "significant forms" and that just these kinds of forms—not anything, and not in any way—elicit aesthetic emotions or responses.[11] "Formalism'" in aesthetic theory, espe-cially in modernity, is a relative to other theories regarding the particularities of form, the "just this" that determines the kind of art one is dealing with. If an artwork is conceptually grounded, one must know what an "idea" is, as opposed to—and limited in relation to—something else. If art involves moving people affectively or (in a wider kind of movement) changing soci-ety, one must be able to define what an emotion is or isn't and what counts as change. Or, in a more classic mode, if one thinks of art as the imitation of nature, one must ponder what constitutes "representation." However one wishes to understand it, a form is a delimited entity that is somehow ordered so as to be identifiable, even if not well understood.

Of course, automobiles are forms; so too are microorganisms, grains of rice, and old clothes. One might wonder whether theories of aesthetic formalism can be applied to this more basic level of reality that constitutes the things of the world. Are we to characterize *everything* that fills the earth by those qualities that formalists like Bell ascribe to art: organic unity, orchestrated diversity, balance, visual or aural dynamism, and purpose or aim? Modernist aesthetics, by the early twentieth century, was struggling with just this kind of question: Where is the line distinguishing artistic form from commercially manufactured objects or "found" artifacts within the world (collages, Dada, collections of dead insects)? The fact that the question is a matter of debate simply points to the more inclusive notion of form qualifying all entities that we can identify, even imaginary ones. We live in a world of forms; for we live as creatures within a creation that has its beginnings and its endings, its names and places, its times and colors.

We might think that the forms human beings create are peculiar; philosophers, in identifying art, can speak of human intention as a necessary element of production, through which purpose imposes a new order on or demands an elicited articulation of order from sets of created realities— molding a lump of clay, tracing a line on an empty surface. Even collections of dead insects have been intentionally laid out in this or that series that involves certain human choices, though a viewer may choose to approach the series in a variety of ways. That said, the intentional order that a human artist might apply to the things of the world cannot escape the nature of their own being, however transformative the artistic action may be; these elements of created reality, pure and simple, have their own form, which both precedes but also survives the work of art itself. Nothing a human being makes is ever independent of the preexisting forms of creation; and these frequently survive the human artistic production (ruins, detritus, decompositions).

Such an inescapable form, which precedes and survives human artistry, may involve the *concreta* of life itself, of which art is their mimetic and illuminating "imitation." The definition was classically presented by Aristotle[12] and was still regnant through the eighteenth century: art is inevitably concerned with matter and flesh, even the temporal interactions of the created world, to which all mimesis must return. Novels, poems, and depictions of one kind or another are based on already-existing forms. These are independent of the work of art, for they finally follow their own history, just as the lithe figure of a human body must finally return to the dust. If not these more complex forms, we can at least say that the ground and end of art may be reduced to the material of its production: stone or oiled pigment, wood or some field of color. There is no human "art" apart from these created realities, which are simply given to us, and are found amid the collection of things that make up our world and the portions of it we inhabit over time. Statues crumble; paintings fade, rot, or burn; objects of one kind or another disintegrate; and sounds dissolve into fading waves. The intentional aspect of human art—its own peculiar formliness—must always give way to the deeper forms of divine intention that constitute their createdness in the first place. We live among and as a set of mortal forms that are simply given us by God, and it is these we feebly order or are ordered by. The interplay between the two—God's giving and our ordering—is disproportionate.

If created life has a form, then, it is a form that follows this divine disproportion, whereby human intention finally submits itself to God's own artistry. If the form of a life is analyzed in these terms somehow—and certainly every human life must be admitted as having a form—that form will be complex and dependent on the fundamental shaping given it by God, one that is metaphysically prior to any human art. The purely human aspect of making "something beautiful" will rely less on its matter or its final destiny—this is always God's in the first place—than on its small human directedness, the "for God," the offering. The result of this basic reality is that, whatever terms we use to describe the matter of a life, its form will be something beautiful as it expresses praise to God for the very gift of its being. Such praise marks the distillation of the divine disproportion, as it were, that describes the form of our life. On this score, the formal criteria will always somehow return to and articulate this disproportioned nature and character of the gift itself: "You made me."[13]

It is important to stress this creative disproportion here: a beautiful life is *not* a life created by human beings. A beautiful life is, in human terms (for God knows the true beauty of all things), a life created by God that is acknowledged as such with human thanks. Such acknowledgment is, to be sure, deliberately offered and thus entails human intentionality somehow. But this human response is a paradoxical, creative act in that its entire production lies in lifting up only what it is already given. The disciplines involved in such a lifting up are real enough. But the offering adds nothing to the matter offered, which is all God's. Milton's notion of the poet who is "himself a poem" is alluring but misleading, unless the language of such a poem be God's in the first place.[14] And so it is, as enunciated in the divine scriptural words themselves: the more we recognize our resemblance to the living forms by which God has ordered the world's life—this is one way of understanding what Scripture is—the more we affirm the beauty of the lives we have. Here we can provide a concluding definition: a beautiful life is one that the Scriptures somehow utter and whose utterances the human creature gratefully assumes. The woman who washes Jesus's feet not only does something beautiful but also becomes the very beauty of any human life wherever and however she is somehow found within our own existence. She lives within the words of the Scriptures: "I am she," we will say at some point, and our attempt at explaining how and where this identity emerges will be the uttering of our gift. "Truly, I say to you, wherever the gospel is preached in the whole world, what she has done will be told in memory of her" (Mark 14:9 RSV).

It is useful to underline this point, since the well-shaped life has often been reduced, even in Christian terms, to moral virtue or obediential achievement. Aristotle and Augustine—to mention again these two influential theorists for our modern presuppositions—had their own lists of characteristics on this score, as we have seen. Aristotle's ordering of the virtues, in their moderated interplay, frames the Good Life as closely as is possible in this world, beset as our worldly existence is with misfortunes and stumbling blocks. While the best life might be the contemplative life of wisdom, that is impossible for most people, as we have seen, simply given the probabilities of suffering. Augustine is quite focused on these probabilities and reckons that the virtuous life, as the philosophers might imagine it, is both practically impossible as well as inadequate, theoretically, when compared to the character of divinely created human purpose. The practical impossibility is given in the misery of mortal limits as we experience them in a fallen world, and the inadequacy in the fact that the traditional virtues simply leave out the central end of love, which permeates all created purpose, given the reality of God's infinite priority. Thus, divine forgiveness is far more powerful in its conferral of beauty than any otherwise defined virtuous life; and the truly good life of any Christian, navigating the miseries of this world as a pilgrim, lies in obediently ordering the love of God and neighbor in the course of mortality's pinching environment.[15]

Augustine's refashioning of virtue in terms of divine grace seems inevitable for the Christian. But the line between his challenge to the philosophers and a reductionistic lapse into law-keeping is easily crossed, and Augustine crossed it himself over and over. The inhabiting of divine command, or adjusting in its shadows, or crumbling before its demands—these properly become the colors on the canvas of a life more often than not, and there must be a way to take account of this in a more central manner, rather than discarding the colors simply as the pigments of sin. Leviticus, in this light, is more than a ritual or moral code (as Christians often read it); rather, it is a book of mortal beauty, just insofar as its intense gaze is aimed at the most proximate sources of human relation and their fragile integrity. The great warnings of chapter 26 are, that is, part of the divine gift even in their imposition, as the striking narrative intrusions into the book (e.g., of Aaron's and Shelomith's sons [Lev. 10; 24:10–23]) seem to demonstrate, along with the placement of the book as a whole within the narrative canon of Israel.[16] Divine judgment received in thanks is just as much a part of the beautiful life as is God's mercy retold.

This is a crucial claim, one obviously not acceptable to everyone. Today's funeral sermons and their eulogies reveal a telling confusion here.[17] By and large and at its best, the tradition has used such occasions simply to reaffirm scriptural claims and hopes, and perhaps to locate the deceased within this larger affirmation. By contrast, modern sermons or remarks at death tend to pursue two lines of reflection. First, they may focus on the dead themselves, offering stories about the kind of person he or she was—quite precisely, their virtues, retold in a small frame. Alternatively, they are often about some single attitude of God toward the dead in general ("life," "love"), evading the quite discrete, hard edges of commands and disobedience that are scattered through the years of the remembered person's existence. One catches glimpses, behind these two tendencies (often mixed up), of the dead person's created—that is, mortal—form: the stories told in modern eulogies that consist of familial moments; divine love is offered to grieving children; the dead person was beset by some unspoken burden; and those who listen realize, unconsciously perhaps, that the life here remembered was mostly made up of the struggle with temporal matter, all of it now unmentioned and left drifting within a scriptural shadowland.

Admittedly, the framework of human virtue and wisdom and of divine judgment, reward, and punishment—all scripturally rooted—has unintentionally sustained this narrow vision. But narrow it is. Obedience is only one aspect, however important (even if often unrealized), of the recognition of divine gift that the offering of our lives entails. Virtue emerges not in the perfection of our following but in the struggle to do it at all. Virtue comes to be, then, usually only in the midst of a difficult and often unrealized attempt to navigate that which *subverts* our obedience—testing, suffering, frustration, anger, and despair. But just here the scriptural center of the good life—the beautiful life—comes into view. For the navigation of evil days, in its details, is itself "beautiful" insofar as these details follow the divine design of the world that the Scriptures themselves embody. The Bible is, in its historical format (which includes the lived realities that form the context of legal and prophetic scriptural texts), the presentation of this navigation, better and worse in its skill and outcome. Cain and Abel, Noah's children, the patriarchs and their families, Israel, the judges, Saul, David, Solomon, the kings and queens of the people, and the prophets in their midst—all these display the shape of engaging the "testing" that comes to all (1 Cor. 10:13). The recognition of these accounts as our own, just in this identification, stamps our lives with the beauty that God would grant them.

Consummated obedience cannot quite fathom such beauty, a point I must continue to press, and an inability to acknowledge obedience's limits in this regard continues to bedevil our vision of the Good Life. We inevitably ask, in the face of the biographies of Ahab and Jezebel or of Jehoram and Athaliah, "In what sense can these be called 'something beautiful,' such that they can stand as offerings to God?" They are so only as they embrace Scripture's own utterance of their forms, something that others may do of them for lack of any such recorded confession from the lips of their own actors. We speak for the dead. For even Ahabs have moments of self-recognition, whose abyssal tremors must rock the depths.

Most lives do not reach the lurid pitch of Ahab and Jezebel; and many quite deliberately strive after the concretely positive scriptural forms that are often lifted up as moral exemplars: "Blessed is the man that . . ." (Ps. 112; or Ps. 1), or "Who can find a virtuous woman? . . . She will" do this and that (Prov. 31:10, 12). These kinds of texts are read at Shabbat meals, for the blessing of husbands and wives. But Ahab and Jezebel lurk about our tables too. After all, the forms involved in these scriptural descriptions of blessing always touch upon *particular* lives, which include marriage and parenting and have in view intricate relational networks and outcomes. Such lives involve, as well, toil or work and even wealth of a kind, and human beings are called to apply themselves in ways that order such relations, work, and possession according to scriptural command. Just such blessings uttered cast their net around a vast breadth of intricate hopes, failures, and evasions. To read Psalm 112 and Proverbs 31 each week, as at the Shabbat meal, in the presence of those caught in this net with us is not so much to render their words irrelevant, as if they had no real referent in our midst, as it is to throw oneself, even with one's dissimilarities to the figure, into the hands of their formative power, which must include the lives we offer in their grasp.

Scriptural formliness is therefore limited neither to commands nor to predictions of the future. The elements of Ahab and Jezebel, or of our dissimilarities with the "blessed man" or "good wife," are aspects included in the comprehensive fit or set of the universe, which takes in the full scope of created experience, much as the book of Job, with its odd avoidance of either law or history, suggests. Lives are beautiful insofar as their fit (a fit that is always actual), along with all these other realities, is *recognized*. All is good and thus beautiful in the eyes of God, even "evil," insofar as it is transformed by God's good doing (cf. Gen. 50:20). The offered life is the naming of that truth, goodness, and beauty. That naming is given in the identification of a life's scriptural form: "this is that," in the great figural trope of Acts 2:16 (where "this day" is the "that day" spoken of in Joel's vision), a truthful trope that includes all the limits of our lives, imposed and unintended, wrongly chosen or not, which are recognized as God-inscribed.

We here come to another important conclusion as to the shape of a beautiful life: lives of obedience or habituated attitude are truly virtuous only insofar as they press our recognitions and naming of this as that, my life as Scripture's life. Such lives are not virtuous primarily insofar as they exhibit principled characteristics, such as justice or love. Rather, a life of righteousness will fit with the justified Zacchaeus's life, and that of love with the woman in the house of Simon the leper. This is why, as we shall see, straightforward practices of reading the Bible, of catechesis, of scriptural worship—practices of recognizing what is beautiful—are all central Christian virtues. Their upholding is therefore, from one perspective, the central political aim of the Christian life. Furthermore, the recognition and naming that the beautiful life involves, whether the life of Miriam or Aaron, goes far beyond the practice of this or that sustaining virtue. It is bound up with all the things done to us, the pressures, the falls, the hard and also wonderful encounters, the sufferings, the judgments, and the tested joys of our lives that mark the contours of providence. If we are to call the beautiful life "virtuous," that character must designate the grand beauty that marks not particular acts, habits, or attitudes alone but their place within the textured event of praise itself.

Therefore, just because it is *these* kinds of lives that scriptural form embodies, that form also engages vicissitude: a future with "evil tidings" that seem ready to invade (of which the man "is not afraid" [Ps. 112:7] and at which the woman "laughs" [Prov. 31:25]). Here one thinks of Job, who, with his wife, might well have found their forms within Psalm 112 and Proverbs 31, even as the corridors of these texts now rumble with details that trouble both the figures of this couple and those who read them. One can also think, therefore, of other lives—shorter, differently ordered: Saul's, Jonathan's, Rahab's, Naomi's, those of the widows and the abandoned that are scattered about the Scriptures. The shape of each life is made beautiful by the recognition of its ordering according to—"perforce," we could say—the law and commandments and their judgments, or to the will of God made clear.

It is this recognized ordering "according to the Scriptures" that constitutes the outlines of the beauty these lives portray and actually embody, in both obedience and disobedience, judgment and mercy.

In each case, furthermore, mortal limits themselves give form to a life, and the "form" of encounter with these limits provides the particular shape of a life span. Whether in regard to Jonathan, Job, or Rahab, the beauty of each of these lives is given between birth and death: amid parental and familial relations, in sexual struggle, in hostile opposition, in uncertain friendships, and in the bodily forms of growth and suffering. As these are *named* before God in a way congruent with the given realities of God's own creation of such a life and its context, all the aspects of each life find their place: learning, playing, dressing, engaging, enduring disease and harm, emotional challenge and debilitation, geographic and spatial location and dislocation. Every aspect ramifies with age, if age is given—into work, communities of various kinds, actions and tasks, roles, new loves and hatreds, subjections and offerings, sexual relations, children, and weakening, even to death itself. Well may it all be very brief; it is also all very complicated, if one were to stop and trace, parse, and follow each element in any given moment.

The "form" here is not the virtuous or vicious making of a human creature in itself. The form is what God has made this person to be within the world. The form's beauty is granted in the confession drawn from the human creature's recognition of Scripture's own description of how the limits of birth and death hold together this infinite complexity somehow, limits provided by the Maker of life and death itself (Deut. 32:39). The psalmist who proclaims, "I am fearfully and wonderfully made" (Ps. 139:14), utters this thanksgiving in the context of blasphemy, hatred, enmity, wickedness, and blood (139:19–22)—a realm explored in detail throughout the whole of the Bible and whose darkness and light, as we would subjectively feel it, together "shine" forth as God's (139:12). To speak in just this way about just this life is the only way to fulfill, as it were, Milton's otherwise sentimental quest for the poetic life.

To offer our lives as "something beautiful for God," then, involves recognizing them as being given in the forms of Scripture and giving thanks. This is obviously quite different from most other common ways that our culture (including, often, our ecclesial culture) identifies, evaluates, and shapes the forms of a good life. For in most contemporary contexts these forms are usually defined in terms of productivity (of some quantifiable good), contribution (to some quantifiable end), and accomplishment (of some quantifiable task). It is all horribly restrictive, reducing the form of a human life to what is left when most of its matter has been whittled away.

The common vision of the Good Life picks out only a small portion of the complex matter that forms an actual life, a life as it is constituted by the created form given from God's hand. In addition, popular notions of the Good Life neglect and often obscure so much that darkens and besmears the forms of human living—the "hidden" truths of our lives. We get prurient glimpses of these failures through the now regular "revelations" of misdeeds and distorted passions on the part of the celebrated, uncovered by an ever more sophisticated investigative technology that we would be horrified to imagine could be turned against us (though it sometimes is). These are techniques and practices whose end is the destruction of all artistry, whether human or divine.

Were David alive today—as he is in our own lives—he would most likely be submerged in scandal, gossip, and widespread repudiation—and not without warrant. Yet the life of David is a beautiful life. The terrible episodes involving Uriah, Bathsheba, David's murderous lies, and the dead child born of his misdeeds are, taken as a string of actions and events, morally repugnant. But woven into his repentant humiliation, which signals their place in his life as a whole—"My days belong to you, O Lord, even as you judge me!"—they take their part in a life that, over and over again, he offers to God in a display of thanksgiving that names his own identity in terms of unworthy receipt. Here is where beauty gleams, as it does for all those who name their lies and their otherwise desultory experiences as joined to David's deeds and humble repentance.

This naming—from one's own lips, from the lips of others, and ultimately from God's merciful decree—is one expression of human dignity. The fullest expression of this dignity is the naming of Jesus Christ, in open confession, as the One True Man whose form holds our own. Our lives, just in their mortality, are given in the forms of Jesus's life or, in Barth's stark assertion, are their "shadows": "All pain, all temptation, as well as our dying, is just the shadow of the judgment which God has already executed in our favour," a shadow (we might say "figure" or created "form") that includes, whether enumerated or not, all the mortal goods of our existence and their design.[18] And the form of Jesus is the most beautiful of all: "And the Word was made flesh, and dwelt among us, (and we beheld his glory, the glory as of the only begotten of the Father,) full of grace and truth" (John 1:14).

"Let her alone; why do you trouble her? She has done a beautiful thing to me. . . . And truly, I say to you, wherever the gospel is preached in the whole world, what she has done will be told in memory of her." Despite the lip service paid to democratizing human value, most of the common cultural forms that measure the Good Life are profoundly elitist: they consign the vast majority of the human race to formlessness and thus to scriptural dissimilarity and therefore, finally, to mute self-possession (versus God-possession). After all, how many lives are filled with quantifiable productivity, contributions, and accomplishments, including those that somehow match the full range of traditional virtues, let alone of scriptural command—smarts, discipline, wealth, sobriety, moderation, philanthropy? Little of this was on display in the home of Simon the leper. Yet it was a home filled with beauty.

By ignoring the rooted, mortal character of what is beautiful, much of our "productive" culture denies to most people's lives their sacrificial capacity, through which, for instance, a psalm is said and one's life is displayed in a quiet epiphany: "I am a worm, and no man" (Ps. 22:6), we may mutter at our most self-critical. "My wounds stink and are corrupt because of my foolishness" (38:5), we may realize with stricken astonishment. "My flesh trembleth for fear of thee" (119:120). "Remember, O LORD, the children of Edom in the day of Jerusalem" (137:7). These are all pieces of a life (and there are many others, like Pss. 46:1; 76:1; 116:1) whose unremarkable and often unwanted ingredients are what elicit such recognitions. No doubt, accomplishments and contributions according to this or that metric *can be* true offerings of beauty. But they have little intrinsic connection to the shaping of the specific mortal forms—how we navigate our births, generations, and deaths "in accordance with" the Scriptures—that constitute the Good Life. For most contemporary cultural forms of the good, in their search for a "future," for something beyond the gifts of everydayness in its constraining grip, constitute instead an orientation unrelated to those limits that both define us and to which we will finally succumb.

If politics cannot make us better human beings or give us a better world, then politics will have to be reframed so as to give us what is already here: our selves, in their true form, their form that is God-given and thus God-taken. "Let her alone; why do you trouble her? She has done a beautiful thing to me." Politics is what the Christian does with others in order to provide such a service of offering, the well-shaped artifact of a mortal life that properly reflects and names, and thus recognizes, what "is," what is true. Every Christian is thus an artist of mortality, and our politics the framing of an art, a true and beautiful offering for one another and to God.

I have mostly concluded the first part of my reflections, indicating in a very general manner the way that mortal goods constitute the center of the good life we seek for ourselves and for those we love. And general my discussion has been, well I admit. Still, the outline is clear enough: while a good life may seem an unrealizable hope in the midst of evil days, I have suggested that only the mistaking of our mortality as itself an evil leads us to such hopelessness. Our mortality and its lived elements, the things we love and let go of, work for and find unachievable, enjoy only to yearn for again, the families that form our world and burden it—all these in themselves *constitute* our creation as granted from God and God alone. I have argued that a beautiful life is indeed possible in any day, for our days are beautiful insofar as we receive them from God as God's own offering. And in this reception we offer them to God in thanks. Such offering is a process by which we come to see our days as ones of God-given miracle (hence as humanly untethered and impermanent), recognizing their gifted form, whatever their mortal burdens, in their simple divine enunciation—that is, in the Scriptures. That is good, that is beautiful, and that is the truth of our lives.

I will end this section in the following chapter by describing what this offering might look like, even in my own life. The act of such personal description is hardly easy, and I approach it only glancingly. My attempt at description demonstrates, at least in my case, how difficult it is to accept my general claims in all this if we have not been *taught* the skills of seeing our lives as God's gift and of recognizing their gifted form as God's scriptural word about them. This incapacity on my part—in both learning and teaching—is one I deeply regret. The writing of a letter to my children, toward which this essay aims, is only one small act of atonement for this lack, to paraphrase Lord Chesterfield. But in the light of such regret, and in deepening this one small act, we can then turn to the more specifically political questions that touch upon those forces that in fact constrain and ought properly to focus our efforts at shaping a good and beautiful life, that one great offering that confesses the true value of our beings and our loves.

Seven

An Incomplete Life

Be silent before the LORD and wait expectantly for him; do not be agitated by one who prospers in his way, by the person who carries out evil plans.

Psalm 37:7 (CSB)

I have been talking about "the beautiful life" and insisting on its possibility for everyone, even the most bereft. "Recognize it as God's gift," I have said, "find it in the great forms of Scripture." I admit that there is something unreal about such counsel, but that is partly because we have been trained to gauge a valued life in other terms. It is not unusual to compare one's own life to that of a recognized, or perhaps only privately acknowledged, saint. Mother Teresa has become both a model but also a proverbial and impossible ideal. In my own case, it is hard to see the beauty of my life in its larger form, in part because the offering of my life's parts seems both so paltry and so grudging. My life has also been shaped in ways that simply render this larger form crooked and broken, sometimes even crumbling, like the few bits of shattered pottery one might find scattered in the soil around some old rural homestead. It would be difficult to put them together into anything identifiable, and the faded colors that still adhere to the surfaces hint at lostness rather than at discovery.

I take solace in the fact that it is Israel as a people, and not Moses only— let alone the common Hebrew slave by himself or herself—who is called to serve God (*avodat Hashem*) on the mountain of the Lord's own choosing.

I come with a host of others, I live with and like them, and the bits and pieces of what is meant to be "beautiful"—in form and offering both—find their integrity only as embedded within this larger gathering of those "just like me." It is not simply that only as a people do we make up something beautiful, but that our essential bondedness to one another, in its own often difficult historical forms, constitutes that which we offer. This fact is inherent in the nature of mortal existence itself—we are "children of Adam" by blood—and this informs the goods that existence involves.

The shape of my life is not, then, only what I do or even what I do to others, as if the meaning of who I am is measured by discrete actions and their cumulative ethical profile. Rather, my life is as much properly described by what is done *to* me, which, if traced out in detail, implicates a breadth of human and created reality within and along each rough edge of the proffered artifact that defines my life span. But, too, what I do and what is done to me by others do not mark a collection of morally quantifiable deeds and responses that "add up to a life." As we know, there is too much in these acts that is unconscious and undeliberated, reactive and confused, to ever coalesce into a clearly delineated artifact of holiness. Even Mother Teresa's life could not manage this, and the disappointment many felt in discovering this failure led them to reject the notion of a life's beautiful self-offering altogether. The poor were not in fact made rich by her work; the integrity and corruption of gift-giving were often indistinguishable when it came to donors; and within her ostensible peaceful trust in God lurked emptiness and sometimes angry sorrow. Yet just this combustion of diverse sentiments and experiences, provided in the intersection of individuals and their groups, including the vague and misted beginning of her life in Albania, were, I have argued, the *actual* offering that Mother Teresa made: what was done and what was done to, all carried to God together, like any sacrificial victim. I do not offer my life alone to God; alone, I offer my life as the work of a people and of a world to God.

The meaning of a Christian's social life has become increasingly and deeply individualized, as we know: social responsibilities are defined in terms of personal deliberation, decision, and commitment, as well as in terms of individual accountability. While there is much talk today of "the common good," it is each individual person who is judged by his or her personal choices in relation to that putative good. Perhaps this is simply the outgrowth of a long Christian evolution.[1] Even Benedict's communal rule was aimed primarily at the individual's own personal salvation.[2] This tendency has drawn criticism, and not only from the ancient world—Christians are "misanthropes" because they are concerned only with their own souls and they withdraw from civil life. It has also been negatively assessed in the modern era, as with political theories like Rousseau's "general will," which stands as a kind of response to a purportedly socially quiescent (and thus individually self-interested and irresponsible) Christian culture.[3]

It would be a complete misconstrual of Benedict's vision, however, to reduce the monastery to a functionalist social organization whose order exists mainly to help this or that individual get to heaven. On such a misconceived reading, the Rule is articulated as a contract, motivated by individuals who determine that they can best serve their souls by providing the conditions of their individual security through common contributions, within which each Christian is thereby free to pursue his or her personal sanctification. This sounds a bit like Hobbes (see the next chapter). It turns out, however, that in Benedict's vision, saving one's soul, as it were, *is* just this life with others, not a common life as a means but as the very shape of "service" (a great Benedictine term) itself. Not only that, but the Rule makes it clear that this shape is colored by all the details of "being done to"—the ultimately joyful burden of submitting to brothers and abbot—as much as by the personal decisions of fidelity the individual monk might make. The Benedictine community is "stable" just insofar as it holds its myriad internal disruptions and failures together and offers these as the sum of prayerful life spans—life spans marked by prayer and toil that are knit into the fabric of others, namelessly.

This is a very different way of looking at the integrity of social life than what we usually assume today. Thus, Rousseau took a Hobbesian claim regarding the usefulness of a social contract in which individuals surrender their personal rights to a sovereign for the sake of peace, and he tried to reframe it according to a purported shared rationality among persons capable of reaching consensus (perhaps) on "the common good." That there is even the possibility of a common rationality, a common deliberation, and a common good that is recognized and articulated out of this is not something Benedict could have envisioned. He tended to trade in realities like the Holy Spirit, humility, obedience, and suffering. These frame and reframe the small catastrophes of life that mark everyone's existence, including those of any monk or nun or of the communities in which they live. However, even though many readers of Rousseau have themselves observed the impossibly vague and unrealistic character of his political ideal—a "general will"!—modern liberal democracies especially have pursued their increasingly dysfunctional processes on the assumption that such purported commonalities, intrinsic to human thinking and deciding, are in fact operable. Some notion of a shared understanding of the common good and of a shared means of identifying and enacting it lies behind almost every political program aimed at bettering civil society. As a result, and because such programs have by and large shattered themselves against the complexities of people, time, and space, fewer and fewer of us believe that our lives are in fact capable of being offered to God in any beautiful fashion at all. Having sequestered mortal goods, with their banal elements of family and toil, in a space of at best uncertain value, and at the same time now having had to face the dissolving specter of common (i.e., ideally immortal) goods supposedly recognizable and achievable by all, individuals and groups have been left in a realm of aimlessness that only confusedly awaits its sojourning purpose.

Certainly, I have felt this, and have felt it just because of my inbred assumptions about making everything better—indeed, about how making everything better forms the core of my value before God. I have spent the majority of my life trying to better, even to save, that which, in other persons and their common institutions, I saw as broken and even lost. That such efforts have missed their mark is no surprise. Yet it is important to see how such failures require significant reframing if they are not, on the one hand, to unravel the true (i.e., mortal) social bonds that we are given by God to tend and, on the other, to persuade us that our vocation of life-service is irrelevant. On their own, our lives are always incomplete in their form, always unbeautiful, even ugly; yet properly viewed as bound to the imperfections of other creatures and given over to God as such—for this bondedness is at the root of God's gift of creation—they can at least gleam with the burnished glow of the widow's mite. Such offerings are not only "all we have," but the exhaustive reach of this "all" opens up to the infinite grasp of its Maker.

From a political perspective, this struggle in offering was forced upon me as a young priest in Burundi, East Africa, in the early 1980s. Not long emerged from a horrendous civil conflict that saw the massacres of hundreds of thousands of persons, the Burundi I lived in for several years was a society held together by the grip of a military dictator, under the umbrella of a single and coercive political party.[4] Criminals of the recent war were protected, survivors and victims pressed into silence. Many of the worst cultural and economic consequences of such arrangements flowed through and encircled the nation. The more I understood some of these currents and was able to see into the otherwise hidden corners of people's lives, the more I began to chafe under the code of silence that kept the political system in place. I seemed to be living in a world that refused to describe the details and shape of its own history, one that coursed through individual and social memory, however repressed. Everything seemed poisoned by this secretive avoidance.

Yet life went on. It was a strange phenomenon, as I looked around me. An outsider, I could not imagine living through this kind of imposed tension, secrecy, and coercively constrained recollection and with the emotions and desires to which this all might give rise. Do something! Speak out! The twenty-five-year-old spirit within me, eager not just for health but for a vigor that could grow and grow, simply pressed against what I felt to be a suffocating social net. This is what I felt, while all around me life just carried on in a kind of sequential stasis: the beans were dug and harvested, wood collected, uninspired schooling pursued, roads cleared, markets thronged, with their careful bickering and occasional outbursts. And, of course, tears were shed in the quiet. Not only that, churches were built and tended, songs were sung, prayers offered. All the while I was allowed to teach the Scriptures with young men and women.

I could not hold my tongue, however, and was eventually arrested and deported for writing a small essay on the need to break silence over the past. There was nothing wrong with what I wrote, in itself; it was all true enough. "The will to silence that characterises so much of Africa must be judged negatively, despite the realistic concerns that underlie it. And so too must those efforts by churches, intellectuals and ideologues who support or acquiesce to the myth of peaceful order that is used as a cover for injustice and spiritual illness."[5] So I wrote. Despite deep, if unfaced, reservations I had about choosing to write and what I wrote, I continued to feel justified in my claims. Analytically, they seemed spot-on, especially as Burundi (along with Rwanda in its own yet more concentrated and horrific way) soon after careened into years of civil war and bloodshed, whose carnage merged with the depredations of AIDS that took away friends and colleagues in a common torrent of loss. As these further events unfolded in the international press, my own arguments for international intervention and democratic nation-building were pursued in a long stream of letters I wrote to political and religious leaders.

The pragmatic lessons of this kind of experience are surely worth identifying and pursuing. Scholars and activists have in fact been doing so for some years now, obviously not just with respect to Burundi but to a host of other nations, each with their own peculiar and similar challenges and travails. How do we heal conflicted nations?[6] How do we intervene to prevent bloodshed? How do we "get" other people to behave decently or morally or at least live the way we would ourselves wish we could live? The beautiful life, politically promoted, seems to demand successful answers to these questions. But in the face of these desires and, in a way, inescapable imperatives, I was forced to learn patience of the deepest—because most heartrending—kind.

Saving other people is something we all want, at least at some point and for some persons. If we are Christians—and even if we are not—such an accomplishment is the most beautiful thing a person might do. Jesus did it! The desire is not a curse. But like love itself, it is never satisfied in this world. In fact, within our created lives, the desire to save is ever wrenched into the form of curse, such that true love takes "curse" upon itself, makes itself one with its burden (cf. Gal. 3:13). Where it all comes from is another matter. I was raised to "make a difference." That is what schooling in the 1960s Berkeley of my childhood inculcated. There were many areas to do this, of course: nuclear war prevention—we still had drills in my elementary grades—civil rights, free speech, emancipation, ending war. At ten years old I passed out flyers on behalf of the Black Panthers; at eleven, I was signing petitions; at twelve, calling into (left-wing) talk radio. But I could also see (or at least feel), even as a child, the toll all this difference-making might take, even in the midst of family and friends—drugs, conflict, anger. Berkeley in the 1960s had its happy-go-lucky breezes; but these often turned into cold and dampening chills and even gales of lost happiness. Still, the prospect of change for the better, with the self in the center of its confecting, was also exhilarating and was bred in my bones.

Was any of it beautiful? The question never arose. But my musical forma-tion, which became a serious part of my young life and continued through early university, for all of its being undercut by the professional and personal realities of competition and regret, at least sensitized me to the substance of beauty and offering in a tangible fashion. The joy I later felt playing the violin in church or with friends or even alone was real and deep. I learned something that partly explains how song can coexist with prayer in the worst of circumstances—a political as much as a religious insight.

Bettering and saving are not the same, of course. The one is more at ease with its purpose, at least for a time, while the other has a kind of finality to it that can tolerate desperation. The two, however, tend to feed off each other. Our desperate attempts to save rise up out of the frustrations of our optimis-tic bettering efforts. My political hopes for Burundi, as a young man, simply emerged from this ravenous circle. My family had long unraveled in mental illness and death, and my making a difference in the world, within Burundi's context of social challenge, was—I realize now—constantly being fueled by my deeper sense that at any moment the whole thing might come crashing down. As indeed it had but a few years before my arrival, and as it did not long after I left. As it did in all the catastrophic turns of my own relationships, riddled by suicide and its bitter debris. I knew from my family's experience that sudden and complete undoings could happen, yet I had never been taught their meaning for gauging the shape of a life. Building a better society in Burundi, something I had at least long been trained to yearn for automatically, was often but the cognitive instrument for a deeper and unfaced anxiety. My mother had killed herself. My sister was on her way to doing the same. I was dragging along memories and motives of my own and in fact simply acting out of a grand insistence: life must be grasped at, no matter what!

But saving a life, while certainly beautiful as an ideal, is not something we can ever do, I have learned. Not only is there in fact "none"—no creature—who "shall save thee" (Isa. 47:15) in this or that circumstance (or not for long!). More sweepingly, it is simply not *possible* for one human being to "redeem" the life of another (Ps. 49:7). God might do it (49:15). But even God will choose his times (cf. Ps. 18:41). As for myself, I have tried and I have failed. To better and to save: if this be the ordering motive of our common life, with its voracious hunger to demand with ever-greater importuning what it cannot have, it is but a worm of senselessness set loose within the body that slowly bores into its sinews, ones wrenched this way and that over our short life spans.

Whatever may be the offering of our lives—lives of things done and being done to—it must include the working of this worm, the things not only left undone but that are in fact undoable. This inclusion of the worm, as it were, comprehends the full scope of what is beautiful before our Maker. For the undoable, that which can be neither bettered nor saved, is part and parcel of what it means to live with others and to receive with them the goods that constitute our lives. All this is what we are given in our essential givenness. I cannot live forever; I cannot always have my way; I cannot eat my fill; I cannot stand upright for long; I cannot create forgiveness in another's heart; I cannot summon up my own. I cannot keep my parents with me or my friends beside me. I am not the engineer whose projects can "let judgment run down as waters, and righteousness as a mighty stream" (Amos 5:24). These impossibilities are in fact impositions of a sort, most often pressed upon us in our lives with others. We cannot live without others; we cannot live with them as we choose.

Early modern political theorists such as Hobbes, Locke, and Rousseau, whatever we think of their political analyses and programs, at least took this reality of inevitable yet impossible communal demand as bedrock and framed their theories around it. The "social contract" was the fruit, after all, of pondering socially charged impossibilities, the fact that other people hem us in somehow. What was seemingly never pondered, however, was the idea that these fences and forces are themselves divine gifts that shape the offering of our lives in ways that make them "good." Tennyson's long poem *In Memoriam A.H.H.* ends by affirming his dead friend's life in God. Love, Tennyson writes, is in fact never lost (despite his famous line about it being better to have loved and lost than never to have loved at all), for life itself is taken up into immortality. But the opening lines of the poem also affirm the author's incapacity to *believe* this, at least consistently. Tennyson simply asks forgiveness of God for feeling the senselessness of death and of love's wrenched disappearance, for living with a worm he cannot kill. Both affirmations go together. It is one poem. Love mourns and hopes, love is what it is because it breaks and disappears and sometimes then is also remade miraculously. The dual affirmation is simply the character of being made a creature and therefore the character, essentially, of grace. To be "done to" is, thus, not a condition to be tamed by politics through contracts or laws and punishments; these political constructs are but a part of the whole baggage thrust upon us. Instead, we come to recognize that "being done to" is itself among the highest goods of mortal life, which politics can at best preserve, though in a fashion that can be rendered beautiful.

For too long I searched for beauty without its God, a quest defined intrinsically by its unsteady gait. Are not all of us carried by the deepest love as it scrapes the innermost surfaces of our being? Yet, unless we know the giftedness of this abrading pull, it seems only to exhaust us in what it removes. Catastrophe is ever lurking, and we always try to stay one step ahead of it; or, once it turns upon us, we seek some refuge far away. Steadiness and endurance keep us where we are, not statically but faithfully. In contrast, I was driven on and on to an array of causes I felt compelled to acknowledge and, to some degree, engage: mental health, refugees, human rights, and economic and racial equity within the US, especially. Whether I was pastoring in churches or teaching in seminaries, my time was filled with newspapers and discussion, my mail with donations and letters of support or protest. Nothing but random turbulence.

The "mystery of senselessness" that all this amounts to seems much like—or perhaps identical to—the mystery of iniquity ("lawlessness") that rumbles about the earth. Yet Paul was able to include that mystery within the telling of redemption (cf. 2 Thess. 2:5–12). In so doing he was only representing what the whole Scriptures have done less frequently—Satan roaming about the earth, as Job tells us, yet still subservient to God (Job 1:7; 2:2). And if that is so, included too are all of us.

The shape of this life, my life, is hardly clear in light of this. But just because of this comprehensive inclusion of us all in the wide spin of God's creation, we are placed within a wider act of God, a defining relationship of receipt. I am willing, therefore, to offer this life, though it seems so formless in its pieces. Grace holds it together, even as the formless "it" is still something given over to me and seems to constitute all I have. Though I alone can offer it, dislocated and incomplete as it is, my life's jagged form is my own kind of grateful gathering of those I live with. My life—and thus my offering—takes in my mother's and my sister's lives (and deaths), my children's and my friends', my spouse's, and all the smaller and greater joys and catastrophes of their existence. My offering rephrases them all, articulates their forms in a singular and intentional fashion.

Thus, when measured against the lives of others, this incomplete life of mine is not so odd. Indeed, my only claim to escaping self-absorption in this recounting lies in insisting that I am talking about others too, whose lives are far more clearly etched in their trouble than is mine. Any offering I might make, if offering it is, takes in all others whom I have done to and who have done to me. And if "all," I am no more than a figure for others, not a peculiar lens. And if figure, I too have a place in something that, taken together, is the most beautiful created form there is—the "best of all possible worlds," as the philosopher Leibniz rightly if perhaps too bloodlessly suggested—in its complexity and luster.[7] If catastrophe lurks and the worm burrows, they do so within *this* form because of it, or at least not despite it. They too are a part of the offering.

Striving to minimize, then, let alone eliminate, the upheavals and catastrophes of existence must seem not only intrinsically frustrating but also morally perverse. Not that the assaults on our desires or that our suffering and that of others could ever themselves constitute the good; but they can and indeed must be implicated within it. They mark the form of the only goods we share with one another, in part because they constitute that sharing. Shall a person make better the life of another? Shall a nation save another nation? When shall we give up bettering and only rescue or vice versa? These are political questions, of course, but they are tethered to the character of human life, which, in putting both bettering and saving themselves into question, carries their unresolved and open-ended—perhaps even impossible—claims on us into the midst of political decision-making and makes them inherent in the commonwealth's very integrity. We shall need to learn to live with all the upendings of our tiny spheres of life, endure them, find light within them, and then offer them up to God. And someone must teach us how. *This* is what any Christian political responsibility bears most heavily as a calling.

I myself was never thus taught, at least not as a young person, or not clearly and openly. I was taught, instead, to make, to produce, to achieve. In my own family this was not seen in terms of material manufacture or money. Yet it was, in the end, not so different: a post-Christian intellectual and moral amassing of "goods." Mine was an academic, professional, culturally sophisticated family in the midst of a culture self-consciously embracing values that could be used as a currency for life: jobs, reputation, self-esteem, and, in an almost instrumental fashion, friendship. (Do not be friends with a stupid person! Do not be friends with the indecent, the aimless, the desolate!) Never was I taught that, not only do friends often contradict our values and our ideals, but they contradict our deepest hope for them: they die. Never was I taught that their deaths are part of the love we are blessedly granted to enjoy at the heart of our spirits. There was, echoing around the boundaries of this ethically rigorous realm of achievement I inhabited, the sound of scoffing at a grace that only reception can recognize.

Never taught, I instead only mysteriously received without asking (which is only a proof of reception's far greater power): the impulse to pray; a church and its modest lights; the gospel's proclamation; the joining of hymns; the repetitions and steadiness that, in their own formal iterations, mimicked the endurance of a soul within the world of created matter and its spiritual inhabitants. Then, more clearly yet, I received the offering of lives as something at last recognized, bit by bit: the beauty of parents, of friends, of bishops and priests, of students, whatever their (and my own) looking away, distractions, and peculiar and often cutting edges, all of which culminated in the piercing beauty of spouse and children.

Being taught any of this is surely safer than being cast into the world to find it on one's own. Indeed, if steadiness and endurance are the distillate of a life-offering's integrity, then models and exhortations, practice and joint exercise are its most fertile ground. That is one reason why letters to our children have flowed from many trembling pens. That is why I write at all.

Offering is a struggle that is bound to what will not give way and what must therefore be faced and embraced in thanks somehow. In a certain fashion, I have continued to tramp along a path I was first placed upon long ago: it cannot be let go of! But my hope has changed somewhat to a survival that can articulate letting go. Who will live to tell this truth? Who will teach it to the great congregation (Ps. 40:9–10)? Each of us is so called. If the mystery of senselessness abounds, yet all the more so (cf. Rom. 5:15, 20) does the creative grace that goes forth within its dominion (Ps. 19:4; Rom. 10:18). Though nothing may improve according to this or that political metric, grace gleams more clearly in this or that time and place where we have survived and learned to tell the tale. That is not so much a "better" place, but it is the best place that our politics can take us. All of us must be content, and privileged, to offer with thanks what is fundamentally incomplete.

Part Two

THE SCOPE
OF CHRISTIAN
POLITICS

Eight

The Conditions
of Our Offering

And these words, which I command thee this day, shall be in thine heart:
And thou shalt teach them diligently unto thy children, and shalt talk of them
when thou sittest in thine house, and when thou walkest by the way, and when
thou liest down, and when thou risest up. And thou shalt bind them for a
sign upon thine hand, and they shall be as frontlets between thine eyes. And
thou shalt write them upon the posts of thy house, and on thy gates. . . . (For
the LORD thy God is a jealous God among you) lest the anger of the LORD thy
God be kindled against thee, and destroy thee from off the face of the earth.

Deuteronomy 6:6–9, 15

I have argued that the offering of our mortal goods to God in thanks represents the fullness of our service of God. Such an offering is "beautiful" in
a way that touches upon the gospel's depth itself. But I have also stressed
how the beautiful life almost always seems stymied by the very limits of our
mortality and their complex, often unexpected, and certainly unmanageable
impositions. Our offerings are always sorrowfully incomplete. Although I
also described how this very incompleteness might be viewed as beautiful
just in its own offering, I rather suspect that this is hard to believe, at least
subjectively. If God asks something of us—"calls" us, as it were, as he calls
Moses and Israel to their worship of his name—and we fail to achieve it,
that failure must seem our undoing. The politics of the Christian is, in

large part, ordered to limiting this sense of undoing—to structuring a space where the offering of our lives is always possible, even in its incompleteness. This could be viewed as a kind of justice, which is perhaps the most commonly articulated aim of politics, both Christian and otherwise. But I doubt that framing a space for the sacrifice of thanksgiving is what most of us think of when we think of justice. The second part of this book is an attempt to describe the parameters of our ordered life and, in this chapter, thus to indicate where justice resides in human terms.

Whatever justice is, however, it must cohere with God's own actions. At the center of God's self-presentation in the Christian faith is his command, as well as his judgments. They seem to go together as a divine version of the claim "What is, is right." One of the unusual features of divine prescription is how it elides into divine prophecy. God commands, and this simple divine act of enunciation carries with it an entire history. Law and directives are asserted by God, and conditional alternatives are articulated: "Do this" leads to "If you do, then . . . , and if you don't, then . . ." And finally, the conditionals take flesh, are lived out, and give rise to a new creation. The historical context of divine command thus turns out to be one of struggle, of constraining and unstable circumstance—reward, punishment, and somehow navigating these—that is, in the end, given over ("offered") to God's creative grace.

Understanding this can ratchet down historical expectations, steer attention to impinging realities ("local" experience), and provide the contours in which the form of a life can be considered more closely and immediately. In political terms, the character of obedience to God's commandments minimizes the space of social action but also lengthens its roots more deeply within the soil of mortal life that marks our created being: we seek to obey, we disobey, we suffer, and in all this we give ourselves over to God's remaking.

Prescriptive divine address, with its history-forming power, is paradigmatically exposed in Deuteronomy, with its extended and repeated instances of blessing and curse that are attached to the enunciation of the law by Moses. In a way, political life has always been built on such a yoking of prescription and conditional outcomes, whether the directives are viewed as divine, "natural" in some way, or simply utilitarian according to some given calculus. We aim at an end or have some overriding value that guides our sense of right and wrong ("justice"), and with this end or value in mind we lay out pathways of enactment or obstruction, blessing and curse. Thus, blessing and curse in themselves are not an unusual framing scheme for political life.

But Deuteronomy and, indeed, much of the Bible, from the Pentateuch through the Prophets, complicates this framework by preempting the simple application of the framework by means of the divine assertion of a given outcome: disobedience by Israel and then, perhaps, forgiveness and restoration by God. That is, the divine prescription turns into a prophecy of popular human failure and then of divine mercy. The failure gives rise to the curse, not as a conditional but as a future certainty; and this certain future is then simply offered up to some new creation by God. Thus, chapters 11, 27, and 28 of Deuteronomy outline the blessings and curses in a standard conditional manner. Yet by the beginning of chapter 30, we realize that the conditionals have *both* been fulfilled: "And it shall come to pass, when all these things are come upon thee, the blessing and the curse, which I have set before thee, and thou shalt call them to mind among all the nations, whither the LORD thy God hath driven thee . . ." (Deut. 30:1). It *will* happen, both blessing and curse, a curse that will scatter a destroyed Israel among the nations. Then will come something new: repentance, mercy, and conversion (30:3, 6).

It is a strange set of directives that Deuteronomy gives, then. They culminate in a song that God dictates to Moses, one that is to remind Israel of her sinfulness and rebelliousness, remind her of God's commands, somehow provide context for her terrible suffering—terrible indeed!—and finally give rise to the most astonishing historical reversal of the book. This reversal is one in which divine violence seems, in one fell swoop, to merge into new creation: "Praise his people, O you nations; for he avenges the blood of his servants, and takes vengeance on his adversaries, and makes expiation for the land of his people" (Deut. 32:43 RSV). Directives turn into conditionals, which turn into certainties, which turn into unexpected novelties created by the God who alone "kills and makes alive, wounds and heals" (32:39).

What, in all this, is Israel's calling? In a fundamental sense, that calling remains steady: obedience, faith, thanksgiving. But what a book like Deuteronomy makes clear is that such a calling must be lodged within a *history* that embodies that calling's assault, obscurement, forgottenness, and reassertion in a way that decouples the calling itself from any conditional achievements. Incompleteness—as in a life whose beauty is ever incomplete—seems to be here intrinsic to the "wholeness" of the life itself. The calling is thus not one of achievement, but one characterized by endurance in and through the turmoil of time. With this in view, Deuteronomy's own obediential focus is upon the practices of endurance: generation, teaching, remembrance, and the social frameworks that make this possible—parents and children, families, communal stability and trust.

Deuteronomy's discussion of diligently teaching God's words to one's children and literally embedding them into the architecture of one's home (Deut. 6:6–9) comes within a long rehearsal of the past, of God's actions of grace, and of Israel's heedless reception of his gifts (vv. 1–25). This rehearsal presents the commandments themselves as part of a long history of sojourning whose shape lifts up God's law through its suffering of blessing and curse together. That is, the law is "fulfilled" in the subjection of Israel to its weight within time. And thereby is Israel's subjection transfigured through its being recounted from generation to generation in a way that lifts up the details of Israel's struggles as the stuff of divine purpose. (This view of "fulfillment," of course, grounds the great epiphany of the Son of God's own fulfillment of the law in his flesh.) Israel's life, death, and resurrection become the fundamental prescriptive *form* of divine command. Furthermore, the elements that determine how to secure a space for such generative retelling mark out the parameters of social action: how to survive, how to teach, how to maintain the temporal form of both blessing and curse as the object of Israel's offering to God. This space-securing, I am repeating from multiple vantage points, is the sum of Christian politics.

In Zacharias's canticle of Luke 1:68–79, the prophetic focus is upon the end point of the Deuteronomic history of blessing and curse: redemption. Such redemption, however, presumes the middle point of this history, the condition of the curse. Here redemption is described in terms of the securing of these narrow social parameters: God fulfills the oath made to a previous generation in Abraham, that he would deliver Israel from her enemies so that she might "serve him without fear, in holiness and righteousness before him, all the days of [her] life" (1:74–75). This service, as we have noted earlier, constitutes the *avodah* that marks the center of Israel's calling. Here it is enacted in a space devoid of fearfulness, in which all the days of a life can be rendered to God faithfully—that is, according to his commands. *Avodat Hashem*, the service of a human being to God, is such a person's life span in its embrace of a comprehensive offering of just this limited and mortal life and its goods. This almost minimalist view of temporal deliverance—some space of quietness or, in this case, unimpeded self-offering—is carried through in the New Testament, for example, in the famous "political" verses of 1 Timothy 2:1–2 and, more complexly, in Romans 12:17–13:7 (which falls under Paul's larger rubric of "offering" in 12:1). As Paul writes to Timothy,

> I exhort therefore, that, first of all, supplications, prayers, intercessions, and giving of thanks, be made for all men; for kings, and for all that are in

authority; that we may lead a quiet and peaceable life in all godliness and
honesty. For this is good and acceptable in the sight of God our Savior; who
will have all men to be saved, and to come unto the knowledge of the truth.
(1 Tim. 2:1–4)

The Christian should not reject Aristotle's argument that the virtues of
"the happy life" are finally political, because the virtues of the happy person
are mostly ones exercised in relationship with other people and are most
reliably *shaped* in association with other people.[1] But Christians ought to
accept this for their own reasons: these relational virtues of the Good Life
are those aimed, not at an ideal ordering of human life, but at our service
of offering our mortal goods to God. This offering, because it is an offering
and not really a human ordering, furthermore can by definition be enacted
in any number of social arrangements (though perhaps not all). Thus the
political scope in which virtues must be exercised is relatively thin. On
this matter, Thomas Hobbes is closer to Zacharias than are the ancient
political theorists and their followers. The promise to Zacharias has little
to do with empires, Assyrian, Babylonian, or Roman, and everything to
do with true divine worship. This worship, epitomized and primordially
enacted by Jesus (Heb. 9:11–14), is, as it were, regime-neutral because it is
cosmically absolute.

Hobbes (1588–1679) is today mostly an exemplar of political narrowness,
bound to the dynamics of inhumane power and reliant on the most stunted
materialism in its hopeless pursuit of social calm. Still, he is also constantly
read, at least because the clarity and consistency of his vision still snags
some deeper intuition that we all share. For Hobbes, the security of the self
constitutes the center of political concern. Human existence, with all of its
goods and struggles, depends upon there being a secure space in which to
pursue these. But because human beings are naturally driven by the need
to survive—articulated as the first natural "law of liberty" that defines every
human being equally—we end up in inevitable conflict, as each individual
pursues his or her own needs in idiosyncratic directions that cross and
bump up against others. Hence, the right to liberty is but one side of a coin
whose other side is the right "by all means we can, to defend our selves."
The world of liberty, unqualified, is a world of war. The preservation of our
lives—our natural right—is thus bound up de facto with their vulnerability
and being under constant threat.

From the fundamental natural right to preserve our lives in the midst of
danger, Hobbes concludes that the fundamental natural "law" of human
beings is to "seek peace, and follow it."[2] And from this law come all the

subsequent natural laws that are instrumental to this end: covenant, justice, gratitude, mutual accommodation, pardon; and then a set of negative natural laws—against revenge, anger, pride, arrogance; as well as more organizational laws for equity, against favoritism, for mediation and arbitration, impartiality, witnesses. Hobbes sums all of these up by the Golden Rule: we do nothing to others that we would not have done to ourselves.[3]

Hobbes's simplification of social duty here is notorious. Moral life and its attendant virtues, as Hobbes himself admits, fall within these limits, as does politics itself: everything boils down to the given realities of life, danger, and desired security. Hobbes's crude though penetrating theory of the sovereign as the necessary instrument of security's achievement grows within this narrow field. The natural condition of human existence—what we might justly call our decidedly mortal frame—gives us no more than this defining range of social movement. Hobbes's famous description of this natural condition of human existence, as it inevitably descends into war, is worth repeating for the succinct way in which he summarizes how social life, in the form of its valued elements, not only depends upon this basic security of life but in a way must also serve it.

> Whatsoever therefore is consequent to a time of Warre, where every man is Enemy to every man; the same is consequent to the time, wherein men live without other security, than what their own strength, and their own invention shall furnish them withall. In such condition, there is no place for Industry; because the fruit thereof is uncertain: and consequently no Culture of the Earth; no Navigation, nor use of the commodities that may be imported by Sea; no commodious Building; no Instruments of moving, and removing such things as require much force; no Knowledge of the face of the Earth; no account of Time; no Arts; no Letters; no Society; and which is worst of all, continuall fear, and danger of violent death; And the life of man, solitary, poore, nasty, brutish, and short.[4]

All that undermines the various natural laws noted above, and that thus aims at the final subversion of peace, must therefore lead us back to "mere nature"—that is, to war itself.[5]

"Leading a quiet and peaceable life," in Paul's phrase, is the goal of political life—indeed, of all human life once it is perceived in its social posture. By contrast, a society divided among opposing factions, especially when it is in fact organized as such and pursued in such contrastive postures, is likely, in Hobbes's view, to slowly (or quickly) unravel the laws and virtues of nature that uphold security. The natural condition of human beings is mimicked or repossessed in such division, which, if left unchecked, will take the form, finally, of civil conflict and even civil war—"intestine" violence. "Rebellion," which is but an initial form of civil war, Hobbes says, "is but [natural] warre renewed."[6] Rebellion reverts society to a terrain in which there is no sovereign and thus no *means* of peace except violent coercion. Insecurity is simply another way of describing a human life of despair, where the fundamental purposes of survival are repudiated.

Regimes of security are multiple, which is why Christians themselves have argued, following Aristotle's loose and adapted typology (one that Hobbes, like others, maintains), about the comparative virtues of monarchy, oligarchy, and democracy, as well as about their peculiar vices and temptations.[7] There is nothing intrinsically Christian about any single regime in this case, since any one might promote or at least provide (intentionally or not) the minimal conditions of security that ground *avodat Hashem*. Joseph can encourage his family to relocate to the despotic realm of Pharaoh as God's "good" will, for the simple reason that Egypt will permit the survival of Israel's generations (Gen. 45:7). Such generational survival constitutes the moral basis for the structure of the ark during the flood (cf. Gen. 6:19). To be sure, the service of God in some regimes may lead to death itself— but an open death, a testifying or sanctifying death, one that Christians call "martyrdom." One of the great political discernments that Christians face is thus not so much how to "further" this or that state of affairs but how to distinguish the fundamental calling to secure peace from the fundamental grace of martyrdom.

Hobbes was not in the end wholly consistent on the matter of evaluating regimes according to their peace-securing character. Nor did he have any room in his theories for the Christian call to martyrdom. His theory of sovereignty at times overwhelmed his more basic understanding of human existence. At one point he argued that loyalty to the monarch, even in the midst of violent conflict, is demanded. The state, embodied in the sovereign, cannot actually dissolve just because anarchy and violence prevail, and duties to the king—including protecting the king through war—are thus obligatory. Upholding the sovereign, Hobbes insisted, may well involve giving up our fundamental right to self-preservation. (Jonathan Swift would later declare that our necessary obedience to the state, even in its unholiness, was analogous to suffering and "submitting" to "general calamity, dearth, and pestilence"—i.e., it was a facet of mortal life itself.)[8] Still, although he may have wriggled out of this at the Restoration, in *Leviathan* (with an eye, perhaps, to his relationship with the Commonwealth authorities) Hobbes seems to think that once the sovereign is destroyed and a new one replaces him (in whatever form) and assumes the duty of securing the state, then

loyalty is owed to this new ruler. If violence is warranted on one side—
the sovereign's—in a civil war, it ends once that sovereign is formally—
practically, mortally—replaced. This was his more logical position.

This logically consistent side of Hobbes could support, in a fashion,
the numerous satirical stabs at religious chameleonism and conscience-
adapting self-protection that followed the "survivors" of war and regime
change in early modern Britain. If personal security is our main existential
end, religious integrity (and other integrities too) goes out the window.
Compromise, of the most craven kind, becomes the overriding virtue. This
worry is expressed in the popular song, perhaps of the early eighteenth
century or before, known as "The Vicar of Bray," in which a clergyman
manages to adapt to every political and ecclesiastical regime in order to
remain in his pastorate. The verses catalogue each change of political
order within which the Vicar adjusts his convictions, proclaiming with
each his immovable allegiance: "This is [the] law I will maintain until my
dying day, sir."

> In good King Charles's golden days,
>   When loyalty no harm meant,
> A zealous high churchman I was,
>   And so I got preferment:
> To teach my flock I never miss'd,
>   Kings are by GOD appointed,
> And damn'd are those that do resist,
>   Or touch the Lord's anointed.
> And this is law I will maintain
>   Until my dying day, sir,
> That whatsoever king shall reign,
>   I'll be the Vicar of Bray, sir.
>
> When royal James obtain'd the crown,
>   And Popery came in fashion,
> The penal laws I hooted down,
>   And read the Declaration:
> The Church of Rome I found would fit
>   Full well my constitution;
> And had become a Jesuit
>   But for the Revolution.
> *And this is law, &c.*

And on the ditty goes, verse by verse, through the accession of George of
Hanover and an affirmation of the "Protestant succession."

And George my lawful king shall be—
  Until the times do alter.
And this is law I will maintain
  Until my dying day, sir,
That whatsoever King shall reign,
  I'll be the Vicar of Bray, sir.[9]

All the while, the Vicar not only survives but, as he insists, he remains to tend the congregation that endures through the various revolutions and changes of society. The stages of vicaring mentioned begin after Cromwell's Commonwealth. The Vicar of Bray is a thoroughly "Anglican" monarchist, for all the changes he embraces. But Hobbes's views might have given some space for a verse about the paradigmatic Vicar's switch to Presbyterianism or Congregationalism along the way. Why not? The commitment to or at least consequence of continuity in pastoral presence in Bray through all these changes constitutes a possible virtue worth reflecting upon.

For Hobbes is probably right that, when it comes to the fruit that human relationships can bear—the fruit of ongoing life in its mortal fragility and beauty—social division sets up a zero-sum struggle: competing *religious* claims, especially, along with their diverse political underpinnings or ancillaries, do not tend toward peace.[10]

Peace can be promoted and lived out through religious adaptation, of course, but whatever the virtues of the Vicar of Bray, the song's satirical tone was not an accident: religious faith itself is defined not in terms of adaptability but in terms of commitment to something absolute, even if that absolute demands compromise. Hobbes could never properly engage this aspect of God within the world. The issue is not whether Hobbes believed in heaven; he may or may not have with vigor, though he certainly affirms a general Christian belief in the afterlife.[11] Rather, his own unwillingness to embrace the sojourning mystery of mortal life—human existence as intrinsically connected to and embodying transcendent life through creaturehood, and thus God-dependent even in its loss—seems to end by banishing God from the world itself.

In the end, "security" is a temporally relative term; and mortality renders its exact meaning for any individual something evanescent. Instead of simply valorizing security in itself, we should acknowledge that the very *struggle* to live faithfully is at the center of human existence, and, as both the receipt and the offering of mortal goods, that struggle is always in a state of uncertainty and vulnerability. Whatever "security" means for the Christian, it can only define the space of this permitted struggle, not be the fulfillment of a predetermined life span characterized by an ideal set of experiences. Thus, in the struggle of offering, God is ever and immediately before us. This is the "secure" space of faithful mortal life.

For Hobbes to say that the struggle itself, which involves concrete realities of body and relationship, is thus irrelevant to the conception of "peace" is to drain creation of its divine significance by decoupling its very limits from divine grace. This cannot be right, and in a way it ends by divinizing the political realm itself—as if politics is the only grace that there is. This Hobbesian claim turns out to be the practical outcome of the ameliorative notion of "betterment" that has so taken over Christian (and secular) understandings of the purpose of existence. By contrast, I am suggesting that the virtues of the Christian political life are bound to the sojourning reality of self-offering and sacrifice that characterizes human creaturehood in God's self-giving. Render this divine reality irrelevant or even unwelcome within political life, and Christians have nothing to offer and no one to offer it to, and hence logically disappear as a referent altogether in any socially significant sense. Such disappearance is something that is exactly the final characteristic of contemporary progressivist and conservative "Christian" political life itself, as their respective goals are measured increasingly by purely civil benchmarks.

Christians *must* hold dear that service of God for which divine "deliverance" is given: the freedom to worship him without fear (Luke 1:74). They must insist on this requirement of fearless worship for their mortal existence since it *is* the very form of that existence. Hobbes, by contrast, ends by deliberately separating the service of God from mortal goods altogether, explicitly locating such service in some inner, "spiritual" realm: faith "is internal, and invisible," he asserts.[12] Hence, given the absolute obedience owed by Christians to their sovereign, a Christian must rightly obey an "infidel" monarch as much as a Christian one. The argument became a standard liberal line as well, taken up in limited ways by Locke and then, in a notorious 1717 sermon, by the Anglican bishop Benjamin Hoadly, who opposed the shape of the Anglican religious establishment on the basis of Jesus's claim that "my Kingdom is not of this world."[13] No one can coerce belief, which is interior. For Hobbesian conservatives and Lockean liberals both, a purely interior faith means that Christians can and must leave everybody else alone. Christian service of God, on this view, is always invulnerable to the world and to political obligation.

What could be wrong with this? Removing faith from the world—that is, from creation's difficult and impinging demands—is a beguiling ideal. One need never fear the ripples, let alone crashing waves, of convictional discent troubling the state. But the ideal is historically unattainable, as both religious and ideological convictions refuse containment, even in the most self-consciously liberal polities. The ideal is also patently false with respect to Christian faith itself, which cries out for the freedom of godly service, a service that, as we have emphasized, is not so much the cause of trouble as it is suffused with the troubling and sometimes overwhelming burdens of mortality. Does cherishing and protecting such a service, however—the sojourning reality of Christian life—not then lead to the fulfillment of Hobbes's worries over intestine conflict, given diverse religious views and thus competing claims to the shape of divine service? My answer would be: it neither leads to it nor prevents it. Christian life aims at security for mortal goods, even as the offering of these goods permits a wide scope of political contexts to exist or unfold and within which praise can still be sung. The beautiful incompleteness that this scope embraces is the basis for its breadth.

Hobbes could have gone this route, logically—peace admits of various regimes in which various religious commitments can be pursued—but his distaste for religious life itself blinded his appreciation of true Christian political humility. The summation of offering in the act of martyrdom, after all, is something that can in theory be embodied in many contexts. But Hobbes himself carefully limits true martyrdom, first to the apostles, who actually "witnessed" Christ Jesus with their own eyes (all other "witness" is thus at best secondary), and second to upholding the single claim that Jesus is the Christ, something that, as noted, he intimates can be believed in an interior fashion anyway.[14] The freedom of Christians to worship God demands that the troubling aspects of life—that is, its mortal goods—be received in thanks and offered in praise, and thus the Christian life, the Good Life, spells a certain kind of "trouble" wherever it goes, and it presses for the broad spaces in which such trouble can be viewed, accepted, and lifted high. The suppression of such receipt and lifting up is exactly where the edge of Christian political life cuts.

Thus, Hobbes also refused to accept that insecurity can be measured and finally politically opposed rightly by Christians on the basis of their vocation to "serve our Lord" in a visible fashion, as God directs (Exod. 10:26), in a way that is located geographically and relationally. Hobbes's commitment to the absolute right of the sovereign to maintain his or her own security—a form of "reason of state"—meant that the security of persons themselves became secondary. Yes, the state's security was, he felt, the only sure basis upon which to provide personal security. But obviously that simply is not true in many cases, and not only in the extreme cases of totalitarian states. We know this too well.

If we take several well-known scriptural promises of security, we see them described in the most concrete, if limited, of ways:

> But they shall sit every man under his vine and under his fig tree; and none shall make them afraid: for the mouth of the LORD of hosts hath spoken it. (Mic. 4:4)

> And Judah and Israel dwelt safely, every man under his vine and under his fig tree, from Dan even to Beersheba, all the days of Solomon. (1 Kings 4:25)

> And thou shalt say, I will go up to the land of unwalled villages; I will go to them that are at rest, that dwell safely, all of them dwelling without walls, and having neither bars nor gates. (Ezek. 38:11)

Each under his own tree at peace, without locks on the door, without fear: it is all a rather modest, peasant view of heaven on earth. It is also a simply realist view shared across cultures. Gilgamesh, the ancient Mesopotamian hero, is taught to give up his hope of immortality, death being the lot of human beings. Instead, he is urged, "Let thy raiment be clean. Thy head be washed, (and) thyself bathed in water. Cherish the little one holding thy hand, (and) let thy wife rejoice in thy bosom. This is the lot of mankind."[15] The nature of security itself is somewhat malleable here: it can be enjoyed in a Sumerian tyranny as much as in an Italian city-republic. But there are also limits stated that seem relatively fixed: the ability to have a family and feed it (along with oneself); the ability to work; the ability to sleep in peace. To this one might add the ability to pray and give thanks, not alone but with others (this criterion is less easily defined than some but probably not as vague as some might suppose). "Ability" here *is itself*, perhaps, the vague term: Is it permission? Scope? Means? "Right"? A combination of some of these? The peasant seeks to be left alone with the goods he or she is given, engages, and offers. And "left alone" necessarily involves other people within the scope of generational survival. Into this place of "peace," however, it is possible and likely that all kinds of troubling things will tumble and invade, for the days are evil: famine, accident, illness, incompetence, the faults and betrayals and loss of others. If getting the better of these invaders is not an essential aspect of *avodat Hashem*, then we can at least say that the peace of mortal goods goes no further than the boundaries of this minimum: being content with what one is given in these realms—for example, food and clothing—assuming that they are in fact given at all (cf. 1 Tim. 6:6).

Such a minimal view of peace will seem to many unduly risky, for it offers room for other central political categories, like sovereignty and authority, to expand and indeed grow into Leviathans of menace. Hobbes's deep anxiety over social instability—making the trains run on time, in one reading—has not without reason become associated with authoritarian tyranny and its attendant injustices and sometimes even horror. Hobbes himself is often linked to this view. Powerful sovereignties can become so inflated, out of this anxiety for stability, as to become invulnerable to righteousness, let alone bottom-up pressures for righteousness. In this invulnerability, wickedness propagates itself.

This is no doubt true. At the same time, a minimalist view of peace like this can also provide a platform for opposing just such wayward authoritarian regimes, as well as for measuring the value of such opposition. Experiences like life in Saddam Hussein's Iraq and life after his fall are now proverbial, as are the attempts to unseat such regimes. If security is a human "right," driven by a "law" for peace, Iraq's, Afghanistan's, and Syria's experience forces a political calculus that, however difficult, is nonetheless inevitable: the peasant cannot survive in any of these settings.[16]

Liberal democratic regimes organized representationally, like Canada's, are by contrast historical oases of material security, even without discounting (not morally but quantitatively) the sufferings of variously identified demographic categories, such as Indigenous groups, the homeless, the mentally ill, and the underemployed or underpaid. One can, in almost all Canadian cities, walk the streets without a reasonable fear of attack; one can sleep through the night without any reasonable fear of arbitrary arrest, assault, or shelling; one can find food in most stores in almost all places; one can even read a book at will. But what shall one say about the room offered, in a place like Canada, to *avodat Hashem*, the freedom to worship or serve God without fear?

In many liberal democracies, the COVID pandemic uncovered worrying dynamics: the closing of churches (in contrast to the "essential" services of liquor stores), the threat of legal action against Christian schools that would teach children and young people traditions deemed essential to the truth of religious doctrine, the civil demand made upon doctors and other professionals to support state-sponsored medical suicide. It is not clear in these cases that thresholds of "freedom of service" have been crossed, but they are certainly being squeezed. And if, on this front, security is being threatened, the political duties of Christians are being tested. Paul's call in 1 Timothy 2 to value the authority of civil political authorities is in fact something he explains in terms of teaching and possible conversion: "For this is good and acceptable in the sight of God our Savior; who will have all men to be saved, and to come unto the knowledge of the truth" (1 Tim.

2:3–4). The peace of the commonwealth, it turns out, is measured in an essential way by this criterion of formation and witness, which coincides in fact with a Deuteronomic outlook.

One might also question whether the extreme cases of Iraq and Syria properly illuminate the intrinsic value of democratic regimes even on a more material basis. The United States, with its divided religions and divided opinions more broadly, is deeply conflicted, with this conflict descending into assaultive confusion, including civil unrest, in a way that mirrors Hobbes's worries about the dissolution of commonwealths. Some of these divisions touch on matters of religious freedom, from public shaming and criticism (see the strong attempts to limit religious schooling), to the injection of civil rights into church employment practices, to the struggle for the right and practice of carrying guns in churches. The United States has also seen its share of anti-religious violence, especially (but not only) against non-Christian groups (Jews, Sikhs, Muslims). But beyond religious matters, one must wonder at whole communities in America where daily life has been rendered insecure through crime and the depredations of a drug economy and gang warfare. Or again, more broadly, one must wonder at the way that the politicization of public health and its access and offering has arguably undermined the receipt of such care for considerable portions of the population.[17]

What we see here, in part, is how social complexities come into play in difficult ways that make even a minimalist understanding of security practically opaque. Although the issue of social complexity will be addressed specifically in chapter 11, I raise it here, if only in passing, for its role in muddying the actual discernment of the most restrictive definitions of peace. The COVID pandemic offers but an opening to the extensive elements in play today with respect to discerning the way that multiple social realities impinge upon the explicitly Christian discernment of political calling. The emergence of the pandemic quickly involved billions of people and hundreds of nations and governments, each with its own economies, resources, and ramified cultural expectations in play, but all of whom, on a number of key levels, had to coordinate and cooperate. Medical and academic institutions and guilds, ordered differently and often competitively around the world as well as within some nations, were immediately brought into a whirlwind of activity, demanding funding and responding to uncontrolled journalistic reporting and media discussion. Entire industries were revamped to respond to a rapidly unfolding crisis; local and national governments were mobilized in reaction; data was gathered, analyzed, debated, and sometimes suppressed; views were offered, attacked, asserted;

health systems were reordered and forced to make provisions for unknown and quickly changing situations; schools, manufacturing, retailing, and transportation were all upended and reoriented in municipalities, localities, and whole countries, with the threads of cause and effect multiplied in literally myriads of directions. No one was in charge, nor could they be; sovereignty and authority were claimed, rejected, shifted, pressed, invented, and reinvented in thousands of diverse contexts.

However complex all this in fact proved to be, there were nonetheless concrete choices that—again, locally—forced themselves upon individuals: where to dwell, how to spend the minutes of the day, what to wear, how to order a family or children's lives, what to say, what to eat, how to work, what to teach, and how and where and with whom to learn, pray, and praise God. Only on this level was the need to keep the Christian political ideal in mind absolutely necessary: serve God without fear through the obedient offering of our mortal goods in thanks and praise. Although haphazard and incompletely discussed, let alone agreed upon, it was clear that specifically Christian service was in many cases being assaulted and confused with regard to, for example, visitation of the sick, funerals, and common prayer. The contexts in which such service could—and can—in fact be pursued were wide-ranging, just as were the impinging constrictions on such service's enactment, and these aspects varied from place to place. When it came to the mortal goods of the Christian life, the political responses to the pandemic were obviously problematic in many ways, although just how problematic was not something people agreed upon, in part because the value of such goods was rarely identified. Had it been, it is quite possible that faithful political choices by Christians would have still been debated; but the often painful pursuit of such debate would have itself proved transfiguring, a part of the sojourning struggle that makes up our human life at its core.

This embrace of open-ended uncertainty as an act of faithfulness is important to stress. The actual and proper realm of "security," in a Christian reformulation of Hobbes's central claim, is simply not definable, according to details, in advance. Yet this realm itself is what defines our political duty. What is at issue politically is whether the Christian has the means by which to engage a struggle with the uncertainties of this realm in their minimal but nonetheless shifting demands. The shape of Deuteronomy's historical promise lays this out: the clarity of obedience or disobedience, which elides with an inevitable inadequacy and failure, leaves us with the obligation to survive into a future of repentance and divine re-creation. From this simple obligation flows the fundamental prescription for generation and teaching in the midst of the mortal pressures of our evil days, a prescription which in turn provides the limits to the necessary security of service. We can, that is, define security not simply in terms of food and raiment but in terms of hearing the Word of God and its communication across time to family and people. The contextual needs of this kind of life—which can be described in terms of "generational catechetics" but also in a way that upholds the Good Life—may be minimal and variable, but they are substantive.

So, for instance, we can begin to trace the conditions of our offering on the basis of these needs. We can identify the Word here with the divine law. Included in it is an array of commands, many of which are tied to what today we call political policy and action (economic relations, criminal codes, justice). Yet this identification alone does not get us very far. For ordering whole civil societies on the basis of the divine law and its commands has proved to be ever incomplete and often unrighteous itself. The great revolts against church and state of the seventeenth and eighteenth centuries in Europe and America were driven, in part, by the experience of such an order's oppressive inadequacies. The reality of "evil days" reframes the context of obedience here, both in the receipt and the fulfillment of such commands, according to the limits of the mortal, the unfinished, the frustrated. Bettering cannot be trusted as a criterion, nor can escape reflect the proper goodness of the mortal life we have been granted. The social elements of obedience to the divine law are always, it seems, improvised, even as the commandments themselves are received as transcendent gifts to be thankful for and to be taught across generations.

Hence, generation and family become the main social context that the Word presses upon our social existence as necessary. There is nothing "private," in a Hobbesian sense, in this view of what God asks of us. It is simply a matter of properly identifying where security finds its defining limit. Social or civil pressures to concretely dismantle the family's generative and nurturing identity are rightly to be resisted; resisted too should be their change ("betterment" in only this limited sense) or the attempt to flee them geographically and so escape them. Modern frameworks of politics have value only as they are constrained to a small area of life and are therein truly or rightly measured by the limits of our mortality, our births, our generations, and our deaths.

Finally, this leaves teaching, in its generational reach—catechesis—as the primary political focus of the church. What permits, enables, and enacts the teaching of the Word across mortal boundaries—generations—is the church's benchmark for political thinking. But teaching is obviously both possible and perhaps dramatically powerful in a host of socially beleaguered and politically troubled contexts: from the uncharted homes and groups of the first- and second-century church, to the catacombs, to village outposts, to the wanderings of Mennonite refugees, to the forests of Cévennes or later church schools in the Vichy-controlled Plateau region of southern France, to Communist work camps, to the family-church networks of contemporary America. In all these contexts, in their varied modesty and in their attempted suffocation by enemies, Christians can still offer themselves to God, if only in the form of pleading before God:

> O God, why hast thou cast us off for ever? why doth thine anger smoke against the sheep of thy pasture? . . . They have cast fire into thy sanctuary, they have defiled by casting down the dwelling place of thy name to the ground. They said in their hearts, Let us destroy them together: they have burned up all the synagogues of God in the land. . . . O God, how long shall the adversary reproach? shall the enemy blaspheme thy name for ever? . . . For God is my King of old, working salvation in the midst of the earth. Thou didst divide the sea by thy strength: thou brakest the heads of the dragons in the waters. Thou brakest the heads of leviathan in pieces, and gavest him to be meat to the people inhabiting the wilderness. . . . O deliver not the soul of thy turtledove unto the multitude of the wicked: forget not the congregation of thy poor for ever. . . . O let not the oppressed return ashamed: let the poor and needy praise thy name. . . . Forget not the voice of thine enemies: the tumult of those that rise up against thee increaseth continually. (Ps. 74:1, 7–8, 10, 12–14, 19, 21, 23)

When the pleading is itself silenced, Christian politics may become indistinguishable from the abnormal politics of the world as it joins in a desperate resistance to death's invasion. A limit might indeed have been crossed in Saddam's Iraq. But even here, perhaps not, especially as horror embraces the work of dismantling such regimes (a sad Hobbesian insight). Just war calculations—for example, under the heading of "proportionality"—rightly demand that the cost of defense not outweigh the cost of patience.[18] In any case, in the face of the possibility that patience overrides self-protection—where, for instance, Babylon unmakes Jerusalem for the sake of Israel's survival—the sensitivities of Christians are politically sharpened. We are always asking, "What will it take to pass my faith along, so that time itself is filled with service?" The teaching of *avodat Hashem*'s underlying condition of endurance demands the formation of embodied witness, which requires some secure space, though how much is never known by formula. Justice is constantly readjusting according to the limits of patience. Where teaching is possible, and where families and ecclesial communities persevere sufficiently to receive such teaching—where their survival and energies are enough for the moment—there justice is or at least can be fulfilled. Everything else is secondary.

The actual service of God takes place in a "now," not in a future. Such a present, to be sure, knows the divine truth of where it has come from and where it is going. This truth is that creation is God's, with whatever pasts and futures define it in his purpose. God's Name is both revealed and worshiped in all times by the creatures he has made and sanctified by those whose lives are given over to him in praise. Hence, *any* present is open to such service, however difficult this must seem. *Kiddush Hashem*, the "sanctifying" of God's Name—or martyrdom, in the technical Jewish sense—is thus also at the root of all faithful life in the present world, a world that comes and goes in the most astonishing and unexpected of ways. We can die for God at any time and thus fulfill our purpose. That the freedom to worship God without fear should be transfigured in martyrdom only means that tracing the boundaries of security is politically malleable, unstable, and tenuous. Just how tenuous is the focus of the following chapter.

Nine

Catastrophe—the Container of Our Politics

> Disaster will come upon you, and you will not know how to conjure it away. A calamity will fall upon you that you cannot ward off with a ransom; a catastrophe you cannot foresee will suddenly come upon you.
>
> Isaiah 47:11 (NIV)

Offering, I have stressed, is the central framework for a Christian understanding of politics. Within this offering is kneaded the limits of mortality. Indeed, these limits *are* the stuff of our offering, the definition of those mortal goods that mark our miraculous creation at the hands of God. These limits, however, are often felt as assaults—feared, resisted, wept over. The Christian grace of their transfiguration, embodied in their offering itself and encompassing the unstable mixture of incompleteness and security that drives our political desires and despairs, somehow coexists, at least in this time and in this culture, with a larger civic judgment about these limits that has come to revile the limits themselves, demonize and evade them. Within a non-Christian context—which Christians themselves inhabit and internalize—mortal limits arise and loom up as the visage of all that is unwelcome within the social sphere. Politics, therefore, as we use it to order our larger lives, whether as Christians or not, is driven by the subterranean threat of catastrophe.

Here I want to ratchet up our discussion of the context in which our politics has any political bearing. If we live in "evil days," these days themselves must continually unmask the pretensions of our political hopes. Besides "offering," then, perhaps we might promote catastrophe to its own central and informing role in a specifically Christian politics, or at least one of necessary ancillary service. For the non-Christian, catastrophe simply obliterates; for the Christian, it can provide a form to service. Let us allow catastrophe to do its own dance on the stage of mortal beauty.

"Catastrophe" is a peculiar lens through which Christians ought rightly to understand their world and their place within it. The term is usually applied to some horrendous event that literally "overturns," in an uncontrolled moment, the way things are. But more broadly, catastrophe is simply the human experience of being born and of dying, the uncalled-for appearance and disappearance, making and unmaking, of life by God. Although "catastrophe" is usually linked with destruction, a tearing down of creation, as a biblical word it connotes the widest range of astonishing and sometimes positively creative acts.

The Greek translation of the Old Testament does, it is true, use "catastrophe" and its cognates to render the Hebrew *hapak*, which is often applied to the destructive overthrow of peoples and kingdoms (cf. 2 Kings 21:13). But "catastrophe" is also used for any kind of sudden change that touches the deepest character of a thing. Thus, catastrophe can sometimes include the sudden movement from bad to good, curse to blessing (cf. Deut. 23:5; Neh. 13:2); sea to dry land (Ps. 66:6); or sorrow to joy (Esther 9:22; Ps. 30:11). The more familiar negative transformation of catastrophe—rivers into blood (Ps. 78:44), love into hatred (Ps. 105:25), health into disease (Lev. 13:3), peace and stability into suffering and ruin (Hag. 2:22)—is thus tied to a deeper divine reality, wherein the power of God flashes across the threshold that separates nonbeing and being and displays his person as Creator with a wonder that causes trembling or—as Job might put it—the "churning" of one's gut (Job 20:14).

In the New Testament, catastrophes should thus be seen as comprehending the metaphysical ground of creaturehood itself. On the basis of the paradigmatic Greek translation, from the Hebrew, of God's overthrow of Sodom and Gomorrah, a literal "catastrophe" comes up in just those contexts of divine punishment (2 Pet. 2:6; metaphorically in 2 Tim. 2:14). The Gospels prefer the term closer to "unraveling" (*kataluō*) when speaking of the end of the temple (Mark 13:2). Yet applied to the human body—Jesus's own and ours (2 Cor. 5:1)—the catastrophe of dissolution is simply the mark of God's miraculous making of our lives, and thus implies or contains their undoing also. Hence, the politics of security, given in personal and communal health, is squarely placed within the humanly uncontrolled hand of God, who mysteriously initiates life and its endings. Even in its negative form, catastrophe at its most explosive in the New Testament, as in the so-called apocalyptic teaching of Jesus (Matt. 24; Mark 13; Luke 21), is always only one side of a larger act of God that creates and reveals his light (Luke 21:27–28).

Trying to read these kinds of dominical teachings for insight into politics makes many people nervous. Jesus's words about wars, earthquakes, sorrows, persecutions, darkened skies, and cosmic disasters—words, it needs to be said, that appear at length in three of the four Gospels and permeate disparate parts of both the Old and New Testaments—have lost the consistent theological context that is needed to be understood seriously in our day. The images are too closely linked to certain forms of (pre)millennialism that are deemed grossly irresponsible by many, stoking, they believe, an almost ravenous desire for nuclear or environmental annihilation. And not only premillennialists: one researcher in the late 1980s, when the issue of nuclear arms control was at the front of public discussion, found that a deep hindrance to such efforts in the US was the fact that many people find the Bible to be, as he put it, "literally true." "For millions of Americans," the author discovered in a complex statistical analysis, "it seems futile to try to reduce the chance of global devastation because nuclear war is inevitable; it has been foretold in the Bible."[1] Not just sociologists but also serious political scientists worry about such popular attitudes. The issue here is not Christian fundamentalists but their secular counterparts: ecological doomsayers, worried economists, and so on. Effective "social revolutionary" politics need different "narratives," as one writer notes in an essay evocatively titled "Dystopia Is for Losers."[2]

In this perspective, Jesus's teaching about the world's catastrophic future is a problem, even a dangerous one and certainly an unhelpful one. If politics—and responsible Christian politics—would follow the early modern and modern project of ordering societies justly through the construction of effective forms of collective decision-making—democratic usually, but perhaps revolutionary—then either we reframe the "literal" sense of Jesus's words or we ignore them. What we do not do is take them seriously as stated.

But perhaps we should. In fact, the concept of catastrophe has received a renewed scrutiny as a political category, mostly in Europe.[3] Some elements of the category have entered into discussions over the past sixty years on regime change, totalitarianism, and theories of authority, such as the great German political scientist Carl Schmitt's concept of "the state of exception," which tried to outline how and when the political sovereign might enact a state of emergency beyond otherwise regulating the laws of a nation.[4] Much of this interest (spurred in part by worries over the intrusion of dictatorships) is about how either to use or to overcome "catastrophic" thinking in order to be more politically effective, on the assumption that catastrophic thinking constrains or is itself a paralyzing attitude.[5]

In the context of the present discussion, however, this is to get things backward: catastrophe is simply, if often horrendously, a form of change that happens in the face of human incapacity, political and otherwise. As just noted, worries over Christian catastrophic thinking associated with late twentieth-century fundamentalist predictions of, say, nuclear "Armageddon" have tended to drive contemporary critiques of catastrophism. But events such as the AIDS epidemic and the Indonesian tsunami of 2004, which have had evident, widely experienced international consequences, have also led to a subdiscipline dealing with catastrophe response. Such studies actually have a long history, dating at least from the time of the 1755 Lisbon earthquake, and focus on how to organize, assemble, and allocate resources for immediate rescue and engage in short- and long-term rebuilding. Catastrophe, that is, is not only a political category but a wider humanitarian one.

Yet, in historical terms, catastrophe is a common feature of human civil life. Jared Diamond popularized the idea that climate change, environmental degradation, and societal conflict have had—and will almost certainly continue to have—catastrophic effects on various communities over human history: the Anasazi, Easter Island, Haiti, Rwanda.[6] For Diamond, population pressures above all stand as the great direct and indirect foundation of the slow or sometimes sudden unraveling of whole societies and civilizations. While Diamond explored interactions between epidemics and catastrophic change, others have more clearly demonstrated their role. Scholars, for instance, have analyzed how the mid-sixth-century "plague of Justinian"—whose effects were comparable to or perhaps far worse than the fourteenth-century Black Death—rearranged the political and social constellations of the entire Mediterranean region and perhaps opened up the way for the expansion of Islam not long after. Vast areas of central Asia were probably affected and, in human terms, reordered by these kinds of events, as were, obviously, the Americas in and after the sixteenth century. The effects of the Great Flu Epidemic of 1918—the deadliest we know of in absolute numbers—are only now being carefully studied, and the AIDS pandemic, I believe, will prove to have had profound effects on culture and the global order, in ways that have only rendered political life more intractably impenetrable.[7]

Catastrophe, whether natural, epidemiological, conflictual, or based on the environmentally corrosive effects of human activity, is thus a given. While proactive political response to catastrophe in terms of preparedness, prevention, and moral demand is a rational imperative, it is also and often more likely the case that, in many instances, political activity is forcibly reinvented only *following* catastrophe, as its unplanned progeny. Thus, while catastrophic violence erupts in the relational deserts left by ineffective or paralyzed politics—as in Weimar Germany or in 1990s Rwanda and Burundi—so political life that has become ineffective and paralyzed is remade, for better or worse, in the wake of catastrophe, as in many African nations after the onset of AIDS.[8] Where difficult and even overwhelming social demands have rendered definitive and effective decision-making impossible, catastrophe is likely to be the inevitable agent of change, whether in the form of the direct fruits of such political failure or simply as an external intrusion into an otherwise incapacitated (or ineffective) political system. While some aspects of catastrophic change are therefore generally predictable, others can never be and must therefore remain unmanipulable ruptures in the social fabric, astonishing, frightening, and ineluctable. The recent COVID-19 pandemic has already challenged political systems in profound ways that, although intuited as to their scope, have yet to be actually identified.[9]

Catastrophic politics—the politics that follows catastrophe or is intentionally in response to it—is therefore a well-practiced set of communal orderings in human history, and in some eras and places the primary set. War, drought, flood, and disease shaped decision-making in Europe throughout much of the Middle Ages and arguably beyond, and certainly in wide areas of the globe until recently, if not even today. To what degree is Brexit the result of the catastrophes of the Middle East and Saharan and sub-Saharan Africa? Decisions are being made in all polities all the time in these contexts, but on what basis and for what reasons? Catastrophe drives and shapes rationality and persuasiveness according to a particular set of pressures and constraints. Catastrophe is a politics of enforced change; and submission to its demands has been universal.

Certainly, many Christian theologians and believers in the past have recognized this on a basic level. What politics might look like in this light is perhaps not obvious, but such a politics will be clearly constrained. We will examine some of Luther's stark thinking on all this in the next chapter. One thing to be pointed out here is that, despite his wildly shifting views over his lifetime, the almost ad hoc variation in Luther's political teaching reflects the way he understood the limits of political agency with respect to ameliorative efforts. Readings of Jesus's catastrophic teaching before Luther, because they tended to avoid reflection on the present and its very real turmoil, also left politics mostly untouched by the Lord's warnings. Not so for Luther. In his vision, politics positively tumbles from its position of instrumental good. There is only so much that political agents of the world—princes, magistrates, church, *populus*—can do to "make things better." Indeed, there is little that can be done at all in the big picture, where catastrophe is not only always around the corner—in the past or in the future—but is actually ever embedded in the present moment. History has a core, and that core is catastrophe.

This is perhaps just the kind of conclusion that contemporary critics of catastrophism decry. But, on purely empirical terms, is the conclusion all that preposterous? And, from a Christian political perspective, is Luther only an unfortunate outlier to readings of Jesus's teaching? Catastrophism before late modernity was bound to a heightened sensitivity to mortal limits and thus to the nature of mortal goods. It cannot be repeated often enough that individual and social experience demanded and honed such sensitivity before the era of extended (and finally the doubling of) average life spans, an extension of human longevity that began around 1900.[10] Infection, disease, nutrition, sanitation, accidents, violence, wars, droughts and famines, floods, earthquakes, and the rest—the numbing list of assaults on human life that were endemic to existence, rather than being only the "tragic" intrusions we see them as today, must never be dismissed in our attempts to understand not only the past but the present to which the words of Scripture point us. Historians, as we will see in the next chapter, can outline some of these realities as a way of elucidating the experiential contours of, say, Luther.[11] The challenge is to embed these particular studies into our understanding of human existence more broadly and thus of the political scope such an existence in fact affords.

One recent and remarkable effort to this end is the demographic historian Walter Scheidel's *The Great Leveler* (2017).[12] The subtitle explains Scheidel's project: *Violence and the History of Inequality from the Stone Age to the Twenty-First Century*. The overall argumentative conclusion is simple: income inequality within societies has never really been significantly mitigated by normal political means; rather, such mitigation has come about only through the catastrophic disruptions in human society caused by what Scheidel imagistically labels the Four Horsemen of War, Revolution, Social Collapse, and Plague. For a host of reasons and in various ways, these disasters force societies into adjusted economic relations in which the gap between rich and poor is narrowed, sometimes even drastically. Yet precisely as peace and stability set in—that is, as societies recover from the disruptions of catastrophe—income inequality reasserts itself.

While Scheidel has as a starting point the various and increasingly unequal economies of nations after World War II, his vast canvas takes in all of human history. With stunning consistency, he documents how the significant narrowing of income inequality within societies—European, South American, Asian—has almost always been confined to post-catastrophic periods following plagues, invasions, natural disasters, wars, violently destructive revolutions, and the political collapse of nations and consequent chaos.[13] These post-catastrophic periods rarely last very long, however, and as political systems are remade, fueled, and oiled for long-term use, the old or perhaps new inequalities (re)assert themselves. In a more popular article dealing with North America today, he writes, "If history is any indication, . . . the resurgence of inequality since the 1980s should not have come as a surprise." In our era, he goes on to say,

> making America more equal again will prove the more daunting challenge. Whereas incremental policy measures to shore up the fortunes of the middle class are both desirable and feasible, the past suggests there is no plausible way to vote, regulate, or teach society back to the levels of equality enjoyed by the postwar generation. History cannot predict the future, but its message is as unpalatable as it is clear: With the rarest of exceptions, great reductions in inequality were only ever brought forth in sorrow.[14]

It is surely "unpalatable" to read this. Interestingly, Scheidel concludes his politically depressing volume by weakly attempting to deflate the practical horror of his larger argument by thinly explaining why the "four horsemen" have perhaps lost their legs in the past fifty years: pandemics are probably no longer possible in an age of global communication and even partially coordinated medical response (how wrong he was there); the threat of catastrophic war has been reined in by nuclear worries, and nuclear war itself is a receding danger (he somehow ignored an era that still contains the likes of Vladimir Putin); and so on. He seems to say that, however inadequate, contemporary politics is at least left with an increasingly noncatastrophic context in which to work.

I doubt it. Scheidel seems to have put aside the realities of how AIDS changed the world politically, economically, and culturally and how economic dislocation, whatever its causes—failed states, climate change, and, if only in perception, migration—is currently upending stable political systems in both the UK and the US.[15] And, of course, the world marches on since the book's publication in 2017 in directions that, after all, are hardly more surprising than they are dispiriting. But his book is less interested in the failures of politics than in the successes, as it were, of catastrophe, and thus he ends up inflating catastrophic efficacy while avoiding an analysis of that efficacy's relative character: it is only because political processes have been intrinsically ineffective that catastrophic social upheaval has been able to provide openings to effective change, and change, at least in terms of this or that measure (e.g., income equalization), for the better. Furthermore, such change has come only sometimes and at costs that in retrospect may be politically unacceptable. The real question, then, has to do with the causes of the ineffectiveness of normal politics and why catastrophe does better. For if in fact "catastrophe does better"—better according to some extraordinarily limited metric—then not only will the political initiators of catastrophe (they exist) be emboldened but, from a completely different vantage, the Christian might be encouraged to see the catastrophic world less as his or her enemy than as simply part of the gift of creation itself, one in which the peculiar graces of faith can find their flourishing.

Here the reasons are clear enough, at least in terms of describing the root of the problem. Normal politics engages in categories that are hopelessly complex and have become ever more so, as we shall see in chapter 11. Catastrophe, by contrast, is effective to the degree that it drastically simplifies these categories, mostly through destructive processes. While it is hard to demonstrate this claim conclusively, it is a demonstration that cries out to be attempted. The argument is straightforward: the problems facing human societies, especially in a world of expanded populations and networks (something that goes back to the ancient world), are too complex to be solved through the application of social analysis. This is so for two reasons: first, the analysis itself will always be inadequate to the problem and, if not outright false, at least misleading; and second, the application of such analysis, given its complexities, is impossible to effect given the multiplication of the players involved.

From this perspective, there is a clear reason why catastrophe is effective in political terms: it destroys complexities. It does so by destroying peoples, their institutions, their desires, and the impossibly manipulated networks of decision-making that gum up the works. Catastrophe does not create good leaders or strong vision in and of itself. In fact, it can crush these as much as it crushes anything. But catastrophe clears the field with its sweeping forces, and the narrative of de novo will sometimes include, as well, new clarities of decision and action. Certainly, in the wake of the Four Horsemen, there are fewer pieces to involve—of persons, interests, pressures.

My point here is not to celebrate catastrophe. God forbid! My purpose in elaborating the ineluctable and incessant social power of catastrophe is, rather, to disabuse ourselves of certain presuppositions about the way politics itself works and ought to be defined. In the light of the catastrophic character of social change—and hence of political judgment, forced or otherwise—we can say the following:

- First, catastrophe is, it appears, the unhappy partner of normal politics. It breaks in, breaks apart, and stirs up political action in ever new ways.
- Second, catastrophe is, even more specifically, an aspect—even a central aspect, perhaps even a necessary aspect—of ameliorative politics, the work political agents engage to make common life "better." We could say that catastrophe is normal politics' stalking horse, behind which our quotidian political efforts work themselves out, often in a desultory fashion. We will look at the relationship of normal and abnormal politics in chapter 12; but here we can simply say that catastrophe demonstrates that abnormal politics is inseparable from the politics of stability, and thus that security, in a Hobbesian sense, is rarely something that can be pinned down and in fact merges, for the Christian, with the possibility of the ultimate offering of *kiddush Hashem*.
- Third, therefore, catastrophe is a normal part of normal Christian politics to the degree that Christians engage politically at all. Catastrophe is not an outlier, nor is it a religiously perverse obsession. Just the opposite: catastrophe, just because of normal politics' bondage to its force, is religiously central.

These points have their practical consequences. They ought to relativize and disrupt, as we have been arguing, the ameliorative assumptions of much modern Christian politics. They ought also to reorient what counts as "the political" in Christian terms toward alternative goods—alternative or in addition to, that is, normal political calculations as they are amelioratively conceived. The goods of this life are in fact other than we might normally imagine. Put in a more traditional way, Christian politics—no surprise—conceives of the "goods" of human life in terms other than those offered by "the world."

From a Christian perspective, we are ever in the midst of catastrophe. More than that, because this kind of history, which is scripturally inscribed, is by definition a divinely wrought reality, catastrophe is a Christian theological category par excellence. If catastrophe is simply, though often horrendously, a form of change, as the word ("overturning") suggests; if catastrophe is something that happens in the face of human incapacity, political and otherwise; then catastrophe's historical meaning for Christians ought to be a central theological concern. To be mortal is to be changed into and from—to be created. All creation is catastrophic.

The Christian faith, for instance, makes fundamental claims about the shape of individual catastrophe in terms of suffering, loss, and death. These in turn have been seen as inevitable aspects of the character of human creatureliness—that is, mortality and, however shaped by sin, human incapacity. But Christianity is also deeply concerned with social catastrophe as well, although this topic, in a way that exceeds the modern obscuring of individual limitation and even evanescence, has been mostly muted in recent Christian discussion, except as a claim to vigorously hold at bay. Leaving aside the catastrophes elaborated in the kinds of apocalyptic description disdained by contemporary critics of fundamentalist Christian millennialism, including that of the book of Revelation, the fact is that the Scriptures as a whole represent human history in extended, variegated, and consistently catastrophic terms, such that Mark 13 is itself but a figure among many. The so-called apocalyptic sayings of Jesus are, in fact, all very familiar in scriptural terms and do not point to a marginal and astonishing inbreaking of terror. Indeed, so-called apocalyptic literature is really very similar to Wisdom literature in outlining the meaning of quotidian "normality." If creation itself is "abnormal"—and it is—then normality is always subordinate to mortality's grand overturning of all things.

From the early chapters of Genesis through the New Testament epistles—including the Gospels—peoples, nations, and of course Israel in particular are subjected to catastrophic experience: floods, droughts, invasions, plagues, pests, and earthquakes. At the center of the Bible, in a kind of supreme catastrophic figure, is the destruction of Jerusalem and the temple and the complete dismantling of Israel's political system. That the cross itself engages this figure explicitly thus locates catastrophe at the center of Christian theology in such a way that apocalyptic cataclysm involving the sudden destruction of large portions of the human race, when it is described in the Gospels and letters, appears as an extension of a Christian theological vision rather than as a novel and extraneous perspective that somehow requires new exegetical tools. As we will see, Luther brings a newly pointed perspective to Christian catastrophe when compared to earlier Christian interests, which tended to decouple the present from the particulars of Jesus's prophecies. But perhaps early Christian interpreters of texts such as Mark 13 did not talk much in terms of contemporary reference (as they didn't) because the connection was so clear as to be banal; and Luther's interests are not so much new as they are newly pressured by a changing set of cultural expectations.

If this is so, then the developing early modern and modern line of Christian political theology, which aimed at engaging the efficacy of decision-making, either positively or correctively, in democratic or revolutionary forms, can at best be but a secondary mode of ecclesial ethics. Rather, the primary mode of Christian politics should be aimed at living faithfully within or in the face of catastrophe, not effectively preventing or evading it.

Catastrophe is often viewed as an "end time" category, and that has in part been the basis for critiquing its usefulness. Biblically described cataclysm is, as it were, a counsel of despair as well as a perverted and ultimately lazy trust in the value of ultimate destruction. Why bother trying since it is all about to go up in smoke anyway? But scriptural catastrophism is not primarily about the end of all things—even if that end is also a given. Rather, catastrophism is about change that lies mostly outside of human control. Hence, catastrophe, in a Christian sense, is not about endings but about the character of the "middle," which lies between unsought beginnings and inevitable endings. That middle is, of course, characterized by a host of smaller, if often wrenching, endings. There is a middle time, nonetheless, and hence a place for living, informed essentially by its borders between birth and death.

How do we live when, as children, our parents die? How do we live when our home burns down, or is blown down or up, or is washed away with everything in it? How do we live when rivers and crops dry up? How do we live when our leaders are arrested and executed and the same fate hangs over our own labor? How do we live when children or spouse fall dreadfully ill? Catastrophe marks the character of change within a mortal existence; but that existence is nonetheless given to be lived. Isaiah tells us, "Disaster will come upon you, and you will not know how to conjure it away. A calamity will fall upon you that you cannot ward off with a ransom; a catastrophe you cannot foresee will suddenly come upon you" (Isa. 47:11 NIV). In this case the Lord is actually speaking to Babylon, not to Israel. Yet Israel is hardly free from this kind of divine assault, whereby the calamities that flow from her sin burst upon her destructively but also "suddenly" and "in an instant," like a collapsing wall (Isa. 30:13; cf. Luke 13:4; 1 Thess. 5:3). Still, all these words of God are given within a larger context of warning and promise both. By the last chapter of Isaiah, these two proclamations are interwoven into the marvelous folds of God's creative miracle, whereby the travails of birth suddenly give rise to life (Isa. 66:7–9): the Lord is in heaven, earth is his footstool, and what have human beings done? "All these things my hand has made, and so all these things came to be, declares the Lord" (Isa. 66:2 ESV). The intrusive, "suddenly" realized boundaries of our lives are transfigured by their Maker. Faithfulness here, in all of its productive accomplishments, its political will and aspiration, is given—reduced to? created? offered?—in "humility" and "contrition," "trembling," as God announces, "at my word." The tenuousness of justice, and the offering that marks its fruit, is given only here.

I realize that, just as with the general affirmation that "the days are evil," the catastrophic context of our service of God is a difficult way to frame a word of counsel for my children's flourishing and a seemingly blighted terrain in which to pursue the Good Life. We cannot evade the landscape, however, and if there be good at all, it will be grasped just here. But evasion is an ever-present temptation, to give into which brings only inconsolable sorrow. How to understand the temptation itself and the character of its resistance is thus a mark of wisdom too. To this end, in the following chapter I will give a bit of evasion's history through a more traditional survey of catastrophe's Christian "history of interpretation."

Ten

Visions of Catastrophe

Watch ye therefore: for ye know not when the master of the house cometh, at even, or at midnight, or at the cockcrowing, or in the morning: lest coming suddenly he find you sleeping.

Mark 13:35–36

.

Catastrophe is at the center of Jesus's teaching: things happen suddenly and often destructively, much like the descent of bandits upon the feasting household of Job (Job 1). Towers collapse, soldiers appear with their deadly weapons, death simply leaps upon the unsuspecting (Luke 13:1–5). And, of course, the coming of the Son of Man (Matt. 24), accompanied by the worst of the unexpected, takes place at an hour no one knows and with a change of cosmic order whose startling appearance is as sweeping as the breadth of its power.

I have argued that all this founds, rather than simply interrupts, the normal course of our lives and hence of our politics. But my claim is, admittedly, not supported by a good bit of the Christian tradition's reading of Jesus's catastrophic teaching. It is worth seeing how and why, and this chapter represents a quick overview of this interpretive history, since that history's very shape is itself illuminating of the ways that, especially more recently, the evasion of a catastrophic vision has obscured the true character of our lives and their duties, in the churches as much as anywhere. I will look at early readings of Matthew 24 and Mark 13, then at Luther and his remarkable refocusing of attention on Jesus's claims—a refocusing with which I largely agree—and finally at the more modern drift away from both the early and the early modern perspectives. The shifting ways of reading Jesus here are all very telling and sobering. They indicate, furthermore, the direction that Christian political duty, which seems to involve mostly teaching about our mortal goods and their offering, must lie.

Premodern Christian Readings of Catastrophe

All three Synoptic Gospels devote large sections to Jesus's words about this upended history (Matt. 24; Mark 13; Luke 21). While each Gospel has its own peculiar details in this regard, the fact is that much of the Christian tradition until recently was less interested in engaging in exegesis specific to a given evangelist and more focused on the larger thrust of this discussion. In the early and medieval church there was, by and large, a steady, tripartite categorization of reference that readers saw in this teaching. First is the category of the Jews, which takes up half of Mark 13—say, verses 1–13. Almost all earlier interpreters were clear that Jesus's remarks regarding the temple, wars, and persecutions are fundamentally aimed at his Jewish contemporaries and at the immediate context in which the apostolic church would be oppressed by both Jews and Romans. This is a historical claim, and commentators link the text to specific events—Roman emperors and the chronology of Judaic demise—trolling writings like those of Josephus in order to emphasize the historical reality of divine judgment upon the Jews.[1] Hilary of Poitiers can stand as an example:

> All this happened in Jerusalem, just as it had been foretold; the city was consumed—ruined by her stonings, by her expulsions, by her murder of the apostles, by her hunger, by war, and by her captivity. For having rejected the preachers of Christ, she was shown to be unworthy of God's message and not worthy to exist.[2]

This emphasis is then often used as a contrast with the unexpected triumph of the church, as exemplified in Chrysostom's habitual practice:

> O strange and wonderful facts! Countless myriads of Jews did the Romans then subdue, and they did not prevail over twelve men fighting against them naked and unarmed. What language can set forth this miracle? For they that teach need to have these two things [i.e., dispossessed vulnerability] to be worthy of credit, and to be beloved by them whom they are instructing.[3]

The apostolic suffering of the early church, Chrysostom says, is what has given us our now relatively peaceful Christian existence.

The second category of Jesus's catastrophic teaching touches upon the referents from Mark 13:14 on: these are almost universally understood to point to the "last days," those leading up to Christ's second advent and final judgment. Antichrist, terrestrial disaster, and so on are all pressed into a future that, whether distant or near, is nonetheless unknown even on Jesus's own terms (v. 32). In general, the interpretive traction here is given in terms of moral preparation.[4] Jesus's catastrophic remarks, then, are temporally divided into two periods: Jewish catastrophe and eschatological catastrophe.

The third category of reference has to do with the inner life of the Christian and of the church. This is the least consistent in the history of interpretation. It involves either taking aspects of the first category and extending them to the church's enemies subsequent to the Jews—heretics and infidels—or allegorizing aspects of Jewish oppression and demise so as to refer "spiritually" to the Christian soul beset by sin and driven to a kind of flayed existence before God. The "temple" destroyed is not only the body of Jesus but also the body of each individual; and assaults upon it are due to sin. Usually, these texts of destruction are linked to John 2:19–21, where resurrection and its hope are then brought in.[5]

Taken as a whole, then, the standard approach is to present this text as referring to three things: a wicked Jewish past containing a virtuous apostolic witness; an unknown future, before which we should be warned; and an interiorized display of eternal life and death, through which we might be prepared. Thomas Aquinas's *Catena Aurea* on Mark 13 as well as parallel texts epitomizes this outline in an exclusive manner.[6] What is missing in all this, of course, is "today"—the historical present and its era.[7] The standard approach is fairly steady, it seems, across the centuries until the Reformation.

Luther, by contrast, marks a distinct change in interpretative custom. The shift is powerful and extensive and deserves focused attention, not so much because Luther discovers something unknown about the text's meaning, but because he articulates something long only experientially intuited but rarely articulated. Later in his life, Luther took over preaching duties in Wittenberg and delivered several long series of sermons, including one on the entire Gospel of Matthew.[8] His treatment of Jesus's catastrophic teaching in Matthew 24 is, in this context, surprisingly elaborated.

Like the tradition before him, Luther maintains a sense of both past historical reference and future reference. Thus, he has no problem—which is hardly unexpected for Luther—in seeing Jesus's initial remarks about the temple's destruction and subsequent war as directly aimed at the Jews and their perfidy. Likewise, the latter part of Jesus's teaching here envisions catastrophic events that must precede the end of time and final judgment. But unlike the earlier tradition, Luther is in fact most interested in "today": all the horrors that are announced in warning by Jesus—killing, division, uproar—apply to us, he says pointedly.[9] And he spends most of his energy, over his several sermons on the topic, outlining the nature of the "today" that Jesus is indicating to the sixteenth-century Germans Luther is preaching to.

Luther is hardly naïve, nor is he unconsciously moralistic in making this move. He underlines the way that Jesus—in Matthew, and in Mark and Luke in their own way, too, he says—"mingles the times" in a deliberately confusing way in his discourse. Jesus speaks of the history of Jerusalem in his own day and immediately after; but he also seems to be speaking of the end of the world at the same time, in such a way as to bring both into the present. "It is also usual for the Holy Spirit to speak this way in Holy Scripture," Luther notes.[10] He then goes on to give a long example of what we would call a "spiritual" interpretation of the Genesis story, in which he explains how Scripture uses a Hebrew word that literally means "to build" when describing how God created Eve out of one of Adam's ribs; that is, God "built" Eve like a building—indeed, like Jerusalem, and like the church in fact. On this basis, Luther argues, Paul's use in Ephesians 5 of the creation story of Adam and Eve, given in marriage, as a sacramental figure of Christ and the church makes sense. "The Holy Spirit often uses phrases like this" in order to unveil how the ages of the world interpenetrate one another. That is, even the initial verses in Matthew 24 about the destruction of the temple are actually also about the final judgment or, indeed, about us. "Thus [the evangelist] also uses some words here [in Jesus's teaching] in the same way to shed light on the world's final calamity, which is signified by the fall and destruction of Jerusalem—for the Church's tribulation will be just like this."[11]

The category Luther uses to designate this form of the Holy Spirit's speech is synecdoche. This literary term refers to using a part to signify the whole or vice versa; the container for the contained; or a sign to refer to the thing signified. A common example that illustrates this today is speaking of "the White House" to refer to the US presidency. Luther employed the category of synecdoche elsewhere in his writings to explain the eucharistic presence: Jesus's words "This is my body" can be applied to a locally cir-cumscribed instance of the Lord's Supper while in fact truly signifying the whole reality of Christ's incarnational self-giving.[12] But in his discussion of Jesus's teaching on the destruction of Jerusalem, Luther uses the term "synecdoche" to refer to the nature of history itself.[13] The "end"—the end of time even—is always "joined to the beginning," he says, both in literary terms (the end of the world is given in the New Testament's opening Gospels) and in created experience (the "last days" are always embedded in the present days). This is how the world is ordered by God, he says.

This way of looking at history sets in motion a thoroughgoing figuralism with respect to Jesus's catastrophic teaching: the Jews, the temple, Jerusalem, earthquakes, mountains—all of these are ongoing historical realities that explain our lives in the present. Hence, Matthew 24 and Mark 13 refer to the Turks, to the pope, and to sectarians (and yes, Jews too) in our own day, whose actions in one way or another will always embody the words of Jesus. "Nothing will change," Luther asserts, "except that new persecutions will arise."[14] That is the meaning, he says, of Mark 13:30: "This generation shall not pass, till all these things be done."

Luther is relentless with his synecdochic reading. Jesus's words refer, as do the persecutions and terror they unleash, to everything that is nearest to us: to neighbors and colleagues in our midst—magistrates, townspeople, peasants, preachers, pastors.[15] On these matters, Luther goes to town in ways that are now notorious. He is also palpably honest and concrete about the elements that mark the terror of Jesus's words. He describes not only from the past but in his own cities and in his listeners' homes what suffering a pestilence will wreak—whether plague, pox, or syphilis—or what a fire will destroy, or a war annihilate, or a famine eradicate. He has seen it with his own eyes and felt it with his own body and heart, just as have his listeners. He even tries to restrain himself from getting religiously carried away: many of our sufferings are man-made, not even divinely orchestrated, he notes—the result of greedy merchants and princes hoarding and fanning inflation, stoking famine because of their manipulation of the markets. As if this helps. For in the end Luther knows that his life and that of his people is catastrophically ordered—that is to say, completely out of our hands to control, because our lives belong to God precisely in their limits—if not today, then yesterday or tomorrow. But, of course, most especially today, since today is the focus of the limits that come rushing in upon us. "To day if ye will hear his voice, harden not your heart" (Ps. 95:7–8; Heb. 3:7–11, 15; 4:7).

"Todays" can be deceptive, of course. People go along with their tasks of tilling, working, eating, raising children, playing (cf. Matt. 24:38). Then "suddenly," as every catastrophe is described, things are upended. Mortality is not simply the liability to such catastrophe; rather, it is the act and meaning of living in a world of catastrophe. Luther's discussion, then, is not one of moralistic finger-wagging. "Today" is in fact the definition of fragility, something he and his listeners understood well because they lived it.[16] Sixteenth- and early seventeenth-century Europeans bore a cascading and cumulative burden of suffering that is quantifiable and stunning: climatic and epidemiological disaster, unending warfare, crop failure, and hunger, even as principalities and nations crumbled, collapsed, and were barely patched back together again on the ruins of their declining populace. Luther was simply surveying the world as it was, and into that world the words of Jesus brought obvious clarity. This is not what biblical interpreters call "tropology," applying a scriptural figure as a moral example. Jesus's catastrophic words apply to today only because history in fact looks this way and in fact will always look like the events and persons described in Matthew 24, since, as Luther stresses, "the Devil still rules the world." The dynamics of this relationship are thus constant for all ages until the end, just as is the grace of God in Christ to withstand this.[17]

Luther's approach to catastrophe, as he exegeted texts like Matthew 24, constitutes an encompassing reading of history and goes beyond a kind of psychic response to social disaster. One could say—in Luther's own terms—that religion is not reducible to a sociopsychological response to "existential insecurity" (a category deployed by sociologists to describe the sense of external pressure that orders human individual and social response within the world[18] and that is a somewhat bland reflection of one aspect of human mortality). Rather, existential insecurity is itself the reflection of religious truth; it is revelatory. Doctrinally, catastrophe given in scriptural terms simply reflects the fact that there is a God and that we are God's creatures, who are both utterly incapable of altering that relationship and utterly, therefore, given over to God's hands for our very breath, expiration, and re-creation. This revelation lies at the heart of mortal existence and thus encompasses the essential character of the goods we are given by God, which are themselves thus "mortal" goods.

When Jesus lays out the catastrophic character of human history in Matthew 24, then, he lists familiar realities: being arrested, being beaten, being falsely accused, being betrayed, being in flight, being cold, and so on. In fact, all this is also part and parcel of mortal reality, all in its own way, from family disintegration to the clear moment of witness. What Jesus says about actual life in these times is simple: endure. "He who endures to the end will be saved" (Mark 13:13 RSV). Endurance is salvation, in a way. Endurance—a word that has at its root in the Greek a steady "remaining in place"—becomes the paradoxical key to life: one "stays" and lives through that which seems to assault the ground on which one stands and the life that one sees slipping from one's hands. The Christian politics of catastrophe—that is, the Christian politics carried out in the midst of the normal politics of complex incapacity—is thus the politics of endurance.

We will look more closely at the political aspects of endurance and how it properly informs the tending and offering of mortal goods in chapter 13. But Luther's synecdochic projection of catastrophic endurance into the normal life of mortal existence was generally not a standard way to read Jesus's teaching. More commonly, orthodox Christians maintained a relatively strict temporal division when interpreting Matthew 24 and similar texts, keeping to the classical distinction between Jewish referents (especially related to the destruction of Jerusalem and its particular Judaic figures within history) and referents to the second coming. "Today" is rarely imagined. Thus "to endure," as the seventeenth-century commentator Edward Leigh noted, is something Jews and apostles do for a time; and "tribulation" is something that falls upon Jewish Israel and on those in her proximity for a time. But the space between this time and Jesus's return, "today," the middle time, is another kind of time altogether,[19] a mortal time to be sure—1650 and the time (in this case) of England's Civil Wars were hardly benign—but not one colored intrinsically by the peculiar catastrophic elements of Jesus's apocalyptic proclamations.

Catastrophe, in a view like that of Leigh, is solely the destiny of the wicked or the clothing of the wicked's final judgment. It looks on human existence from the prophetic outside, leaving the theological construal of normal time to the cultural pressures exerted upon theology more generally. The classical sequestration of catastrophe to Jews, heretics, and historical endings left the meaning of mortal life to just such larger social reframing. If catastrophe remained "special" in orthodox Christian thinking—as it remains to this day for most people, believers or not and excepting extreme pessimists of any kind—then the subjective mitigation of existential insecurity that began its slow (and then suddenly rapid) advance in Western Europe in the seventeenth and eighteenth centuries recalibrated the character of normal time into a mode that had little room to understand Luther's vision. So too, the political character of endurance seemed too meager to the theorists.

Theory, in fact, proved a major part of the demise even of the classical Christian notion of catastrophe. As temporality, under the press of natural science, was more and more reimagined as a uniform continuum—even a kind of container, in Newton's estimation—even beginnings and special judgments, let alone final ones that could wrench time from its confused slumbers, seemed less compelling. In the place of demanded preparations, adjustments, watchings, and endurings were placed strategies, plannings, and utilities. For these, a different kind of politics, detached in its essence from the mortal goods of precariousness, was needed. Here we come to the larger cultural pressures that have strangled the ability of contemporary folk, including the young, to grasp the central good of their mortal existence.

The Early Modern Marginalization of Catastrophe

Catastrophe itself never disappeared, of course, nor did Luther's own way of conceiving its informing power. The imposition of incompleteness on anyone's life is inescapable. Although commentaries on Matthew 24 and Mark 13 mostly steered clear of Luther's reflections, mortal life continued to be recognized and confronted in terms of its divine grace. Thus, while Luther's exegesis may not have been broadly embraced, many shared the existential intuitions that partly shaped it. The offering of difficult lives, incomplete lives, even mistaken lives depends on this catastrophic obbligato to existence as a created good. But as the express sound of catastrophe itself recedes and endings, upendings, the imposition of limits, and hard change become incoherent with the habits of continuity and stability, these habits themselves exhaustively shape our desires as they touch on mortal goods. Continuity and stability are projected more and more onto the fullest scope of the universe, and when this happens, the mortal good simply becomes the Good, itself immortal, that all of us can or should or could touch, if life were properly organized.

One can observe this shift from a sense of the revelatory nature of catastrophe to one of distracting irrelevance in the early modern debate regarding terrestrial geology. This proved a central topic whose origins were driven by both dogmatic and naturalist ("scientific") concerns. The naturalistic proclivity to view the world's functioning as temporally uniform—how else describe natural "laws"?—would inevitably rattle rigid biblicist accounts of creation, with their seeming chain, however unpredictable, of divine interventions and often violent rearrangements of matter: creation itself, the flood, the sun standing still, mountains smoking, and the rest. All these scriptural stories were fuel for catastrophic conceptualizations of "nature," though, as we pointed out in the last section, they were hardly necessary to orient most people to the quotidian character of existential upheaval. For Robert Burton, writing in the early seventeenth century, the world looked much like Luther saw it, a fact that, for lack of the latter's incandescent christological motive, left mostly a landscape of "melancholy," as Burton entitled his famous book.[20]

This version of experientially negative uniformity would have its own trajectory down to our era. But uniform it was, in its creationless continuity as well as in predictive certainty, just as much as with the developing natural philosophy of Burton's period. An orthodox Christian reading of human history—perfect creation, fall and disruption, emblazoned transformation in the end times—left most of that history within a single and metaphysically flattened container of normal existence, one in which religiously interesting "catastrophe" is aimed mostly at Jews and other wicked persons; and that existence, whether judged good or bad, was thus subject to a stable scrutiny from which the laws of regularity could be distilled and then perhaps applied as levers of practical utility. This last possibility would be seized with increasing optimism, so that, however catastrophic might be the bookends of history, its main story could be read in terms of a rational program and thus be, in theory, manipulable.

Thomas Burnet's *Sacred Theory of the Earth* (*Telluris Theoria Sacra*)— published in Latin and English between 1681 and 1690—offers a window on the first glimmerings of such an envisioned program. Burnet's work proved enormously popular and controversial, going through numerous editions well into the eighteenth century.[21] Today, studied mostly for its role in providing the early Romantic movement with images of the terrifying sublime, *Sacred Theory* is really a rather straightforward attempt to apply the classical vision of catastrophe to the new sciences of geology that were being pursued in Descartes's wake. Burnet famously proposed that an originally "smooth" (and ovoid) earth, ordered to fertility and meteorological perfection, was so wrecked by the universal flood as to be rendered the broken, jagged, and often breathtakingly uneven landscape in which we find ourselves today, surrounded by cliffs, peaks, and canyons. From one perspective, the fallen earth is one big catastrophe. But Burnet in fact saves this category for only the flood itself and for the earth's final unraveling and remaking at the end of time, when the mass of geological confusion that is ours today will once again be returned to its smooth perfection.

Burnet is often viewed as an early advocate for restricting geological, and in a sense even existential, particulars to a paradigm of natural causation. Even the divine catastrophe of the flood was explained in terms of a theory of terrestrial hydrology, and to this extent his view of catastrophe was closer to a modern model of geological "catastrophism," according to which changes in planetary makeup may be sudden and vast but are nonetheless tied to otherwise naturalistically explainable and ultimately predictable phenomena (e.g., asteroid impacts). But Burnet was also a fairly orthodox biblical Christian, and though his was a search for continuities in terms of naturalistic description and explication, he was relentless in demanding that these categories be subject to scriptural pressure and demand. The latter was proving increasingly difficult to satisfy, however, and even Burnet was forced to fudge a bit and speculate that Moses had adapted his creation narrative, which was void of clear references to naturalistic mechanism, to cruder minds (an argument that brought Burnet some heat). This scriptural attenuation, however slight, was nonetheless significant: catastrophe is a natural figure for Burnet. He can describe normal time in its continuous if terrifying way because mortality has become a factor of natural history rather than a divine token of creation itself. The world's natural form, post-flood (i.e., in normal time), is disintegrative. He can argue for the catastrophic "end" of the world by analogy to natural death: the world is "dying," just as individuals "die." This is all driven by naturalistic observation. Thus Burnet (in his later, private writings) seems committed to anti-annihilationism: matter is never extinguished, as it can never leave a realm of uniform laws. And in this way God's creative initiative is already fundamentally restrained.

Where is the cross? Where is the transfigured this-world reality, however tenuous, of creation? In place of these Burnet presents creation as a sign of imperfection that demands mostly a *future*. Burnet's only posthumously published reflections on the state of the dead and eternal punishment—he was doubtful of the latter's justice—sit, if not logically, at least in a moral congruence, with his compartmentalization of catastrophe's religious value: God's character must be discernible with the same kind of consistency as the natural world's forms.[22]

Burnet, despite some of his later ruminations, was quite orthodox. His *Sacred Theory of the Earth* fits well with a whole range of classical exegesis of Jesus's catastrophic teaching, and indeed has little to do with Luther's. It was, however, but a short move from this position, now entangled with naturalistic concerns, to one in which the classical exegesis itself had little purchase or interest. Soon after Burnet's work was fully published, the naturalist and early fossil collector and theorist John Woodward offered his own attempt at integrating the great flood into ongoing geological research. His *An Essay towards a Natural History of the Earth* (1695) simply takes Burnet, as it were, and lops off the catastrophic bookends to history that the latter had retained in his classical exegesis.[23] Woodward's theory retains the reality of a massively disruptive flood (this helps explain fossils) but reverses the moral character of the normal world that results. Indeed, the flood was not so much punishment—human beings were no more sinful before than after the flood—as it was simply the next step in God's merciful leading of humankind. Everything after the flood is now beneficently ordered to human betterment, so that work demands discipline and virtues can result from effort. Though the earth is less fertile than in its antediluvian form, it is better suited in its scarcer fruit for the divine pedagogy that a challenging existence permits. Furthermore, and contra Burnet, fossils seem to tell us that the earth was not, in its basic forms, fundamentally altered by the flood; everything functions as before, but now with greater aim at human flourishing.

What is odd here is Woodward's paradoxical vision of "the goodness of the fallen world." Is this a triumph of Christian hope over observation? Or is it not rather the triumph of observation itself as a religion—transferring hope to the accuracy of stating "things as they are"? Woodward's use of fossils to argue for continuity in the shape and makeup of the ante- and the postdiluvian world is precisely what makes this possible: despite the decrease of the earth's fertility after the flood, all the mechanisms and shapes are exactly continuous (and Woodward uses Scripture to show this—seas, marine life, mountains, etc.). In this scenario, moral life must properly adjust to the natural world.

Woodward's reflections are but an example of how, with eighteenth-century thinkers especially, continuities become absolutes and God's personality is injected into and elided with the hopeful evolution of the world. Catastrophe is an ideal, not a concrete, reality; catastrophe is made into a benign principle. Hence, betterment is established as the dynamic of catastrophe, not only in a limited pedagogical manner but in terms of a progressive movement. The search for universal laws and truths, which motivated Leibniz's life project, aims at discovering and laying out realities and patterns whose transhistorical applicability, in temporal and natural terms, does not present a static world, but rather one that, once these patterns are discovered, can be rightly ordered to an increasingly better-functioning set of social arrangements, measured according to an ideal.

The modern exegesis of Jesus's catastrophic teaching revolves around this larger dynamic. Historical criticism is based largely on the premise of temporal uniformity and the steadiness and predictability of the natural processes that are apparent within this uniform temporal landscape. The "historical" aspect of "historical criticism" derives from the coordinative application of this regulative order to the referents of the scriptural text and, in their interpretation, to the composition of the text itself: referents must cohere with natural laws of temporal experience, and the illumination of this coherence is necessarily bound to the laws of human composition and their own historical character. Not only are the referents of the Bible things that "really happened," according to the new historical critics of the eighteenth and nineteenth centuries—this is a traditional claim—but what it means to "happen" must be coherent with all the happenings of our experience as they are systematically coordinated. If biblical events seem incoherent in this sense, then the interpreter must explore more finely the (expected) order of their historical ingredients, which can reframe a textual referent within a larger natural scheme (e.g., cultural, psychological, and so on).

The development of historical criticism in this larger sense is a lengthy though discrete process that began in early modernity and continues to be carefully assessed in our day.[24] But we can see its fruit in the interpretation of the Synoptic "apocalyptic" discourses. In a manner similar to Woodward's approach to post-flood existence, modern exegetes of, say, Mark 13 tended to drop the classical temporal markers of catastrophe and to locate the meaning of Jesus's teaching here in limited historical terms that were continuous with normal experience. Thus, in a popular scholarly commentary of the late nineteenth century that continued to be used well into the twentieth, we see an emphatic and explicit commitment to dissolving any reference to "the end of the world" and to limiting the "prophecy" solely to the singular event of the Roman destruction of Jerusalem.[25] Jesus's use of "end of the world" imagery is explained in terms of his (or Mark's) deployment of Old Testament figures regarding the general principle of divine engagement in the affairs of Israel. But that is the point: the catastrophic tropes are common literary figures that have little to do with unique events, instead signaling certain states of mind on the part of authors and believers. Jerusalem's fall, to be sure, is a real event, but its shape is no different from any other civic disaster of the kind that marks human history. Its meaning, however, is now tied to Jesus's claim that a new "kingdom" is established "on earth" by and in him—a kingdom that, because of the grip of uniform historical existence, must be located within the spiritual consciousness of his followers rather than in reordered material existence.

There is a paradoxical consequence to this widely shared exegetical development. On the one hand, Jesus's teaching in Mark 13 is, we are told, indeed aimed at the hearer's "today," one now placed within the realm of Jesus's spiritual "kingdom." On the other hand, actual catastrophe, as depicted scripturally, is in this case limited to first-century Palestine. This is a far cry from Luther's synecdochic quotidianizing of catastrophe itself. Rather, catastrophe is now but one element within the large classificatory system of historical permutations. In a way, this modern development has looped back to earlier pagan and Christian attitudes of denigrating embodied mortality in favor of spiritual immortality. The difference in this modern version, as contrasted with an earlier commitment to postmortem immortality, is that it quite deliberately is aimed at clearing a historical space for the ideal of this-worldly "kingdom life"—that is, the building of a better world. Catastrophes are one regular item, among many, in a regular history; they are themselves without revelatory power. Similarly, the regular order of history is basically mute—neutral "stuff"—apart from the inner insights of spiritual men and women.

The epitome of this development—something like Rudolf Bultmann's sophisticated systematizing of this coordination of regular historical event and historical composition—is to concentrate divine scriptural meaning into the moment of this insight ("faith") independent of this or that actual catastrophe, whether in fact expected or only figuratively construed.[26] For Bultmann, Jesus may have believed such and such about "the end"; the Gospel writers may have believed something else; Paul something else again; and so on. The distinctions here can be identified on the basis of careful historical-critical analysis. The Christian challenge is to get at the core insight of these diverse attitudes gleaned from the confused text and to seize (or be seized by) the divine claim to which they all point: only God is true, and only God saves. There is a compelling power to the cumulative argument here, born of the sweeping range of human hopes and fears that, in this case, Bultmann traces through the layers of the scriptural text, now interpreted through his own existentialist lens. But for all that, the result is to confine God's life in the world to the interiorily instantaneous, leaving the rest of creation still to the whims of human experiment and failure. The political potentials left open here were and remain chilling.

While mid-twentieth-century European social experiments now seem unbearably frightening, they took their form within the same cleared space that progressive hopes were inhabiting. When catastrophe is no longer the very shape of existence but purely a kind of alien but bounded intrusion or, less insistently, the identifiable rough edges of an explainable universe, it too can be assuaged, choreographed, and even applied to making the world a better place—hence, internment camps, torture, eugenics and euthanasia, and the technology and techniques of extermination. Progressive hopes—whether liberal, fascistic, or communistic—all aim, on one level, at the mitigation of catastrophe, a possibility dependent on its reduction to other classifiable natural events. Such mitigation, certainly in modernity, has been tied to advancing the kinds of science that aim at "betterment" itself (as we saw with the concept's seventeenth-century invention by Joseph Glanvill). It is not simply that natural science and physics generally become sites of putative progress; rather, their applications in medicine and engineering, in particular, are seen as the shock troops against catastrophe's predations and perhaps the means for its ultimate elimination.

John Wesley could still see earthquakes, with all their horrific and sudden spoliations—as in Lisbon's iconic disaster in 1755—as clearly linked to the pattern of divine providence and punishment and thus as woven into the fabric of a human existence at the mercy of God's will. The world, he wrote in a pamphlet shortly after the earthquake, was riddled with disaster or, as he put it in an earlier hymn, with "impending plagues and woes." Though someone—a person of wealth, perhaps—might hire a carriage to escape a ravaging local epidemic, there is no exit from an earthquake that simply opens the earth in a moment "to swallow you up." Even the rich are "not out of all danger yet; unless you can drive faster than the wind." The image is rich and resonates with Old and New Testament figures of futile escape. Wesley is attacking what he sees as the atheism of the new science, which attributes all events to theoretically identifiable causes. Rather, since nature is nothing but "God's art," as he puts it, disasters must be seen as part of God's own purposeful "artistry," however terrifying. With his brother Charles, Wesley even authored a collection of hymns about earthquakes, in particular, which was devoted to this pattern and its clear demand for repentance and faith, whereby a person might grasp the divine promises of immortality beyond this world.[27]

All this was a classic, if constricted, Christian vision. Yet it was one that, in Wesley's own era, was under tremendous pressure to be re-formed.[28] The very concept of "catastrophe" had begun to migrate into discourses not only of natural science but of literature, philosophy, politics, and medical and social welfare. Wesley himself was fascinated by natural phenomena and their mechanisms, however divinely grounded, and his manuals and discourses on medicine, physics, electricity, and economics, though religiously infused, were driven by a conviction that God's beneficence, worked out in a uniform history, provided the means of alleviating human misery and that these should, in thanks, be taken up.[29] In this regard, Methodist "synergism"—the coworking of human and divine energies in the service of salvation—was laying out a social program.

Lisbon's immediate rebuilding, after all, was driven by a precise view of human ingenuity's capacity to thwart future catastrophe, in terms of both "reconstruction" and mitigation as informed by up-to-date natural science and engineering. Furthermore, these were tasks now viewed as lying squarely within the purview of a national government—that is, organizations that could deploy vast material resources and labor. Coercive impositions of betterment, from revolutionary to utilitarian-reformist, are all parts of this practical thrust that harnesses larger political forces to achieve their goals. However blinkered and psychologically self-serving were Michel

Foucault's judgments about the development of "bio-politics," his particular studies—for example, on the modern organization of prisons and mental institutions—properly uncovered the central link between technology, control, and the values of existential improvement that characterized early modern and later Western social policy.[30] These values ran across a range of ideological commitments, including the liberalism some have viewed as opposed to governmental regulation and management. Modern politics, and the outlooks from which it is derived, flows from the fantasy of assimilating catastrophe into the calculus of improvement.

The Catastrophic March of Progress

Within evolving Christian spheres, particularly in Anglo-America, the evangelical desire for individual reformation tipped, by the nineteenth century, to one side of Wesley's tottering balance—from a pure dependence upon God to an increasingly assertive commitment to social betterment as a human vocation and possibility. It was a commitment that, in all its complex forms, lay behind the great missionary expansion of that century, which was as much technological as it was religious. Glanvill himself had referred to the "discovery" of new worlds as a spur to scientific growth, and his contemporary Thomas Sprat, of the Royal Society, had identified these new lands as a destination for the "spread" of "mechanick genius," a trajectory that Wesley's own call for the "spread of the Gospel" mirrored in its movement. In the words of one 1865 paean to the contributions of the telegraph—an invention that Samuel Morse himself had famously christened with biblical gravitas ("What hath God wrought!" [Num. 23:23])—the progress that Glanvill had first identified as one of mostly theory now clearly and concretely included catastrophe's taming. Commenting on Morse's work, the contemporary journalist W. H. Russell wrote,

> Next year will see the renewal of the enterprise of connecting the Old World with the New by an enduring link which, under God's blessing, may confer unnumbered blessings on the nations which the ocean has so long divided, and add to the greatness and the power which this empire has achieved by the energy, enterprise, and the perseverance of our countrymen, directed by Providence, to the promotion of the welfare and happiness of mankind. Remembering all that has occurred, how well-grounded hopes were deceived, just expectations frustrated, there are still grounds for confidence, absolute as far as the nature of human affairs permits them in any calculation of future events to be, that the year 1866 will witness the consummation of the greatest

work of civilised man, and the grandest exposition of the development of the
faculties bestowed on him to overcome material difficulties.[31]

The taming itself was still, for most people, a hope and not a reality. But
the hope colored how reality was increasingly described. The history of the
concept of "progress" is well-worn. J. B. Bury's celebrated 1920 study *The
Idea of Progress* articulated the still-current paradigm that contrasts a premodern view of the world as generally in "decline" with a modern view that
sees human history as, more or less, a succession of civilizational improvements in terms of knowledge, culture, and perhaps even morals.[32] Greek
religion and ethics, with their stress upon the dangers of human pride, had
no room for any sense of human progress, and even a self-congratulating
Roman imperial outlook still faced the reality of its own brevity and the unrelenting changelessness of human misery. With Christianity—Augustine
being a key theorist here—human history was conceptually tethered to a
providential divinity whose promise of final judgment was also tied to the
uniqueness of a divine intervention in Christ, both of which relativized any
sense of historical permanence. It was a vision enshrined quite distinctly in
the catastrophic teachings of the Gospels themselves. If the world was soon
to end, the world was also in its final era; it was aged and mostly enfeebled,
a *mundus senescens* (a world growing elderly).[33]

Bury's sharp contrasts have been contested, and there have been subsequent histories of the idea of "progress" by prominent scholars—Christopher
Dawson, E. L. Tuveson, Robert Nisbet, Margarita Mathiopoulos—that have
refined and even rearranged his genealogy, both in earlier periods and in
more recent ones.[34] But whatever the details, Bury was right, it seems, in
stressing how the intellectuals of the seventeenth century, in both Britain
and France, reinterpreted the "aging" world and gave rise to new Christian
views of history, now sharpened by novel political arrangements, missionary
endeavors, and scientific experiments. The watchword became "novelty":
if Christianity itself was new in its appearance on the historical stage and
thus refreshed the world, so too would the Christian church and civiliza-
tion set in motion a movement of constant renewal. The issue wasn't the
valorization of spiritual youthfulness, but rather a newly positive judgment
on the value of temporal accumulation: like money, knowledge and experience could be gathered, year by year, grown and furthered, simply by the
passing of time. "Now" is thus always wiser than "yesterday"; and if it is
not, "now" is being unfaithful to its calling.

In this framework of expectation, God's ending of the world could only be
a kind of gracious surd of supererogatory beneficence. Postmillennialism,

as it came to be called—a scriptural theory that placed the millennium of Christ's rule on earth before this end—was the perfect container for such Christian progressivism: things would get better, and humans (or Christians, in particular) would lead the way until, at some point, perfected existence under Jesus could be experienced.[35] Only then comes the end, no longer catastrophic but a glorious crown to a well-run race. The issue is continuity of human effort, and the expected advance in the accumulation of human wisdom and skill (all things being equal) remained lodged in the postmillennialist vision. "The end" became a mostly indefinitely deferred, perhaps even "mythologically" useful, literary figure for this vision. Here the specifically Christian attenuation of catastrophe merged easily with more explicitly and areligious political theory. Bury was himself a liberal whose view of progress fell into the category, as he explained it, of "indefinite" improvement, uncertain in its ends, driven by individual liberty, trial and error, and hiccups and surges, pressing forward with normal human effort as well as genius—but progress nonetheless, however humanly fueled as well as resisted, and measurable on any number of levels.[36] It is a view that remains relatively entrenched in Western societies and has widely permeated Christian churches in such contexts. Wesley's later and more benign, though highly moralistic, views of human history have been largely secularized, with social opprobrium and shame, even repression, replacing the divine agency for judgment that Wesley certainly retained, even while demanding that social improvement remain the essential vocation of human effort.

Obviously, catastrophe as a discrete and punctiliar event does not fade from the experiential scene just because of the rise of a political culture of progress. We shall touch on catastrophe's insistent role upon the historical stage in the next chapter. Here it is enough to have sketched the conceptual and social terrain in which catastrophe became finally a politically dangerous category, the tool of religious fanatics and their destructive pessimisms. Curiously, however, contemporary critics of "catastrophic politics" share more with their purported enemies than one might imagine, precisely because our common life has been shaped by a shared sense of human existence as in fact *not* defined in its fabric by catastrophe essentially, but only occasionally.

The most usual bogeymen of contemporary anti-catastrophism are certain popular Christian dispensationalists, who are viewed as irresponsibly consigning the human future, and thus contemporary political effort, to the literal flames of nuclear war or ecological disaster, in the sure and certain expectation of the imminent return of our Lord. Here, to be sure, lies a contrast to the postmillennialism of early modern Christianity.[37] In fact, though, dispensationalism has little to do with Christian catastrophic thinking, whether quotidian (as in the traditional petitions of something like the Anglican Great Litany) or explicitly theorized (as with Luther). Indeed, dispensationalism trades on the kinds of temporal compartmentalizations—each with their own internal uniformities and all within a single temporal frame—that permit catastrophe's containment within certain (in this case) scripturally defined periods and peoples. The Babylonians have their dispensation, Jewish Israel its own; Jesus too has a particular time with a set of moral constraints within it, as does the church, and so on; and each of these is carefully laid out in scriptural order. The dispensationalist world has its succession of disasters, but their divine designations do not, in this case, upend the laws of uniform experience by which the Bible itself is read in a very modern fashion. The world may not be getting "better," in this perspective, but it is advancing in a measurable way to its divine end, and each step marks the "ever closer" attainment of that goal. The whole outlook is upheld by its own kind of de-volution from an exegetical honesty that confronts the challenges of Matthew 24 and Mark 13. That my own family might be a referent of Jesus's words of sudden demise, in any "now" of our small lives, is as strange a thought to the dispensationalist as to his secular political critics.

Certainly my family should not be so cursed. On this score, all of us think the world *should* be getting better, at least for me; and that wish makes a certain kind of politics at least self-interestedly progressive in its logic. Who-ever we are, our default political ideology is betterment, tied most assuredly now to the fabrications of scientific or technological application, as we noted earlier. These are not without measurable ballast: life span, wealth, physical security, and so on. When in 1961, as an outgrowth of the post–World War II Marshall Plan, the Organization of Economic Cooperation and Develop-ment (OECD) was formed, the goal was to coordinate data, knowledge, and policies that would promote "development" among European and Anglo-American nations. The organization has since grown a bit to include other, mostly "democratic" and economically well-functioning countries, and for decades now the group has marshaled its research resources for the sake of encouraging what is now simply called "progress" among its members and the larger community of the world. Among the OECD's ongoing pro-jects is its survey of what is called "well-being," which has used an evolving set of metrics and statistical methods in its analysis.[38] By all measures, in 2020 the OECD was certain that things were getting better and that social politics was happily at the root of these improvements:

> The good news is that well-being has, in some respects, improved relative to 2010—a year when the impacts of the financial crisis continued to be

deeply felt in many OECD countries. We are living longer, safer lives. Across OECD countries, life expectancy has increased by more than one year, with the average baby born today living to over 80 years of age. The OECD average homicide rate has fallen by one-third since 2010, road deaths are down, and people feel safer when walking alone at night in their neighbourhoods. One in eight households live in overcrowded conditions, 3 percentage points fewer than in 2010. Income and jobs are on the rise—with both the employment rate and average household incomes increasing since 2010 by over 5 percentage points. Today, almost eight in every ten adults are in paid employment. Recent surveys suggest people are more satisfied with their lives, relative to how they felt in 2013.[39]

This judgment, based on a historical canvas upon which one could trace a nicely, if relatively recent, rising curve of happiness, has been shared by many,[40] such as the cognitive scientist and public intellectual Stephen Pinker, in a widely cited volume whose title places the argument squarely within a stream that Bury might have sketched: *Enlightenment Now: The Case for Reason, Science, Humanism, and Progress.*[41] While not everyone is comfortable with the almost glib certainty of Pinker's assertions, his general thesis is mostly accepted, even if only as an aspiration whose motive values are now part of a common stock of assumptions. Even if, as one major 2017 volume on the topic has concluded, we are now at a crossroads of decision with respect to the "remarkable social gains [that] have been achieved over the centuries," these have left "humanity . . . in a much better position to advance individual and collective well-being than ever before." That is, even if there are clouds on the horizon of our progress, "working together, we can inspire, innovate and accelerate sustainable social interventions that promote human well-being."[42] As Charles Taylor has argued, the elimination of "pain" has gained ascendency over the past centuries as a prime moral imperative—every calculus is now "utilitarian" in a basic sense. Not only that, contemporary culture's self-description is as a force for accomplishing just this demand, whether or not in this or that instance achievement has been won.[43] This self-description is the important feature of much of today's political life, by which rival utilitarianisms can be sustained and extended in a way that leaves little room on the field simply for learning how to live with quotidian catastrophe, let alone considering seriously its endemic nature.

While philosophers have distinguished a range of approaches to "welfarism," as the driving social value of well-being has been dubbed, the attempt to create lists or categories is pervasive. OECD has its own fairly unexceptional elements: income, housing, work, health, education, environmental quality, safety, and then a range of more "subjective" measures such as feelings of satisfaction and purpose, work-life "balance," social connections, and perceived "civil engagement." By these measures, OECD nations had made a good deal of "progress" in the seven years between 2013 and 2020. Of course, then came 2020 itself, with its pandemic. Within a year, OECD had determined that "the [COVID] virus caused a 16% increase in the average number of deaths across 33 OECD countries between March 2020 and early May 2021, compared with the same period over the previous four years. Over the same time frame, survey data in the report reveal rising levels of depression or anxiety and a growing sense among many people of loneliness and of feeling disconnected from society." Life span had decreased by almost a year, and employment, housing, health, and many of the subjective aspects of OECD's snapshots had tumbled.[44]

That none of this should have come as a surprise is itself surprising, whatever one's religious commitments. We will note in a moment the progress of "progress" after its flourishing political assertion in the nineteenth century. The notion that one might be moving into, perhaps even attaining, a world where tears are wiped away and catastrophe but an occasional and muted accident—the gate left open now and again for the devil to sneak in at night—was refuted by historical experience over and over again. Still, the culture of progress has barely relinquished its grip on political thinking. It is the only way we know how to think, even if we don't like it. As with C. P. Snow's grandfather, who had moved from his own unnamed grandfather's rural existence to the drudgery of an industrial tramway laborer, there is little means by which we can look to the past with any practical positivity. As Snow writes in his now-classic discussion of the "scientific" and the "humanistic" mind, "To people like my grandfather, there was no question that the industrial revolution was less bad than what had gone before. The only question was, how to make it better."[45] From a purely scriptural point of view, this is simply incoherent. The Bible's discussions of catastrophe, with their complete disinterest in outcomes of betterment, are clear enough on this score. They are clear because of the fundamental nature of creation, which has no clear movement across the uniform landscape of space and time, only the dynamism of fits and starts that mark what any created world, simply because it is distinct from God, could ever be. Catastrophe, that is, is an essential aspect of our mortal being, unveiling the nature of those mortal goods that human creatures are called and privileged to tend, engaging as necessary a politics not of betterment but of limited and gratefully informed survival. Why we cannot ask for anything "more," and the increasingly anxious refusal to accept this, is the topic of the next chapter.

Eleven

Infinite Finitudes, Desperate Complexities

O Lord, how manifold are thy works! In wisdom hast thou made them all: the earth is full of thy riches. So is this great and wide sea, wherein are things creeping innumerable, both small and great beasts.

Psalm 104:24–25

As Wesley noted, if we can run "faster than the wind," then perhaps we can escape the enclosing and catastrophic frontiers of our lives, singly or in common. But we cannot. While the sea has its boundaries, its greatness is such as to swallow us up. One of the reasons it is perhaps impossible to run from catastrophe is because the course of such a flight is endless. Flight must mirror progress, in human terms: each is an attempt to get beyond limits—limits that, because of our creaturely status, have their being only in the hands of the infinite Creator. To reach God or to run from God and the character of his work is essentially without human definition. To move on is as impossible as moving away. The reality of being a creature assures us of this odd proportion: mortality is not simply a limit upon biological life; rather, it describes the fact that created life is utterly given in terms that are not its own, that are therefore nonfinite in every way, and that the creature cannot identify, understand, or effectively grasp. Though constituted by finitude, mortality is given as an infinite gift that is ever beyond

151

our control, negatively or positively. Dying—born of the gods and reflective of their laws, as Sophocles said, or better, the shadow of God the Almighty as our creator—is the great complexity that swallows up human genius at every turn.[1]

The political consequence of this is that, pragmatically, creaturely life cannot be bettered or changed at root, and attempts at change must always set one adrift in the unending expanses of the unsortable. Thus, in Scripture, sins and the calamities of divine punishment are often described in images of boundlessness, uncountability, or numberlessness: they are heavier and more numerous, in a favorite trope, than the sands of the sea (Job 6:2–3; Jer. 15:8); or, evils are more than the hairs of the head (Ps. 40:12). This abyss of creaturely suffering mirrors the infinity of divine life: God's thoughts are innumerable and past understanding (Ps. 139:17–18; Isa. 55:8). Hence, the sand's extent can characterize good things, too, like descendants (Jer. 33:22). So, when Paul tells the Galatians that, in assuming some portion of the law, such as circumcision, one is obligated and bound to keep the whole law in its fullness (Gal. 5:3)—a calling that is in fact impossible, given that all are sinners (Rom. 3:23)—this playing with the infinities of demand, sin, and divine grace forms the basis for Paul's handing over of complexity to the miracle of divine justification. So Anselm intuited in his famous outline of the atonement: only God can sort us out.[2]

This dogmatic connection, exemplified in the concept of justification, is an important one to bear in mind when thinking of Christian politics, which, for understandable reasons, has tended to treat complexity as a problem to be solved rather than one before which we bow. Critics of modernity whose analysis is based on social organization—brilliant thinkers like Ivan Illich—can appear to be Luddites largely because of their failure to engage complexity. Organizing billions of people to some common end requires the imposition of unnatural structures upon and within life, humanly fabricated structures, "advanced technology," to which a human life must be subordinated. There is no point, one might say, in being nostalgic about a past whose social breadth was much easier to manage. But there are many progressivist versions of the same failure, which assume that difficult social challenges can be resolved without confronting the implacable and impenetrable reality of large numbers as a reflection of human life and its challenges.

The organization of common life, and thus of life within this network of numberlessness, cannot finally be manipulated instrumentally in a successful fashion because it is too intricate. What we can call "biblical managerialism"—Scripture's accounts of the organization of vast numbers of people—is almost always associated with tyranny and oppression. Assyria and Babylon move in hordes, with huge armies compared to swarming locusts and ordered to projects of outsized human self-assertion, like Babel (Joel 1:2–7). The sins of Solomon explicitly mirror these imperial forms (1 Sam. 8:10–18; 1 Kings 5:13–16; 9:20–23; 10:14–19). Inflating size, in human terms, is always a descent into misery. But such forms, in turn, pale before the "numberless" armies of the Lord (Job 25:3). By contrast, Joseph's small family perdures far beyond the crowds of Egypt and fulfills the promise of a bequest beyond the number of the stars (Gen. 15:5; Deut. 10:22). Modest hopes uncover infinite promises.

Large numbers, then, while morally ambivalent, exist in a clear dichotomy. In human terms, they are signs of pride; in divine terms, they are marks of grace and power. Thus, "numbering" in the Bible is always only something God can do or command; for only God can make sense of and orchestrate the boundless reality of his own creation. When vast numbers are manipulated by human beings, it brings oppression; when a census is pursued on human initiative, as famously by David, it brings with it destruction (1 Chron. 21:1–27). The technological society is no different: taking up and trying to use immense numbers is always a sign of irresponsibility, of sin. For this is in part what sin is: the attempt to grasp what is ever beyond the human hand and mind (Job 38–39). We can only confess our complete incapacity before the scope of divine creativity.

While J. B. Bury focused initially on seventeenth-century discussions, including the central arguments regarding the relative value of the past and the present, tradition and novelty, more recent studies and critiques of the ideology of progress have looked at its connection to specifically economic forms of life mostly tied to quantification, to numbering. So, in a well-known, late twentieth-century discussion, Christopher Lasch reflected on the wellsprings of eighteenth-century liberalism and its theory of human desire, which demanded an openness to an inflationary, productive satisfaction. Human desire is ever-expanding and requires the space to expand; and with this growing space comes the need and possibility to produce more and more to meet our novel appetites. Lasch's study was mostly negative and sought to identify the (widely forgotten) richness of political movements, in America especially, that countered progressive thinking with a kind of traditionalist democratic populism. Lasch, like Karl Polanyi and E. P. Thompson with respect to market economies, was also attuned to the realities of progress's ignored masses as well as its victims. Given the atrocities of the recent past—the mustering of millions for invasion, war, relocation, economic transformation, and reeducation, and with it the deaths of further millions—how, wondered Lasch, can anyone responsibly believe in "progress"? Yet here we are: a society entranced by promises of well-being upheld by material and conceptual devices that have transformed the Good Life into successes measured by standards of acquisition and indulgence. The motor of "ever more," facilitated by "ever easier," fuels a political sphere manipulated by the expertise of a technocratic "elite" who claim the savvy to deliver on these promises, even while controlling with ever-greater rigidity the terms in which the promises are made.

So, writes Lasch, as he ponders the country his children are growing up in at the end of the twentieth century, we now live with the following store of habits and attitudes:

> our obsession with sex, violence, and the pornography of "making it"; our addictive dependence on drugs, "entertainment," and the evening news; our impatience with anything that limits our sovereign freedom of choice, especially with the constraints of marital and familial ties; our preference for "nonbinding commitments"; our third-rate educational system; our third-rate morality; our refusal to draw a distinction between right and wrong, lest we "impose" our morality on others and thus invite others to "impose" their morality on us; our reluctance to judge or be judged; our indifference to the needs of future generations, as evidenced by our willingness to saddle them with a huge national debt, an overgrown arsenal of destruction, and a deteriorating environment; our inhospitable attitude to the newcomers born into our midst; our unstated assumption, which underlies so much of the propaganda for unlimited abortion, that only those children born for success ought to be allowed to be born at all.[3]

The link in social experience between the ideology of progress and economic "growth," with its attendant cultural challenges, is important to consider. Progress is not simply an idea; it is an idea that has thrived on the quantifiable expansion of things, including living things and most especially people. The Edenic vocation of "multiplication" and filling the earth turns, in its postlapsarian enactment, into an ever-increasing social threat. The attempt to resolve this peril must necessarily put in play strategies of organization that involve multitudes, crowds, peoples in their hordes. The efficient outcome of these strategies, however, must always shatter upon the complexity of causal networks that human life, just in its created limitations, embodies.

Interestingly, one consistent thread of explication for mortality, which crosses different religions and epochs, is the need for a way to control population growth. Death, in this case, has long been viewed as a useful mechanism that the gods—or a providential God—imposed to keep the world from being overrun by people and animals.[4] The idea—only seemingly odd for premodern people who lived long before human sprawl but who in fact struggled consistently for sufficient resources for survival even among small groups—has obviously had a modern revival in more fatalistic and species-oriented terms. There are too many people, and the human race will not only kill off most other living beings but will take itself with them. The mechanism is, we are told, inbuilt. But more than that, the threatening catastrophe of too many people is also, intrinsically, a barrier to its own resolution. How can we possibly respond to the menace, politically, in a world of billions of individuals living in myriads of communities and hundreds of nations? Walter Scheidel's thesis regarding efficient political change being tied only to cataclysms derives from the grinding dynamics of this impossible-to-resolve challenge: if we cannot manipulate multitudes into life, the internal disasters of social dysfunction will pick up the slack.

Thus, the concept of the Anthropocene and its referents has become almost a (anti-)religious symbol of incapacity.[5] Since the 1980s, some scientists have begun to speak of the earth as having entered a new geological epoch, beginning perhaps in the late eighteenth century. The previous epoch, known as the "Holocene," is usually said to have begun thirteen thousand years ago. These are the most recent slices of the Cenozoic era, which started over sixty million years ago and saw the rise of mammals and birds. The new epoch, dubbed the "Anthropocene," also involves major changes in the earth's life forms, mainly the explosive increase of the human population and the radical contraction of nonhuman forms of life (the loss of "biodiversity"). Those scientists who have followed this framework for charting the earth's history have been mostly interested in broader geological changes that have taken place in the last two hundred years, almost all human-influenced: changes to the earth's atmosphere, to the distribution of water on the surface of the planet, to the chemical compositions of water and soil, to the structures of subsoil layers, and so on. All these are correlated to the shifting distribution of life forms on the earth and are causally tied to the expansion and activities of the single life form of human beings.

Most of us are familiar with aspects of these discussions, which have entered into the mainstream of popular ecological and environmental debate. But the fact that some of these elements have fueled an intellectual/political movement known as "posthumanism" should point us to the peculiar challenges of this biophysical moment.[6] "Posthumanism" is a term that generally describes a sense of reality—a kind of metaphysics—as well as a political ideal in which human beings are viewed as pretty much like everything else: matter in motion for a little while. The intense anti-anthropocentrism of the outlook is defining and in large part a response to the degradation of the biosphere that the Anthropocene era constitutes: we are to see ourselves as no more important than pigs, chickens, starlings, and finally trees and streams. Social policy consequences flow from this materialist egalitarianism, although exactly how they are to be determined seems intrinsically obscure: only human beings, not starlings and streams, vote or impose their wills. Apart from some universal code of decision-making, there is no reason to think that posthumanist egalitarianism would be anything other than Hobbes's state of nature writ large. Posthumanism, in any case, has no theistic, let alone scriptural or Christian, interests. Adam and the dirt from which he is made are equal, but only Adam makes choices, for good or ill, and there are too many Adams. Yet posthumanists rightly intuit the linkage between human beings and the dirt, however nihilistically assessed. The linkage itself, with its overwhelming imposition upon human beings of unresponsive forces that total up to death and disappearance, indicates how hard it is, by definition, to engage the breadth of our existence through the narrow means of human deliberation and decision. How do we vote to save ourselves? And if we do not vote, who exactly will decide?

So while the Anthropocene moment is politically charged, it has also exposed politics to its flailing inabilities, as it is faced with responding to events and realities whose character, we realize, reaches into the depths of matter and to the distance of stars in ways we have barely begun to identify, let alone disentangle. In particular, many of the concrete issues that exhaust our political debates are now shown to be caught up in these vast networks of cosmic reality—that is, they are in fact bound up with, from a human point of view, infinite complexity. "Anthropocene," from a social perspective, is a code word for "more than we imagined," "so much," even "too much to deal with." Anthropocene social realities and topics of contestation are all characterized by their dizzying extent.

Thus, the *geographical* element of our epoch's sociocultural transformation involves what is today the complete intermixing of peoples around the world. It includes transportation, communication, mobility in work, immigration, religious encounter and interrelations, and the disappearance of group isolation. The *health/life span* element includes the general doubling of the human life span in the last century, as we have indicated earlier, and a range of medical responses to human disease, accident, and frailty. Within this category is also a host of other revolutionary changes: fertility rates, child-rearing, sexuality, family order, gender character, and the nature of work. Included too is the paradoxically deliberate rejection of life through the veiling of death and the embrace of suicide and euthanasia as morally neutral or even positive human choices. The third cultural category of the Anthropocene revolution involves *social identity* and is obviously related to changes in the other two categories. This category is overtly political but also involves how individual persons relate to others. What is a nation? To whom do we bear allegiance, and hence what constitutes "loyalty" or social "commitment" even among smaller collectives? What does it mean to educate a person, and to what end? The social identity category also includes basic aspects of social ordering: the vast urbanization of the world's population and the changes in the way people relate to neighbors (if they are viewed as such), to work, and to the earth and sky, which are increasingly difficult to touch, see, and hear, let alone manipulate or refashion. The economies, in the technical sense, that maintain these shifting orderings have been the subject of much debate and conflict; but how these are intrinsically related to other aspects of our changed circumstances is rarely confronted.

Lasch's litany of social confusions turns out to be simply "what it is like to live in complex human societies." But what we see in our polities is not a doubling down on problem-solving. Instead, we encounter inarticulate surges of popular and fractured discontent that horrify in their sudden manifestations of violence and that baffle political commentators, who try to explain neatly the sources of polarizations and dissatisfactions within societies. If fixing matters here seems unachievable—that is, if social progress is a fiction—it is because the task of getting things done is being pursued in the face of a sheer numerical inundation. The extent of today's intertwined global network of political challenges represents a size of a kind Aristotle could hardly conceive, except perhaps in the almost biblical terms of the subjugated masses of Eastern (i.e., non-Greek) peoples, bound to the tyranny of a compressed, absolute will and power. Multitudes and multitudes, not really people.

The brute challenge of numbers thus emerges again in this discussion, and with it the issue of complexity as it touches political life and decision-making. Single cities now, like London, let alone Cairo or Lagos, driven by all the same forces that have been attached to the emergence of the Anthropocene era, have populations larger by multiple factors than the whole of early modern Britain as a nation. If the English realm of the sixteenth century was a place where political and religious clarity was hardly easily attained—due to religious conflict, popular unrest and misery, and violent regime change, all stoking the embers of what would become a civil conflagration in the next century—what dare we expect from today's struggles? Issues of resource usage and allocation, which are at the heart of contemporary planetary concerns, have become, in these contexts, simply baffling to political systems. How decisions get made within communities is always a matter of debate, but in today's expanded and ramified population centers, these debates are now exponentially complicated.

One might think that Christians would be attuned to these problems. After all, the attempt to make effective decisions within churches has been, perhaps, at the center of ecclesiology from the start: authority, office, process, discernment, judgment, and decree have all, at least by implication, hovered behind and informed the great debates over ministry, teaching, and sacrament, as well as mission and service. But this ecclesial experience, given its often dismal outcome and its landscape of divided Christian bodies, mirrors the dynamics of the larger contemporary political world. Conversely, this modern world and its decision-making framework of, finally, representative voting arose from the struggles of the church and from her extended incapacity to make "definitive sentence" in the sixteenth and seventeenth centuries, as Richard Hooker noted.[7] We are at a standstill with respect to critical decisions over climate change, for instance, in part because it is a challenge that demands the engagement and finally assent of dozens of nations and, within them, of myriad interest groups and billions of citizens. Even mathematical attempts to sort this out dissolve into dizzying claims whose actual political traction seems to melt in practice.[8] How to "decide," and what would such decisions entail in any case, in terms of efficacious knowledge and practice?

On a smaller scale, even tiny nations like Burundi—with around eleven million people—remain paralyzed but also violently conflicted because of their inability to find ways of making definitive sentence with respect to nation-building and ordered polity. In each case the issue is one of social and epistemic complexity driven by size and ramified relationships that do not permit knowledge mastery, consensus, and participation together. For some time now, secular social scientists have been aware of the limits of "participatory" democracy—lack of interest, expertise, and competence of expression and function (how even to manipulate the means of expression).[9] Political representatives, even professional ones, have some skills in this regard; but their road to election and tenure is also tied to embedded dynamics of corruption, whether deliberate or habituated. Yet all this has been faced and tried within the ecclesial context for centuries, with little obvious consensus, let alone common action, about how to resolve disputes and divisions. In some major respects, the tireless work of ecumenists and a few church leaders over the years has narrowed, to a previously unimaginable extent, theological and structural differences between certain major

Christian traditions—Lutheran and Catholic, say. But practical common-alities have been grasped mainly through the pressures of the churches' own social diminishment, and thus in ways that do not carry with them renewed evangelical vision or vigor. New and deep divisions, themselves now politically characterized in terms of "progressivism" versus "tradition-alism," have arisen in the wake of the old ones and are often just as pas-sionately defended.

Economists especially have wondered about these broad questions and have attempted to identify and analyze what can be called "optimum-size countries"—optimum in terms of social and economic benefits. A com-mon approach here engages what some have called "trade-offs" in size (a big country benefits from a wealth of diverse social engagement and skilled heterogeneity).[10] That said, the current world order seems to be favoring, in terms of economic optimality, "small-sized" countries, who are able to gather information efficiently, adjust viewpoints and practices, and make definitive decisions much more readily. After a certain point (fairly quickly), diversity is a drag on economic and political action. The benefits favoring small countries may not always be in place, especially in contexts of preda-tory or geographically extended warfare. But it is all relative: what counts as "small" today—a country like Switzerland has eight million people—is really quite large in the comparative sweep of world history.

Indeed, nations of one million citizens today, as Dag Anckar writes, "are by any conventional measure small members of the international com-munity"; nonetheless, he goes on, "the one million ceiling is not a valid indicator of democratic capability. Rather, states that are close to this ceiling appear over-sized within the microstate universe from a democracy point of view." Indeed, some have argued that the ideal population size for truly democratic interaction hovers around one hundred thousand, with five hundred thousand being a cutoff (that is, over five hundred thousand, size makes no positive democratic difference).[11] Which means that only smaller cities and towns—and what are called "diminutive micro-states," like Iceland and Barbados—are really capable of fulfilling the political form of life that constitutes liberal society's vision for human flourishing. This is something that should worry us.[12] Christian politics, after all—in both the ecclesial and civil spheres—has long been bound to an early modern project that has now become a fantasy: the integration of political participation, persuasion, and consensus. For the project itself, arising from a numerically constrained context of a very different era, simply makes no sense any more, if ever it did.

Britain and the Netherlands were key areas where this project took delib-erate form in the search for counsel and representation and their enabling scope via constitution and guaranteed freedoms. Philosophers and politicians drew, some have argued, from several late medieval discussions and experiments, many of which were lodged in the church's own attempt to sort out its common life—for example, the conciliar movement.[13] The basic categories of liberal political thought—whether more radical or more conservative—were laid out here in this British-Dutch matrix.[14] With the revolutions of the late eighteenth century, the constitutional bases for future liberal societies were established, including their linkage to a framework of fundamental political, and later "human," "rights." These projects and their enactment made enormous human sense. They were literally driven by social dynamics, not simply by individuals, and they ended—in the Anglo-American and then European scene—by staving off larger forms of conflict and violence through expanding political participation and agency.

But once articulated and politically established, these liberal frameworks continued to dictate ways of engaging social relations, even as their originating social dynamics changed radically—certainly in the twentieth century but arguably even earlier. The American Civil War ought to have been a key warning about the already-strained capacity of the still-young constitutional framework the country was working with. Some today, such as the writer Omar El Akkad, rightly apprehend the political analog between climate change and the American Civil War.[15] El Akkad's recent dystopian novel, *American War*, imagines what happens when US states and regions cannot agree on an energy type and its usage and draws on the impulses of much deeper cultural differences and memories. His narrative traces a descent into drawn-out and brutal violence within this fictional version of America, one that has grown from a population of 2.5 million in 1776 to over 330 million today.

Leaving aside imaginative speculations like that of El Akkad, we can ask what happened between 1600 and 2000 that began to cause the buckling of liberal political frameworks. In Britain, for instance, the population grew from four million to fifty million. And today, a single city like Lagos and its country of Nigeria now dwarf all the individual and regional players involved in liberalism's invention and rise. The driving issue behind participatory liberalism's demise over this period wasn't the drying up of natural resources, although that was certainly an element at work in terms of provoking economic instability. The issue had to do with how decisions get made about things *like* resources, given (1) this kind of population expansion; (2) all the other developments that have gone on in tandem with—and in some major respects have permitted—this demographic expansion: in science, technology, medicine, universities and education, and mobility and communication; and (3) the cultural ramifications and convolutions that have arisen both around and within these other dynamics, shaping attitudes and habits of individuals and groups, such as value pluralism, consumable leisure, choice, and multiplied and conflicting optionalities.[16]

The totality of these developments can be described according to empirical standards for measuring human-global interactions—the "Anthropocene" era, for instance, in which it is possible to quantify and analyze the degree to which changes to the earth's actual structure (surface and atmospheric) are now mostly tied to human influence. But these quantifiable changes are themselves expressions of all these cultural shifts, even as they increasingly drive these shifts in new and challenging directions. Overall, we can speak of new complexities of human interaction that have shaped the range of decision-making, especially political decision-making, in critical ways. "Complexity," and in particular increasing—perhaps overwhelming—complexity, is therefore a central aspect of the political shift from 1600 to 2000. Complexity is overturning what we have all assumed, for the past five centuries, to be "normal politics."

How should we approach this reality? Complexity, and complexity theory, has been a popular topic of study and discussion in all kinds of realms, including the social sciences. Most of the interest has been driven, however, by the business community, which has attempted to engage the challenges that firms face in a globalized economy, itself ordered by rejiggered and enfolded international systems of law and cooperation, including the European Union and large organizations like the World Trade Organization. In general, these studies aim to provide positive, and sometimes almost soothing, suggestions about the way forward through the increasingly labyrinthine corridors of national and international legal and commercial demands. The general orientation here is to outline managerial strategies that count on complex systems finding their own equilibrium and to identify habits or virtues that permit open-ended and adjustive navigation. "Boot camps" dealing with complexity and uncertainty are offered around the world for business leaders; newspapers produce podcasts for "global success in your business in the face of complexity"; and so on.

Few in this burgeoning field have engaged the basic issue of how complex societies can make decisions that matter positively in the long-term, but there are some initial studies that have been undertaken. The well-known legal scholar Richard Posner, speaking about this new research, says this: "[It] confirm[s] rather than undermine[s] my suggestion that, thus far, the application of complexity theory to social life has produced retrospective rather than prospective illumination" and appears unable to offer predictive models of any usefulness. That is, social complexity is just too complex to map out *in the present* and thus to navigate or manipulate through a formal decision-making process.[17]

Obviously, decisions get made. But not in a way that is encouraging. Some studies, for instance, seem to show that voters tend to rely more on representative expertise and leadership in the face of increasingly challenging complex issues.[18] This is hardly hopeful, as the turn to the limited knowledge and wisdom of a few, often not very well informed, representatives does not promise deeper or steadier understandings. As a result, focused political representation lays the groundwork for a dynamic of quick disaffection and repudiation by the public. Many political writers, as we noted above, who take seriously burgeoning social complexity nonetheless continue to search for avenues by which better democratic tools and systems can thread the decision-making needle: more direct democracy, more grassroots ordering of discussion and choice.[19] Others simply appeal to some kind of radical democratic reordering—"revolution"—as the solution to political paralysis and its embedded dysfunctions.[20]

But paralysis seems to be the order of the day, and it is not clear how we are going to get out of it. We are all mired in the midst of current impossibilities around participation, persuasion, and consensus (marginalization/exclusion; polarization and polemic; coercion), with the United States as a prime example. There are those who think that simply a regime change, as it were—a new president, Supreme Court, or party in power—will bring clarity and stability and will put effective and wise decision-making into play. This view has partly fueled the remaking of American party politics in the past decade or so, both on the Right and the Left. Regime change will indeed bring a host of related "changes." It is highly unlikely, however, that it will bring the resolution of contested and ineffective decisions. Not only are the ideological differences too great and too broadly dispersed across the nation to permit an emergent consensus, but the actual ability of politicians, even within a single party, to effect significant change is fundamentally constrained by the complexity of the issues they face and by the multiple demands and allegiances—cultural and economic—of individual lawmakers. The COVID pandemic, on this score, does not seem to have been a catastrophe sufficient to wrench the system significantly, on the Scheidel model.

Even "good" politicians tend toward paralysis, as has been shown, in the attempt simply to win reelection in the face of worse possible candidates.[21] While term limits can mitigate this, some argue, term limits also enhance political ignorance and ineffectiveness. The fact that various nations—such as Australia, Canada, the UK, Sweden, Italy, and others—are themselves struggling with analogous political standoffs indicates, not some new rise of ugly nationalism or craven political/economic self-regard, but an embedded political dysfunction now slowly surfacing as a problem in its own right. Within the present political frameworks of most national arrangements (and mostly liberal ones), there will never be consensus around fundamental disagreements about human life itself—for example, regarding assisted suicide, sexual identity and purpose, and the relationship of toil and leisure. The ability to effectively respond to looming challenges like climate change is a victim to the forces that have made consensus about human life itself impossible, as a number of scholars have suggested: there's too much to know, to do, and to coordinate, and the problems are growing too swiftly.[22]

If this doesn't sound good, that is because it isn't good, at least in a world of instrumental values. Complexity, in practical terms, simply means that we cannot know everything and certainly not the most important things; hence we can change very little without altering everything in ways we cannot predict in advance or even understand in the present. Political change is an exercise in control, but of things that are bound to what is always outside of our control. The result is always uncontrolled change, which means consequences that often contradict our goals. This is especially the case in the face of problems whose scope demands effective response—for example, national security, climate change, and demographic social therapy, as it were (i.e., things like the US prison fiasco)—even as their complexity precludes clear political resolution. But since change *will* necessarily happen; and since radical changes will happen in the case of large-scale problems like climate change; and, finally, since these changes, bound to enlarged social entities, as Leopold Kohr has argued, will prove "miserable"—the more people involved, the bigger the countries involved, the greater the perceived stakes, the more aggressive the reactive responses, the more difficult the resolution—the likely alternative to deliberated political change will indeed be undeliberated "catastrophe."[23]

Politically, we should not expect anything other than this. In terms of our faith, we should assert such catastrophe as the obbligato of our social duties. In speaking to our children, this is among the hardest things to share. Perhaps it is simply something only aging can illuminate. Yet I worry that such a view lodges the fundamental truth of this political incapacity in a corner of wearied existence, a place it goes to wither. As a truth, rather, it should be apprehended, faced, and grasped with a sense of sober energy, learned from the start, explored throughout one's years, and allowed in the course of a lifetime to reveal the tremendous being of God. The letters of advice that parents offered children in the early modern period rarely spoke about the political incapacity that complexity engenders; but they did often speak of rightly judging the relative importance of tasks and hopes. Framed, as most of these letters were, by the shared, constant, and acknowledged experience of mortality, such judgment often moved in the same modest direction that I am outlining here.

Christians, however—and certainly in our era—are deeply ambivalent about complexity, perhaps just because, in the lived sphere, it seems to be the cousin of catastrophe. We seem willing, on the one hand, to accept the impenetrable complexity of God's cosmos, metaphysically speaking: angels, spirits, cherubim, demons, Satan himself, perhaps even the dead. All of this is beyond our ken, we admit with awe, and although scholastic traditions have enjoyed the attempt to peer into the world of, say, angelic movement, location, and subsistence, we have never worried much about how it all fits together or how we might help that fit to happen better. Instead, we trust in God's rule over this opaque and manifold larger world within which we live. Yet when it comes to the material and human setting of our earthly lives, we seem certain, on the other hand, that God's ordering of their forms is but *vaguely* trustworthy, and thus that their complexity is and ought to be a manageable obstacle to be overcome by our own calculations and pragmatic strategies. "God helps those who help themselves" (there is even an entire Wikipedia article devoted to this trope).[24] Both attitudes are probably misplaced: we should dread the larger cosmic theater's inhabitants as very much mysteriously yet concretely impinging on our own small stage, and we should much more humbly offer the fundamental impossibility of our lives' manipulation over to God's ordering spirit. In both cases, "the fear of the LORD is the beginning of wisdom" (Ps. 111:10). That is a supremely political claim.

The claim is political because the scriptural enunciation of godly fear, as in the saying's assertion in Job 28:28, is aimed at a very practical posture within the world, a posture of absolute relevance and efficacy. Godly fear is commended not in order to engender despair but to encourage living the truth. Our contemporary epoch, whether we call it "the Anthropocene" or not, has hardly given rise to a new human being. That is precisely this epoch's false claim, driven in its overly optimistic form toward transhumanism and in its despairing form toward posthumanism. Human beings remain exactly who we have always been, the created "children of Adam," with Eve, drawn from Adam's side, as our mother (Gen. 3:20; Ps. 115:16). From these both, "to dust we shall return" (Gen. 3:19). Nonetheless, to be true to who we in fact are, we must be alert to false promises and mistaken paths.

While we muck about—as we should!—with this or that issue, we must understand that "fixing" the problem or "winning" the legislative struggle is only a small plank in a larger structure of witness. Furthermore, what it might mean to "fix" or "win" within such a larger structure is not clear; the victory could simply be illusory because it is shaped by false pressures and premises. The load-bearing beams of this structure are the ones we should at least make our priorities, not because they are newly discovered but because they have been recently forgotten. The old must appear new in order for the one truth to be spoken.

What is old here is what is divinely permanent in its gift, staked out in the midst of the complexity of our creation, which we cannot otherwise understand. What is permanent here is our mortality, and thus our social aims can focus on this immovable ground, one that, in its political and catastrophic sense, is geared to the endings of all our efforts. One thing that talk of an Anthropocene epoch properly implies is that our human lives are limited, vulnerable, and ultimately finite: the world as we know it may be coming to an end, our species itself vulnerable to unimagined assaults and perhaps to imminent disappearance. Even though Christians may rightly fear such endings, we cannot be afraid to name them as intrinsic to our hopes. But Christians must agree and take up this claim with articulate fervor and theocentric focus: everything created will end, including the earth and its inhabitants. "The form of this world is passing away" (1 Cor. 7:31 RSV), and there will come a time when the elements and the earth and all its works will be "dissolved" (2 Pet. 3:10). This is a figure of our own individual demise, when, without warning on any given night, our "soul is required" of us (Luke 12:20). We "know not when the master of the house cometh" (Mark 13:35). It is no surprise that the Anthropocene epoch has spawned its own empty apocalyptic fantasies, bound to dystopian anxieties and threats—postnuclear holocaust, untamed viruses, agricultural disaster. These fantasies are empty not because they are implausible, but only because they exist in a completely godless context. The rise of Christian apocalypticism since the nineteenth century, thus, moves in tandem with rising atheism.

Rather than dismissing all this as fundamentalist raving, however, we should reassert the basic Christian claim—continuous from Scripture through the early church, Middle Ages, and beyond—that our world, and the human race who dwells upon it, exists by God's good pleasure, and only on that basis; and that, embedded in our existence as individuals and as social groups, including churches in their human forms, is a radical contingency whose end *is* final dissolution. From this, and in response to this, is a promised new creation from God, as the Scriptures insist. But such a hope is molded by the reality of our endings and thus by the goods we are given to tend "to the end" (John 13:1).

We cannot understand any of this in such a way as to order it to our betterment. "Such knowledge is too wonderful for me; it is high, I cannot attain unto it. . . . How precious also are thy thoughts unto me, O God! how great is the sum of them! If I should count them, they are more in number than the sand: when I awake, I am still with thee" (Ps. 139:6, 17–18). Even if we were immortal, we would not be able to unravel the threads of God's purposes and their forms within creaturely existence. But immortality is not, in any case, the basis of our social existence. We are born, and yet we then die, with a certainty that is universally shared and that therefore founds our common life. Our deaths are not a denial of the goodness of our creation, but are in fact the only means by which our births are possible. The importance of being born as an informing character of social existence—"natality," in Hannah Arendt's language, the "miracle that saves the world"—has tended to be affirmed only in an intuitive sense.[25] Arendt herself seemed uninterested in the linkage of natality with mortality, assigning the birth-death limitation of human existence to a "mere" biological sphere shared with all unthinking creatures. While not exactly a progressive, her intellectualized approach—thinking, acting, changing, doing new things—saw death as a kind of closure to that which is good rather than as a good in itself to be affirmed so as to shape our active life. It is our mortality—which includes our coming to be from nothing, our births as a gift from God, as well as our deaths—and the entrenched limits to our understanding and grasp of the world that mortality imposes that sustain our very social existence as it comes to be.

We are born and we die as creatures of the Most High, solely through his grace. Our endings tell us of the gift of our beginnings and of the source of our beginnings and our endings together. Hence, what is good is that we should tend the shape of this coming and going since it is the gift of the Almighty, who will shower it with his greater goodness as he sees fit. Such tending is neither passive nor quiescent. As Peter writes, the clear Christian attitude, just because of this ending built into the nature of things, is a "zealous" pursuit of godliness, holiness, purity, and peace (2 Pet. 3:11–14), as well as a thirsting orientation to God's promised world of righteousness. These priorities derive from knowing our certain and immovable limits. Their apprehension cannot be had in a world governed by steady-state expectations of whatever kind, let alone by the assumption of progress. The latter is nothing but an illusion that, for Christians, has ended in nostalgia, anger, and bitter retreat—and for all in positions of power, vanity and overweening pride.

Our finitude is our hope, since it marks our fundamental openness to God. The very reality of created things, massed together and visible in their profusion, is the premise of complexity, which is why the rich can never sort out their duties. Clarity emerges only when it is all given up, taken away, left behind for or passed on to others. Who then can be saved? "The things which are impossible with men are possible with God" (Luke 18:27). But what, then, is possible for the children of Adam? For, after all, *Die Politik ist die Lehre vom Möglichen*: politics is the art of the possible. There *is* a good life possible within the limits of catastrophe. The next two chapters attempt to trace its political contours.

Twelve

Normal, Abnormal, and Charitable

When they came to Capernaum, the collectors of the half-shekel tax went up to Peter and said, "Does not your teacher pay the tax?" He said, "Yes." And when he came home, Jesus spoke to him first, saying, "What do you think, Simon? From whom do kings of the earth take toll or tribute? From their sons or from others?" And when he said, "From others," Jesus said to him, "Then the sons are free. However, not to give offense to them, go to the sea and cast a hook, and take the first fish that comes up, and when you open its mouth you will find a shekel; take that and give it to them for me and for yourself."

Matthew 17:24–27 (RSV)

This wondrous event—a fish that pays one's taxes!—is, in its recording by Matthew, too complex in its own way to unpack clearly. For one thing, Jesus seems to think that paying taxes (in this case probably for the temple's upkeep) is not really necessary. One can speculate as to why, theologically (the temple is no longer itself needed in the face of the incarnation's true temple? the rejected nature of the temple's keepers?). The speculation carries its own moral risks. In any case, Jesus defers to the requirement to avoid scandalizing others, and he depends on a divinely miraculous provision of money to solve the problem. With Paul, of course, the idea seems to have evolved beyond offense avoidance and become a moral demand: "For this cause pay ye tribute also: for they are God's ministers, attending continually upon this very thing. Render therefore to all their dues: tribute to whom tribute is due; custom to whom custom; fear to whom fear; honor to whom honor" (Rom. 13:6–7). Political duties here resolve themselves into a rather simple, certainly *un*complex range of imperatives. The resolution is a suggestive and finally helpful one.

My purpose in this chapter is to outline, in light of the mortal world we live in, the shape of our political duties. These are duties, as I have been indicating, that are really aimed at tending the mortal goods God has given us, whose tending itself makes up the Good Life we are privileged to live out—no more, no less. But tax-paying fish do not seem to be a firm basis upon which to offer the generational counsel that would explicate such goods. Furthermore, there is much modern discomfort with Paul's assertion about authority, and in North American cultures this bristling is deeply informed by partisan ideologies with respect to freedom, private property, the needs of the common good, and more. For all that, the explosive emergence of complexity as a social condition has transformed, at least in our consciousness, the character of political ordering in its lived habits, in ways that simply stand to the side of these ideologies, concerning taxes as much as anything else.

Normal and Abnormal Politics

Let me return to a set of categories I laid out early in this volume: normal and abnormal politics. "Normal politics" means playing one's role in whatever system of governance one finds oneself living within, according to the rules of the system. When I first introduced this category, I did so with the suggestion that Christians can and should engage normal politics with a certain indifference, though that doesn't mean not engaging it at all. Letting fish pay taxes may fit into this. The second category, "abnormal politics," comes into play for Christians when they are pressed by some threat to their mortal goods to take on a political role that either stands outside their normal political functioning within whatever system of governance they happen to find themselves within, or that moves beyond individual political avocations. Abnormal politics, for Christians, emerges as an imperative to action on their part when there arises a need to reorder the system of governance *for the sake of* mortal goods. Neither normal nor abnormal politics, however, holds some intrinsic capacity for betterment, whether aimed at its citizenry or simply at its own functional integrity. Perhaps a few tweaks may be made here and there, but only a few, and only sometimes. And while political change is certainly always a possibility, this is something quite distinct from amelioration.

Thus, it is hardly possible any longer to "reinvent" politics or governments or nations, short of catastrophe's merciless imperative and its irrational brutality of outcome. "Reinventing" the way that large societies order themselves has been a common hope for both Left and Right. *Reinventing Government*, a 1992 bestseller, was based on privatizing elements of public governance; and the trope of "reinventing politics" has been applied in ways that are sometimes democratically hopeful, sometimes pessimistic about the revitalization of authoritarianism, and sometimes radically aspirational.[1] While anything is possible—especially in its catastrophic arousal—for all the talk of new things, governance has become more and more the same, more and more one embracive reality: a function of management; and the politics of sustaining and guiding governance has become a function of certification in managerial expertise. We pay our taxes so that the trains run on time—even more so, so that there can be trains at all. With the payment of our taxes, furthermore, we hand over political action to the managers. There is no alternative in a world of great numbers where some semblance of "peace" is desired (1 Tim. 2:2–3).

The fundamental elements of social survival more broadly—and thus of individual and local survival—are today mostly dependent on the choreography of complex systems: food production and distribution; water systems; construction; energy sources and applications; and modes of transportation. From the intricate, and often only partially integrated, infrastructure and communication networks that enable these systems to function derive the host of particulars that make up the shape of our individual and public material and interactive lives, from housing and neighborhoods, to food, clothing, and medicine, to schools and books or computers, to the full round of quotidian pursuits that include the goods of our households and common spaces. While individuals and groups may argue over school curricula or consumerist values or medical care and insurance, ultimately even these freighted matters trace themselves back to managerial issues: How do you come up with *a*, and how do you get *a* to *b*?

Thus, electric or other energy grids and water systems—two of the most fundamental grounds of social existence—generally grow and function purely on the basis of managerial wisdom and skill. Normal politics, then, is aimed at keeping these systems working as smoothly and efficiently as possible, and the policy questions that might shape the growth of these systems are mostly argued on the basis of this kind of wisdom, which is the domain of urban planners, engineers, and environmental scientists.

There is no escape from this reality. The law of large numbers, in a biblical sense, demands that this be so. To dig cisterns, channels, sewers, canals; to erect big buildings; to import and export resources; to marshal large populations—all this requires the organizing force of what is usually viewed as an oppressive system of imposition, more or less (and the difference between these degrees is mostly a managerial matter). Israel chafed under such a system, as do most peoples. Today's anti-liberal revolt against the "technocratic elite" and "neoliberal globalism" is but one version of this chafing; but there are many versions of it throughout history. Both conservative theorists, like James Burnham, and those on the Left, like Willard Enteman,[2] have attached to the "managerial class" tendencies to hierarchical self-interest, the formation of dangerous ideologies, and, finally, actual tyranny: for examples, see Google, Amazon, General Electric, the Department of Education, and the Centers for Disease Control and Prevention.

These critics and their contemporary followers may well be right on all counts. From God's perspective, however, it boils down to a kind of "What did you expect?" response from the one who had always warned against a human king, yet who finally offered one up to the unquenched thirst of the people for ever "more." Normal politics, whether we like it or not, has become the process of raising up, ordering, and trying to hold accountable (or simply criticizing) the management (i.e., the managers) of complex systems, which includes (often well-founded) worries over unintended consequences. There is no point in complaining about this; there is no alternative, and Christians need to be clear that such a narrow range of normal political concern, with all its intrinsic and profound frustrations, appropriately frames the tending of their mortal goods. The whole astonishing argument, often vicious and on both sides, about "what the science says"—about vaccines or climate change or guns—derives from the inflated political value attached to keeping complex systems of social survival running. "Science," in this context, is no more than good management and should be judged accordingly, but also left in the hands of those who are trained to manage. Citizens should be concerned with the training our social managers receive, of course; although mostly this can be assessed only by those trained to manage training. The idea that millions of people would constantly vote on managerial decisions is, were it not constantly being attempted, prima facie absurd.

There is a sense in which all modern societies are drifting toward a "Chinese" system on this score: vast populations organized by necessity through centralizing mechanisms, so as to mostly stay alive (even while the pockets of a few are lined). There is resistance, as well there might be, with respect to questions of personal freedoms in a number of areas within this general framework, as well as with respect to the integrity of overseeing the managers of our complex systems. Most of this resistance comes in the form of social restructuring: erecting smaller governmental entities, whether in terms of federated nations, as in Europe, or intranational states, as in the US ("states' rights"). Neither of these examples represents a stable alternative, in part because "smaller" here is still enormously large, as we have noted, and still engages the impossibly complex. We no longer live in Athens. Lichtenstein cannot survive on its own in Europe, and California is no more than a giant and unwieldy nation, not so different in kind from China. Both alternatives—federated nations and federated states or regions—committed in different ways to upholding certain freedoms from managerial drift, are riven by the dynamics of group violence (internationally in Europe, and intranationally in the US). Ordering the drift into managerial normal politics—an inevitable movement, as I have said—is one area where occasions for abnormal politics assert themselves, helpfully ("rightly") or not.

Managerial governance thus becomes an object of intense political debate and action when it fails to function. Examples of this might include the collapse of the Texas power grid in the ice storms of 2021; the near collapse and, certainly, deadly constriction of the medical system in many areas during the COVID pandemic; and the inadvertent poisoning of Flint, Michigan's water supply. None of these matters were in fact addressed in a "revolutionary" way; nor have they been definitively solved. So far, the avenues of normal politics remain the preferred pathway of response. But the pressure to pursue them with a more active involvement has been driven by the existential realities at stake, which touch directly on mortal goods. One might say that, in these and similar situations, Christians, along with their cocitizens, are only being "abnormally" pressed, not hurled, into engagement with normal politics. At least for now; abnormal politics, in a full-blown sense, may yet emerge.

What might that look like? Convoys, marches, lawsuits, strikes—these are common instruments, short of terrorism and civil war, that mark abnormal politics in the modern world, and Christians sometimes have a role in their deployment. To this degree, the consideration of normal and abnormal politics for Christians is no different than it is for anyone—one "goes along," in whatever system one finds oneself, until one feels one can do so no longer. However, it is important to stress that the Christian political vocation in these situations is measured quite strictly in terms of mortal goods and their flourishing or being threatened—not in terms of principles, let alone ideals—and that this measure is not without discerning limits. It is not as

if the instruments of abnormal politics are always legitimate: only sometimes, perhaps rarely. It is the responsibility of Christians to identify these
times according to the criteria of their own service of God. Abnormal times,
in this sense, are probably far fewer than we are commonly led to believe
by the debased—because inflated and unaware—politics of our era, and
Christians of both the Left and the Right have fallen victim, in their political
decisions, to this debasement. Furthermore, the frequent consequences
of abnormal politics—for example, the destruction of familial livelihoods
that has sometimes flowed from protests turning into riots or economic
unraveling, let alone civil war—mean that the embrace of abnormal politics
can itself be, and more often than not is, an attack on the gifts of God. At
that point, the weighing of relative ills "for the sake of something better"
descends into madness: everything falls apart.

Certainly, such calculation will descend to the level of offense, and offense
and scandal tend to breed disorder and violence, which is why Jesus seems
to advocate simply letting things be when it comes to political arrangements. Normal politics remains the norm, and the "children of the King"
are to rely on miraculous fish to keep their place within the daily round of
normality as long as possible since, eventually, kingdom will be set against
kingdom (Matt. 24:7).

The critical question around normal politics, of course, remains: Is it
up to resolving major social challenges in the face of, for example, climate
change, campaign finance reform, immigration, and a host of other matters
that, arguably, are or end up being threats to the mortal goods entrusted to
us? Catastrophes are not to be desired, even if they are the inevitable motor
of real political change; and normal political efforts therefore need to be
pursued to avoid them. But one can only hint at the proper place of normal
politics in the shadow of catastrophe, knowing that the latter will upend in
a moment the always inadequate and sometimes intolerable systems that
keep social life moving along in relative calm. Normal politics, to use the
analogy Thomas Kuhn applied to the development of science, is what one
does between catastrophes (Kuhn's revolutionary moments of "paradigm
change"), when that is even possible.[3]

Hence, it seems that normal politics continues to make demands on
Christians in impromptu and provisional ways. Christians—in but not of
the world, as expressed in the often tiresome (because practically nondirec-
tive) but nonetheless unavoidable descriptor given them by their Lord (John
17:14–18)—properly continue to respond to the ongoing requirements of
system sustenance that normal politics serves. They do so, however, in ways
that ought to be anti-theoretical and only loosely strategic. What Christians

offer to the practice of normal politics is the focused recognition of the mortal goods that all human social life is ordered to serve. Christians are, in theory, trained by faith to indicate the range of mortal goods that call for their political attention. At the same time, Christian catastrophic politics and its subcategory of ad hoc responses ought to press the church herself away from too close an attachment to normal politics in her civic location, and certainly from practicing normal politics in her own life. That is not what the church, the true "children of the King," is about in essence. Alas, in this regard, ecclesiological habits have been frequently tied to Christian political habits, and mostly for the worse. But that is a concern for another discussion.

With respect to the first element that Christians bring to normal politics—indicating goods and their range—there are some obvious domains in which the Christian's normal politics will demand a constant attention and at times active engagement. These have in fact proved to be fairly standard domains, not only over longer periods but still quite recently, in—perhaps especially in—developed liberal democracies: laws and policies that make possible and support marriages, families of two parents and children and of multiple generations; that protect the conception and birth of children and the nurture and care of the ill and the dying; and that prevent the imposition of actions that overturn the created bases of this generational extension and arc of life (e.g., interventions in sexual refashionings, assisting in self-murder, the promotion of abortion). Since children, short of abnormal social arrangements, are formed in a variety of settings outside their immediate home, promoting or repairing larger contexts of security—from violence and drugs especially—fall within the domain of normal politics, as Christians engage it, in this regard.

Unfortunately, there are no simple means by which to achieve some kind of optimal and normal political ordering in these matters. They are, like so much in our world, too complex to orchestrate well. These domains remain those of normal politics only so long as the basic tending of mortal goods they promote is not noticeably subverted in a way that brings with it existential threat: the death of the young or the old, the destruction of families, the attack upon generation, the fundamental ability to feed a family and care for them. Individuals will differ on when, exactly, normal politics in these domains has crumbled in its relative efficacy. They will also differ on how the policies necessary to maintain or repair the politics of these domains should be implemented, and they will do so because these policies will never achieve their goals and thus must always remain in the realm of the largely speculative. Finally, for these reasons and because the capacity for mortal sustenance will vary for individuals and their families—policies will affect different persons sometimes in radically different ways—people will differ on what constitutes acceptable or tolerable repair at all. Even reasonable but significantly different and sometimes contradictory approaches—for example, to "family friendly" or "pro-family" public policy—show this, as divergent attitudes to fundamental issues like reproductive rights or the value of targeted aid and state intervention in family life demonstrate.[4] As these differences accumulate, normal politics will perforce shift into the wilderness of the abnormal. And no one knows what will happen next because, in fact, the abnormal is the realm of the catastrophic. It is a realm we often cannot escape, though one we rarely seek to enter.

Charity and the Neighbor as the Christian's Peculiar Politics

One can and should go beyond these normal domains of interest *and* their abnormal invaders when it comes to the particular Christian gift of indicating mortal goods and their range. For it turns out that there is a long tradition to this focusing and limiting with respect to the church's genuine (as opposed to corrupted) political interests on this score. The more modern inflation of these interests, by contrast, has been informed by ever-expanding social theories and calculuses that track instead with the relatively recent rise of the ameliorative politics of progress. Historically, ecclesial political action aimed at the limited scope of mortal goods has been consistent and has fallen into rather distinct areas: almsgiving (food, clothing, shelter), tending the sick (e.g., hospices, hospitals), the care of orphans and prisoners, schooling, and the support of widows. This limited range of action was also a basic element of most missionary work by the nineteenth century.

It is true that the history of Christian charity is hardly straightforward. Ever since Gerhard Uhlhorn's pioneering history of the charitable work of the early church, written in the mid-nineteenth century, scholars have traced the development of Christian charitable practice with increasingly sophisticated social-scientific tools.[5] Not surprisingly, questions of ideology and political control have arisen around the evolving but also comprehensive charitable work of the church and her members, which was carried out by a wide variety of lay and religious groups and organized and funded through a variety of means. Critics such as Ivan Illich have decried the surprisingly quick "institutionalization" of Christian charity in the church's early centuries as a subversion of the gospel's spiritual immediacy, an evangelical gift that was originally ordered to the responses of free personal encounter.[6]

Illich had concerns from early in his career about the church's co-option by larger political forces. But the root of her corruption, he later argued, lay in the first years of the church's organization. For all these debates, there is a surprising consistency in the church's approach and practice across the centuries, through the end of the Middle Ages: the "poor"—the indigent, abandoned women and children, prisoners, the sick and dying—belonged to Christ in a special way. The possessions of those who were wealthier, including the context of their enjoyment (meals, prayers, songs), belonged to the poor just because of their Christ-bonded identity, in a way that could provide some basis for a wider distribution, as it were, of mortal goods. Along with consistency of practice, however, is the local diversity of ways in which this enactment of *caritas* was carried out, ways that probably mitigated its rapid or even gradual rationalization and institutionalization, *pace* critics like Illich.

"Charity," understood in this way, is bound up with one of the key elements in any politics and not just Christian politics: the neighbor. The poor or the otherwise needy person belongs to the realm of the "given"—that is, the "gift"—that mortal life entails. The poor are given insofar as they are neighbors, those who are "nigh," close by, in our midst. His or her encounter, therefore, participates in the revelation of God that mortal life embodies and that is given most fully in Jesus Christ. There is no simple moral logic involved here since, if taken as a metaphysical principle, Jesus as the God-man, the Second Adam, carries in him all the peoples of the world, the political corollary of which would "simply" be our moral bondedness to every member of the human race, equally and without reserve. This is both true (cf. Acts 17:26) and impossibly enacted in a limited life. And, in fact, Jesus comes to us as a single individual, carrying with him the individual in need, the one who finds us close by and before whom we are found— that is, the neighbor. What has been called "the preferential option for the poor" is compelling precisely when and because it presses us in terms of mortal encounter, the nearness of flesh in its need.[7]

The neighbor is thus not everyone, though the neighbor may imply everyone, or at least the "everyone" who stands before God just as we do and thus through whom the fullness of God stands before us: "Thou shalt love the Lord thy God with all thy heart, and with all thy soul, and with all thy strength, and with all thy mind; and thy neighbor as thyself" (Luke 10:27; Deut. 6:5). This is a command that is then confirmed by the proclamation of the one God, "I am the LORD" (Lev. 19:18). There is a sense in which this is a universal imperative. But its scope is always given in proximity. For, by and large, the term we translate in the Old Testament as "neighbor"—a common term, *rea'*, along with some other words—has a mostly locative connotation: someone who is near us, with whom we associate, rub shoulders with, bump up against. This in turn can imply affection, as in "friend" or "intimate" (cf. Ps. 35:14). Whatever exactly is meant, we are told that God spoke to Moses face-to-face, like a "neighbor" or, in many translations, "friend" (Exod. 33:11). Yet neighbors and strangers share something. Moses's son is called "Gershom" because Moses "was a stranger [*ger*] in a strange land" (Exod. 2:22), and Israel as a whole is reoriented toward others on just this basis: "Also thou shalt not oppress a stranger: for ye know the heart of a stranger, seeing ye were strangers in the land of Egypt" (Exod. 23:9). A "stranger" is one who sojourns among others. But to these others, the sojourner becomes, if not a neighbor in origin, at least one who is treated as a neighbor: "Ye shall have one manner of law, as well for the stranger, as for one of your own country: for I am the LORD your God" (Lev. 24:22).

The distinction between neighbor and stranger is blurred just because of this sharing of space near to me, a space that is both circumscribed in its boundaries yet filled with the often confusing currents of shifting identities. Whoever is near to me is unveiled as one with whom a livelihood is shared. This is why the incarnation of God brings both those near and those far into proximity, for all people now are revealed together as being within the same space shared by the Christ. As Christ, the sojourner, comes near to us, he brings with him those who are bound to him, from far to near, from strangeness to fellowship (Eph. 2:17, 19). The need of the stranger— Israel in Egypt—becomes the petitioning or perhaps sustaining touch of the neighbor.

This blurred line between neighbor and stranger is deeply important to grasp insofar as it illuminates our own personal identities as generative creatures, giving and receiving, doing and being done to, and finally offering all to God as an expression of the truth that it is all his from beginning to end. All is given to us (strangers made neighbors), all is shared (to be a creature is to be what others are, no more and no less), all is offered (that which is closest to us is given away to that which is farthest from us). The central energy at work in this area of blurred personal demarcation is generosity, the great enemy of political calculation yet, at the same time, the fuel of that which permits politics to have any value and purpose—that is, to sustain the space of mortal goods and their tending. The spirit of generosity is what reveals to the human creature the gift of being a creature in its larger enjoyment, its life with other creatures; and that enjoyment is the realm in which stranger and neighbor appear to us.

The scriptural vocabulary of generosity (as we translate it in English) is varied and gives rise as well to a range of other English words—"compassion," "grace," "mercy," in addition to the "liberality" that we associate particularly with sharing money. Those who are "generous" in lending to the poor (Ps. 37:21) are (lexically) at one with the God who is "gracious" to the sick and persecuted (41:4). The generous mercy of God that reflects his utter grace in giving life and death (Exod. 33:19; Rom. 9:15) is also expressed, somehow, in the generous contributions of the saints to the work of the church (2 Cor. 8:20), the kind of concretely financial gift that is bound up with "thanksgiving to God" (9:11). Just this diverse dynamic of generosity marks the divine compassion behind the creation of the world itself, of human beings, and of this or that context of national and local life that forms the contours of mortality: persons among persons who together are the multiplying inhabitants of the world (Gen. 1:28; 9:1; Acts 17:26). That I am alive means that I am alive with others, and they with me—with just this person near me, or the one who comes close to me from afar—and all this embodies divine generosity. Furthermore, this givenness of "withness" remains steady in both normal and abnormal times—that is, within the full gamut of the catastrophic ordering and disordering of the world.

As just stated, the reality of charity, neighbor, and generosity remains abstract. The parable of the good Samaritan is, however, a parable of "being a neighbor," not abstractly but in the face of abandonment and the threat to life—that is, of being a stranger who is revealed as one brought close, and brought close in the quite particular forms of personal and financial sustenance for the sake of life. The parable presents us with a man who is far from home, attacked, stripped, wounded, and left "half dead" (Luke 10:30). Left where? Left in the path of others. The question the lawyer poses to Jesus (10:29) is one of the neighbor as a general category, to be distinguished from the stranger. "Who is a neighbor, such that I might love him as myself?" Jesus responds in terms of particularity, in the demand to be a neighbor among various persons who are all strangers in origin yet who are in fact brought together, put in my path, such that stranger becomes neighbor through the demand of proximity. "Here" is always the place where the neighbor appears.

The demand to "be a neighbor," then, is given in a particular context as well, that of life and death, the common space where the one God acts for those who are near and those who are far (Isa. 33:13). The neighbor always appears "here," where his life is at stake. The neighbor embodies the life that God gives us as creatures; and that life is indeed *ours* to give away generously and a life in which theirs is entwined by stark proximity. That the

Levite, the priest, the Samaritan, and an unknown traveler, strangers to one another, converge in this place of life and death simply represents the fact that each life is wrapped up in a mortal commonality. There is no program here, only the establishment of, the naming of, a reality to be approached with the full range of the commands of God. "Be generous," "lend freely," "be compassionate," treat the stranger according to your "one law." The neighbor—whom we meet repeatedly throughout life—is thus a sojourning element essential to the traversal of life, which is itself a constant passage within the blurred space of strangers on their way, sustained generously by the Word of God and also subject to that Word as the source of their continued movement. Neighbors are mortal goods, related to parents and children (Eph. 3:15). It is easy and quite proper to rationalize this: we "depend" on each other, and the "prudence" and "wisdom" commended by Bertrand Russell in his advice to the young (see chap. 2) derive from this reality. There is, furthermore, much in the Bible—for example, Leviticus 19—about this. But the generosity that informs the encounter of stranger and neighbor is best seen not so much instrumentally as it is in the stark nature of createdness and its locality: this is where we find ourselves, and we find ourselves just here, with this person, because of the grace of God.

If care for the needy—charity—is singled out as a particular duty of the faithful in Scripture and ecclesial tradition both, it is because the poor and the neighbor are basically one (Prov. 14:21), and they are one because we live in a given creaturely space that is marked by the miraculous existence, just here, of human lives embodying in the flesh divine generosity. For centuries, the charity of the Christian was shaped and expressed within this limited but miraculous space. What is clear, however, is that a significant shift in the forms and also the meaning of Christian charity *did* take place in early modernity, a shift caught up in emerging patterns of social betterment, with northern Europe moving ahead more quickly than in the south. By the late eighteenth century, a more general and notable transition had clearly taken place, from ecclesial and more locally arranged forms of charity to civic and politically organized modes driven by new motivations. If not exactly a singular moment, the great Lisbon earthquake of 1755 marked a paradigm shift from ecclesial to civil response, with the whole activity of rebuilding now left to (or deliberately taken over by) the hands of the state. At the same time—again, using the Lisbon paradigm—we see a new sense of the neighbor as a broad social category, not as an encountered person, to be addressed by the application of comprehensive policies, though now subject to new moral demands framed in terms of "humanity." Hence the organizing of international "relief efforts."[8] In this way, catastrophe *did* wrench into being new social forms of existence, which themselves quickly inhabited the corridors of normal politics. The tradition of Christian charity, however, was always ordered to both normal and abnormal political situations, stable and catastrophic in their ways.

The modern forms of civic betterment (as distinct from the forms of Christian charity), ordered by refashioned politics, were responses not only to sudden catastrophe but also to the slow catastrophic creep of burgeoning populations, increasingly complex economies, and the unstable regimes governing them. At the core of these responses lay the desire to create better-functioning social systems, upheld by a more efficient citizenry (including the managerial citizenry). One early proponent of organized civic poor relief, the somewhat avant-garde humanist Juan Luis Vives, who was then living in the Flemish urban center of Bruges, argued that education in employable skills should be provided to the indigent. These kinds of proposals involved a new application of the concept of "reform"—as in reforming others, making them better people (and in so doing becoming better oneself). To be sure, earlier Christian charitable attempts sought to provide both spiritual goods and material provision to the poor—prayers, teaching, and the like. But "bettering" was not the goal, and the difference is profound. Premodern charitable pedagogy marked a sharing of life and hope from a common store of grace within a common mortal matrix. This is precisely where the locative force of the neighbor had its influence. Developing modern forms of charity, by contrast, have been marked by the application of an apparatus of improvement applied to increasingly large or distant spaces and aimed at an existence in which, however obviously finite, limits are themselves constantly pressed further away.

In this effort, mortality itself is less salient. The contemporary apex of this movement is exemplified in the transformation of medicine from an act of "caring" to one of "conquering": conquering disease, conquering disability, conquering aging, and finally, of course, conquering death. In some sense the transhumanist motive is deeply intimate: immortality for oneself or for those one loves. But, in fact, the transhumanist practical framework (and the social context of its main proponents shows this) is one of computer networks ordered to the extirpation of locality and finally of localized bodies themselves. Transhumanism is thus not an outlier to the transformation of "charity" but one direct consequence of that transformation's unconscious presuppositions.[9]

While the "slippery slope" argument has been decried as a historical "fallacy," I would disagree. Slippery slopes may not be inevitable, but they point to probabilities. Transhumanism represents a good signal of a particular slope's nadir, and it is useful in this regard to consider elements of the na-dir's prior trajectory in just the terms set by mortal goods and their political import. If the Christian life is a vocation through which God is served by offering to him in thanks the mortal gifts he has graced us with, then transhumanism, as a set of commitments, is by contrast aimed at holding on: holding on to the gifts of God in a way that in fact transforms their very giftedness—their mortal character—in the process. This transformation itself involves many threads, and it points in its own way to the manner in which the revolt against mortality carries with it an intricately unresolvable range of destructive effects, "complex" in their own terms. To hold on to life, to extend its reach more and more in temporal terms, is to weaken the giftedness of natality itself and thus of generation, of children, of parents, of families. It is also to weaken the giftedness, however difficult to receive, of suffering and thus of the whole relational character of weakening, aging, and dying. Holding on to life denies the beauty lodged in a limited life's ordering of self-commendation to God, a beauty that responds to the time given by God by both finding ways to accept it as it is and letting go of it as it is taken. All of these elements in the contrast between receiving and offering versus holding on relate to the mortal goods that Christians see as directing the discernment of their political tasks, distinguishing normal from abnormal duties, and staking out the encounters and relations with neighbors and one's charitable response to them.

To put it crudely: the expanding of moral space is mostly imaginative, and when promoted concretely will lead to that space's dissolution. Charity—the generosity of life that is shared among neighbors (and that turns strang-ers into neighbors)—is obviously part of the peculiarly Christian political posture. While not political in itself in a civil sense, the charitable life is a response to the larger impositions of mortality in their full catastrophic reach, to which politics, both normal and abnormal, partially contribute through their own demands, contested discernments and implications, and sometimes catastrophic outcomes. The life of charity provides a lens through which to interpret and sometimes navigate the uncertain burdens of and difficult transitions between normal and abnormal politics. To re-peat, however: normal and abnormal politics cannot order Christian charity, largely because they have little to do with the actual life of that small space in which generosity between mortal creatures is embodied. Such a small space of encounter and the shape of our small lives are where the funda-mental forms of mortal goods are given: generation, meals together, sleep-ing, toiling, encouraging and suffering, praying and teaching. The space in which charity takes its forms and energy, then, comprises the home and the village and the people of home and village: family, friend, and neighbor. In an essential way, anything beyond this is, for the Christian, a matter that is politically "indifferent" except as a threat to the gift that this space encloses.

I am inching closer and closer to the children I would write to because I am approaching their address, the place they live. This place is their home. Here, teaching happens. And such a place of teaching must, at all costs, endure.

Thirteen

Nazareth,
an Enduring City

And he went down with them, and came to Nazareth, and was subject unto them: but his mother kept all these sayings in her heart.

Luke 2:51

The Lord God, King of the Universe, came to live among the children of Adam and so became a human being, a "Second Adam"; though in another sense Christ was not really "second" but was truly the First Man of all, the image of the Father, in whose image we are made (Gen. 1:26; Heb. 1:3). Coming among the children of Adam, as Adam, and given the name Yeshua or Jesus, he became obedient to the death that is the destiny of all Adams (Ps. 90:3). Paul, in Philippians 2, lays this out in a classic text that is among the most used of all scriptural verses in discussing the character of the incarnation, from Athanasius and Augustine on. What has been less emphasized, though hardly unnoticed, is the shape of Jesus's "form" as a "slave": death, yes, but also a life, a good life, a beautiful life.

With this life, I come to the end of my reflections—as indeed, all our reflections upon our lives must end in this life. Jesus's beautiful life was spent mostly in the shadows of normal existence. Whether or not we attach great significance to the "tabernacling" or "tent-dwelling" image of the incarnation (John 1:14), its vague connotations of sojourning or impermanence, though also of protective cover, are suggestive. Jesus dwells in a world that he shall leave; but, in this regard, he dwells in it like any other human being. To "dwell" on the earth is an act of grace; but if so, one's habitation is contingent—like any dwelling. To this degree, God's love for all the world (John 3:16) is no different, in its lived forms, than the charity by which divine generosity is enacted among the children of men.

This is, admittedly, the stuff of pious sentimentality: the "Holy Family," the "hidden life of Nazareth." Sentimental or not, however, it is a fact. Jesus spent the majority of his relatively average life span (for the era) like most of his male contemporaries: he "came down" with his parents, "went to Nazareth" and was "subject to"—subordinated to—his mother and father, like all children (Luke 2:51; Eph. 6:1). We next hear of him in the "fifteenth year of the reign of Tiberius Caesar" (Luke 3:1), when he is "about" thirty years old (3:23). How long he preached publicly—that is, the time of his life to which the Gospels are almost wholly devoted—is not clear, but certainly no more than three years and probably less. In terms of human experience, Jesus's life seems to have been mostly one of local, familial labor and relations, carried out in the compass of a small town or village. His ministry is summarized prophetically by the aged Simeon when Jesus is still an infant: he is "set for the fall and rising again of many in Israel" and will become the object of calumny (Luke 2:34). Yet Simeon brings his brief foretelling to a close with the simple note that Jesus's life is ordered to his mother's own deep grief: "a sword shall pierce through thy own soul also" (2:35).

Confusing the folk of his community, being disliked, a culminating maternal sorrow—there is a brutal modesty to Jesus's political fortunes. I realize that much has been made of Christianity's social influence over the centuries, including its power to reshape political life. This story is mostly told in terms of quasi-miraculous, certainly astonishing, effects. Or, more recently, it is told in terms of the effects of a finally embraced rationality wondrously grown from the minuscule seedlings that emerged in an ignored corner of the Roman Empire: twelve crude fishermen multiplied into a worldwide church (or set of churches) that changed global history:

> Had the followers of Jesus remained an obscure Jewish sect, most of you would not have learned to read and the rest of you would be reading from hand-copied scrolls. Without a theology committed to reason, progress, and moral equality, today the entire world would be about where non-European societies were in, say, 1800: A world with many astrologers and alchemists but no scientists. A world of despots, lacking universities, banks, factories, eyeglasses, chimneys, and pianos. A world where most infants do not live to the age of five and many women die in childbirth—a world truly living in "dark ages."[1]

But what, in the end, was the great *political* influence of Christianity? At best, a humanizing of Roman and of other antique political arrangements and strategies, expanding the boundaries of participation, softening the impositions of political authority. The imperial character of the material that Christianity worked with, however, had its own effect on the church's view of her political vocation. For, at worst, Christian politics was but one more form of war carried on by other means, usually with these means descending quite directly into war itself. The history of Christian Europe after the disintegration of the Roman and then Byzantine Empires is one, especially in the West, of key political refashionings, most especially in terms of ideological rationale—the humanizing aspect. This history is also one of ongoing violence that simply extended the habits of the past. The rise of constitutional forms of government, expanded franchise, and applied rights that marks late medieval and early modern Western Europe made use of Christian insights and values but also was spurred by the failure of long-standing Christian institutions themselves. The entire period, to the present, is littered with ongoing assaults on human life carried out by Christians themselves. It is hard to say in any defined way that, in the course of the subsequent centuries, the brutally modest political life of Jesus was ever really transfigured. His life ends with the commendation of his bereft mother to the care of his disciples (John 19:26–27); perhaps, in its call upon family and neighbor in the midst of a small catastrophe, this is the sum of his politics.

After all, the endings at the center of our lives, the life that was Jesus's own, have to do with the fact that we are no more than creatures who exist solely at the behest of God, who created us and sustains us as he wills. "Not as I will, but as thou wilt" (Matt. 26:39). This is also true of governmental rulers: "The king's heart is in the hand of the Lord, as the rivers of water: he turneth it whithersoever he will" (Prov. 21:1). Politically informed creatureliness, therefore, is about the ordering of our lives in a way that is proper to our limits and to the fact that they are God-given and God-taken—the service of God in the offering of a life of beauty. We call this ordered finitude "godly worship," or *avodat Hashem*. This worship or service is given in the tending and offering of those mortal goods that constitute our being. Jesus gives his widowed and soon-to-be-childless mother to his friend's care; he gives his own life over to God. We are no different, more or less. The mortal goods of our offering are contained within the history of Jesus's life: conception, social confusion and its navigation, paternal embrace, birth, rearing and growth, prayer and learning, toil, a constrained and brief vocation, joys and disappointments, knotted relationships, singleness in this case, fervent trust, betrayal, suffering, astonishing hope and its assault, familial concern, and finally death, accepted and offered up. The thirteenth-century Stabat Mater, with its call to join in Mary's sorrow, is thus not simply the depiction of the special mourning that belongs to the Mother of God; because the mourning is hers on behalf of her son, it is a grief that both embraces human life in its finitude and demonstrates that embrace's opening to God's eternal life: *Quando corpus morietur, fac, ut animae donetur paradisi gloria,* "When this body dies, so make my soul the recipient of paradise's glory." Mourning itself elides the traditional body-soul dualism here in a way that is centered in a parent's love.

What does one *do*—or what does Jesus do—with all this beyond its offering? Once generation has a goal beyond itself—beyond its miraculous founding of created existence—it must lapse into the instrumental forms of Promethean hopes. Human beings in the Anthropocene epoch have lost all sense of generation in the sense of conceiving, in the sense of obligation for and interaction with those who come before and after us in lines of ordered relationship, and in the sense that this is the central "good" of our creation, even when its hopes are frustrated. Worries about ecological disaster that are not informed by generation and its responsibilities are thus morally stunted, and it is no surprise that, devoid of their creaturely and hence genealogical context, they serve mostly to paralyze. There is a deep contradiction at work, a self-immolating confusion, among those who decry environmental degradation even while they pursue the destruction of ordered human creatureliness. Nations that, for instance, legalize self-murder—among other life-assaulting projects—will never be able to have an effective environmental policy. That is, if you will, a political axiom.

Christians, more than anyone else, have been gifted with the knowledge of what it means to be a creature and to live faithfully as creatures. From Genesis to Revelation, we have been given a picture—complex and sometimes uncertain to our logical minds—of how the human creature is set to live. We have also been shown the precincts of life in which we fail in our creaturely integrity. Male-female marriage, procreation, patient singleness or barrenness, child-rearing, learning, toil, poverty and wealth, friendship and generosity, suffering, self-giving, sacrifice, difficult love, disappointed illness and death, as well many of the social elements that grow up around these responsibly—all these mortal goods are laid out in the face of God's grace and calling. The catastrophic nature of existence in Christian terms— existence's creaturely fragility and mutability—is less about well-being than about these "goods," these specifically mortal goods, and their offering. These are part of the larger and fundamental reality of our created nature and its relationship with God. They constitute the shape of a life that is, in its essential identity, "all grace." Mortal goods, then, are given, tended, and offered rather than acquired, constructed, or possessed. There is nothing acquisitive about Nazareth; its form is, instead, unmeasured but given in an assumed, though perhaps fluctuating, sufficiency. Jesus is a peasant.

Well-being, by contrast, in contemporary social and psychological science presents one developed line, however peculiar, in the tradition of tracing the "happy life," of defining happiness itself, *eudaimonia*. Part of well-being's peculiar development in modernity is to focus upon cumulative aspects of existence, on things that can be quantified and measured (and that includes metrics of psychological attitude across populations and eras): life span, literacy, physical and mental health morbidities, and group disparities in these and other matters. These stand behind the national and global "measures of well-being" that we noted in chapter 10. Like wealth, well-being "grows" and, in moral terms, *should* grow. This is called "progress," and it drives most political programs in our era, if only as slogans. But, as Ellen Charry has argued, the Christian tradition, even in its diversity and constraints, emerged within and remained shaped by the Jewish (and scriptural) value not of well-being but of blessedness, what she calls "asherism" (after the Hebrew term for divine benediction, *asher*).[2] The term is reflective of the fundamental divine grace that constitutes created existence, and a life of blessedness is one therefore that is ordered to the demonstration and recognition of such blessing: obedience to God, repentance for disobedience, and thanksgiving for all things and in all situations (Phil. 4:6, 11). "Blessed is the man . . ." (Pss. 94:12; 112:1). This kind of blessed life is the vocation (in the sense of a gift to be gratefully received) of any existence, in any situation, in the midst of being done to and of doing, that defines the life span of a human creature. Blessedness is embodied in both the receipt and the offering of the forms that mortal life provides. Thus, Simeon blesses not only Jesus but Joseph and Mary with him, on their way to Nazareth (Luke 2:34).

I suppose that one could call this receipt and offering of God's mortal gifts a "happy life" or a "satisfying life," even "well-being." But the words apply only if one completely redefines happiness and satisfaction as currently understood within the practice of social science. For at the base of a blessed life is the reality that life is given and taken and is thus brief and buffeted, that it contracts as easily as it expands in terms of quantifiable measures, weeps as much as laughs, trembles as much as sleeps in quietude, appears mysteriously and fluctuates wildly before disappearing, in trust, into the hands of the Creator (1 Pet. 2:23). *How* this could be the case, within the causal network of human relations that is otherwise applied to the discernment of "well-being," is the Christian political challenge in its unique character. Christians must take up this challenge in a way that is not, in the end, driven by the metrics of progress in a modern sense. Rather, the description of the blessed life of the human creature will be pressed by the purely mortal forms that embody and thereby permit the thankful offering of our lives as such. As simply mortal in the sense of "creaturely," then, the measure of Christian political duty is indeed given, and hardly in a sentimental fashion, in the form of Jesus's life: going down to Nazareth. Such "going down to Nazareth" means living and toiling with parents, only briefly offering this garnered wisdom to a small world of family, neighbors, and strangers, and finally providing care to those most bound to one's affections—family and friends, Mary and John. Such a life also means giving all, inclusive of "going down" to God, in the form of a comprehensive "commendation" (Luke 23:46). There is nothing unduly timid in all of this; it is the act of the very Son of God. In this way such a blessed life can take in the entire world.

"Now in the fifteenth year of the reign of Tiberius Caesar, Pontius Pilate being governor of Judaea, and Herod being tetrarch of Galilee, and his brother Philip tetrarch of Ituraea and of the region of Trachonitis, and Lysanias the tetrarch of Abilene, Annas and Caiaphas being the high priests . . ." (Luke 3:1–2). To be created by God and to live faithfully as such a creature, as an image of the first Adam, is patient of a vast spectrum of political regimes, economic conditions, social positions, and psychological characteristics. The reign of Tiberius is only one example. It might also be Henry VIII or Calvin Coolidge or Mao; and it might embrace the myriads who lived within these datable networks. But in themselves, these contexts cannot provide fundamental benchmarks of creaturely value. What of the date and place of Pol Pot? Or of West Garfield Park, Chicago? The reality of extreme conditions is exactly where the political test of blessedness comes into play in a clear fashion—that is, where going down to Nazareth is threatened, where Nazareth becomes the Bethlehem of Herod the king (Matt. 2:16), where normal politics slides into abnormal politics, and where catastrophe lurks in a publicly striking way. I have noted the difficulty of precisely measuring or predicting this slide, let alone its outcome; and in so doing I have also favored a chastened Hobbesian account of security and its moral burdens and limits. Let me list, again, a few examples where "Nazareth" as the Christian political space—that is, the space for peculiarly Christian politics—unveils often unexpected and sometimes overwhelming political duties in a more civil sense.

Nazareth means that the highest goal of political action, at least in Christian terms, is not the preservation of democracy in Ukraine. There is a fundamental equivalence, in terms of providing a container for the ordering of mortal goods, between the regimes of Russia and of a Western-aligned Ukrainian government. War was never inevitable, though regime change may well have been the alternative. Once war comes, however—and God forbid that Christians initiate or enable such war!—the Christian is indeed called to gauge the protection of those mortal goods to which he or she is privileged: the lives of family and children; the freedom to teach them; the integrity of a home, with food and work; the ability to engage neighbors and friends with generosity. Here, though flight is possible for a few, struggle—abnormal politics—emerges, a struggle that could prove deadly (or "mortal" in a nontheological sense); though, within the context of a clear witness of faith, the sacrificing of self in the face of such struggle may well be the offering that true worship of God embodies, *kiddush Hashem*. A time and place may put a sword within our hands; but those who take it up, however rightly, are just as likely to die as those who do not (Matt. 26:52; Luke 22:36). That it is Jesus of Nazareth who tells us *both* these things is but a sign of the catastrophe whose abnormal demands we simply cannot escape and whose endings are given to our faith.

Nazareth means that the coerced imposition of residential schooling upon Indigenous children and their families in Canada over the years was a blasphemous attack on the gifts of God, a kind of pharaonic assault on God's creatures, aimed at the center of divinely given human life. The recognition of that assault—and repentance for it—is a political act, and a demanded one, by churches (and governments). The awareness and identification of colonialist depredations is not, thus, the result of an ideological perversion, as some politicians and Christians of the Right have asserted. But is repentance more than an act? Is it a political program of sorts? Zacchaeus restores those whom he has defrauded "fourfold" and gives away half his fortune (Luke 19:8), and John the Baptist commands the sharing of clothing and food. When it comes to tax collectors and soldiers, men of fearsome violence for the common people, John tells them to keep to their contracts and instructions: "Be content with your wages" (Luke 3:11–14). There is both extravagance and restraint in these penitential responses, but hardly a program defined by policies. The schools were to be resisted and finally torn down. In their wake, politics takes perhaps another turn. Now, going down to Nazareth becomes an imperative, not a distraction.

But Nazareth means that the homeless people who line and wander the streets of so many of our cities—conservatively numbered, there are well over 300,000 of them in the United States and eight times that number in the Philippines alone[3]—are properly the object of Christian political concern precisely because of the dissolution of those precincts of mortal goods that their condition represents. Normal politics here is driven by the reality of charity in a concrete if now expansive way, only because the proximity of the neighbor in need has gone over us like a flood. The transformation of this condition, however, is hardly obvious, given that the causes of homelessness are both varied and intricate: lack of employment and affordable housing, natural disaster, mental illness, family breakdown, drug use, domestic violence, and more. Formulating solutions to any one of these causes, let alone many of them and in their related effects, enters into a realm of complexity that has defied human ingenuity on a large scale and that presses the challenge not only into normal politics but into its difficult constraints. That said, Christians are compelled by the force of their own created being to share housing, food, and clothing and to aid in the securing of families and of individuals within them. The charitable forms of this generosity, if not some greater reformation of society, are indeed within the purview of the good Samaritan's encounter. Homelessness is always localized and shaped by encounter. Nazareth, though, in its trajectory of a life, does not determine the means or the organization of such efforts—only that they happen somehow, with the same struggle and, finally, humility that characterize the life of one who had nowhere to lay his head (Luke 9:58).

One could extend such a list of the benchmarks of extremity, in the United States as much as anywhere: incarceration, hunger, violent crime; unemployment and a low living wage; but also absent fathers, ignored children, untutored adolescents, insouciant market indulgence. The list is not as long as one might suspect, however; and it includes items often judged as morally indifferent by electing majorities. What Nazareth points to are those areas of concern that must be identified and focused upon in terms of common decisions—politics—as well as to the limits of response. Nazareth alerts the Christian to the frontier where normal and abnormal politics merge in an often dangerous mist. On the one hand, Nazareth indicates the kinds of mortal goods to be tended and thus determines the range of tending itself; but on the other hand, Nazareth determines the precincts within which this tending takes place—that is, the way a life is ordered as a whole, its character and shape. In this regard, the political form of Jesus cannot be reduced to the teachings or actions of his last two or three years of life ("principles and policies," in the eyes of some); rather, this political form is coincident with "about thirty years" of a village existence, several decades of a peasant moral economy, assumed by the Son of God.

We have spoken of normal politics—political systems in place, problems, proposals, policies, campaigns, voting, legislative struggle, or executive imposition—as an ongoing round, a round that, in our complex societies, is at best managed, rarely invented anew or drastically refashioned. Christians are inextricably a part of this round as managers, trainers of managers, and participants in the ongoing oversight of training and, rarely, of overhaul. But much of this is *just* this, a "round" of social interaction and expectation that one engages as the being-done-to of being born and living. Nazareth had Herod, tax collectors, wells and fields, adjudications, occupiers, and the rest. Like Edward Banfield's "backward" peasants, most inhabitants of Nazareth probably kept to themselves and their families, although they seem to have known Joseph and Jesus and his brothers in some real fashion, for at least they met in the synagogue (Mark 6:3). A few were more forward. Today's Nazareth, located in the midst of an Israeli-Palestinian conflict, is caught up in an ongoing struggle of property, representation, administrative legitimacy, and violence. Like Jesus's family, some have simply fled. Others grit their teeth. Some press for change. A church stands there . . . representing what, exactly?

If nothing else, perdurance. Nazareth is a place that proceeds through the generations, struggling over the mortal goods of its inhabitants and neighbors. To *last*, in this way, is its vocation.

We spoke in the previous chapter of Christian charity as a political act. But charity is so only insofar as it is historically bound up with its *Christianness*, its conscious subjection to the limits of grace and thus to its concern with the character of mortal life before God. Even more than this, the catastrophic character of life, which subverts our hopes to penetrate the complexities of personal, corporate, and broadly human existence in every direction, has meant that the actual elements of Christian politics, charitable and otherwise, can be tended to only through a process of Christian "survival" itself. Survival is thus one of the key aspects of charity's spiritual pedagogy—survival, that is, not only of the common life of Nazareth but of the means to explicate its gift, something that the church herself had been given the calling to provide.

Nazareth is both a place and an ethos of formation, then, such that Jesus can, when he is about thirty years old, stand up in a synagogue and read the scroll handed to him before his neighbors, who know both him and his family (Luke 4:16–22). We have mentioned "schools" as a central part of Christian charity, but related to these were oratories, sodalities, catechetical functions and locales, and family networks of instruction, both formal and informal. Nazareth included all of this somehow. It did so as a village, as a community, and as a gathering of families for the sake of human endurance across the harsh terrain of mortal life with its abrupt assaults and inevitable endings, nourished by springs, if only here and there, of joy. If Nazareth lays out the terrain in which normal and abnormal politics can be charted; if, within this, it locates the neighbor as an integral part of Christian politics; then Nazareth also provides the context in which the church's own vocation, politically, is to find its aim: the endurance of teaching.

In this light, a basic argument of this book, and one with which it ends, is that the church's political vocation is to keep the embers of faith alive, such that her members can both understand and tend rightly to their mortal goods. The context of such a vocation is the mortal existence, of generation and death, that marks the miracle of our creation. The entropic version of natural time, the time of this world, is that of a love that "grows cold" (Matt. 24:12) and of a faith that dissolves altogether (Luke 18:8). At least three points about Christian politics thus emerge, ones that, though evident only in the corners of Nazareth, were never really ignored until recently, with the spreading glow of ameliorative hopes. Throughout this book I have hammered away at the delusion of such hopes, simply in order to make more visible these elements, now so overgrown. Each of these elements—the ascetic, the catechetical, and the familial—necessarily help us to grasp rightly how our political calling as Christians is to live in such a way that we can write letters to our children that celebrate the joy of Nazareth.

Ascetic

Within the catastrophic framework of mortal life, Christian politics must obviously take on, first of all, an ascetic orientation. Catastrophic time, by contrast with natural time, marks the overturning of all continuities that we, lulled by our illusions of being "settled," are prone to project onto reality ("I said in my prosperity, 'I shall never be moved'" [Ps. 30:6 RSV]). Catastrophic time offers instead the virtue that accompanies a bare kind of survival that Jesus himself names as "endurance": "The one who endures to the end will be saved" (Mark 13:13 NRSV). "Endurance" or "patience"—*hypomonē* in the Greek and *patientia* in the Latin, as well as related terms used elsewhere in the New Testament and the Septuagint, like *makrothymia*—has a profound role to play in the scriptural vision of social survival. Nazareth remains as a place to which one can return after a flight to Egypt, after a Roman occupation, after waves of various imperial onslaughts and modern nationalist conflicts. The return to Nazareth moves from the pilgrim Egeria in the fourth century to the twentieth-century soldier-turned-hermit Charles de Foucauld and, in his wake, to the renewal of one of the most profound expressions of

Christian politics, the Little Brothers of Jesus.[4] The profile of endurance, a virtue drawn from a divine source yet wholly ordered to created existence, gave rise to a great spiritual tradition that remains mostly unmined in our day, even though it was central to the church from its beginnings to the early modern period. From Tertullian and Cyprian and their linkage of endurance to martyrdom, to Cassian and his identification of patience as a central communal grace and virtue, to Franciscan discussions of the nature of service, *patientia* and its formation became a central lens through which to view the Christian's relationship with God, church, and world. As is clear in Mark 13's figural threads, endurance is a centrally christological reality. Curiously, social scientists have been orbiting around this unknown planet more recently without realizing it, focusing on the character and shape of things like resilience, loyalty, and constancy in situations of communal chaos and trauma.[5] One way or the other, endurance is clearly both the goal and the form of Christian politics. One can neither move through "about thirty years"—an adult life span in Jesus's era—without endurance nor face with hope the catastrophe of life's gift unmoored to its roots.

Endurance means "staying while letting go" or "staying with what is most important, while letting go of the rest." The ascetic character of endurance is given, not only in the "letting go," the divesting of sin or passion or temptation or pride; it is also given more deeply in the struggle itself to be faithful *while* all is being "taken away"—indeed, to be willing to receive God's gift of life with thanks, even as that life returns to its Maker. This can only be taught.

Catechetical

A second major point follows from this larger framework of endurance: Christian politics is catechetical and formational in method—that is to say, according to those few principles one can identify as constant—covering responses in Ukraine or northern Canada or on the streets of Los Angeles. Endurance is a grace, as the tradition has insisted; but it is also learned, in the sense of being bound up with discipleship, of watching, following, being shaped. A Christian cannot survive without such learning, which is part of the offering the Christian gives in the face of created life's fragility. The cross and its verbal and gestural articulation is the outcome of "about thirty years" in Nazareth.

To recall our previous discussion, Luther himself explicitly grabs hold of the issue of formation in his discussion of Jesus's catastrophic teaching.

His vision may seem paradoxical. On the one hand, Luther sees Jesus's articulation of history's ordering as driven by a deep relativizing of all worldly goods: peace, health, harmony, subsistence, security—the kinds of things normal politics aims for and whose failure to grasp pushes us into the abnormal. All these are physical goods, Luther says, that are bound up with the figure of Jewish blindness, the "Jews" themselves figuring the false valuation embodied in things like temples, sacrifices, and great cities. The line between these worldly goods and the mortal goods that determine the gift of life itself is often blurred in Luther's discussions. From his perspective, the historical destruction of all of this, something that Jesus predicts, is real enough; it came under the Romans.[6]

Luther's anti-Semitism in these remarks is grotesquely traditional and should not be excused; but our repugnance for it also should not obscure his larger point. For, in the synecdochal way we outlined earlier, the destruction of our worldly goods continues to come, in Luther's view, under Turks, popes, and the broader array of the devil's minions who populate contemporary life. All our worldly goods are useless, Luther insists, and in the most tangible of ways: today, Luther writes at the end of his sermons on Matthew 24, "many good-hearted people say and desire, 'Come, dear Lord Jesus Christ!' For there is no government; everyone does what he wants. Our preaching will not help, and the secular authorities are also lax. So let the thunder and the lightning strike and throw it all into a heap"![7] Into a heap! This theme is a Lutheran staple, consistent with his famous verse from "Ein feste Burg" ("A Mighty Fortress Is Our God"): *Nehmen sie den Leib, Gut, Ehr, Kind und Weib*—"Let goods and kindred go, this mortal life also" (in Frederic Hedge's well-known translation, in which "mortal," interestingly, is provided as an explanatory detail). "Kindred" refers to children and wife in Luther's German. "Goods" here is indeed "mortal goods," for after all, "the good," in Luther's view and following a traditional strand of Christian thinking we have criticized, is always "spiritual," and in human terms this ultimately comes down to faith itself. It wouldn't matter if the pope were just a thief, Luther says; we can live with that.[8] The problem is when our *faith* is destroyed by bad people.

Yet here is the paradox. For although faith is a spiritual good in contrast to what we have called "mortal goods," faith is given, Luther says, in very concrete ways: in the Word preached, in the sacraments performed, and, finally, in catechism. If, Luther says, "the devil and the heretics constantly boast that they are bringing the truth," the answer is clear: "Let everyone work hard at learning the catechism well and properly."[9] All the real, physical catastrophes that Jesus talks about—and they *are* real—are also figures of spiritual destruction as well, and that is what we should worry about. The way to deal with this "properly" depends upon this-worldly responsibilities, ecclesially defined, as he has emphasized: sacraments, preaching, and teaching.[10] There is nothing here about withdrawal, and of course Luther is the last person to be read in a sectarian manner. Rather, "spiritual" goods are grasped, for Luther, through vital communal existence: social life, political life, and family life, all ordered with regard to the common life of the church of Christ, to be sure, but ordered publicly and tangibly.

All this is, in part, the tenor of his Small Catechism, and it informs large parts of the Large Catechism, especially but not only in Luther's treatment of the Decalogue. However much Luther knew that, in the end, one must "let goods and kindred go"—that is in part what makes mortal life "mortal"—these realities find a redeemed, godly, and historically necessary use when applied to the Christian faith. Furthermore, that application is given through the means of thoroughly mortal goods: let kindred go, but *first* let kindred teach you.

The picture Luther leaves, then, is not exactly asocial or even apolitical in any normal sense. The question has to do with "ends." What are our social and political efforts finally aimed at? Our earlier discussion of Deuteronomy and the "conditions of offering" comes into play here, and in a way that elevates Israel to a level Luther himself would probably have resisted. In the context of Jesus's words in Mark 13, the end here is "endurance," by which Luther means, as he explains, faith itself, faith that lasts "to the end," when everything else falls apart—in his list, when Germany itself crashes down (just like Egypt and North Africa crumbled earlier, he notes), when the church disintegrates, when Christendom goes up in smoke, the whole lot, annihilated by Turks or whomever else.[11] Politics, that is, exists "for the faith" or "for faith," not the other way around. As a result, a Christian politics must aim at the kind of endurance that comes through the faith's profound teaching and inculcation within and informed by the mortal goods of Nazareth. These may be fleeting, but they are utterly critical just because of their transience.

Familial

In the end—and this follows from the catechetical insight of someone like Luther—a Christian politics *is* familial. We have touched on this point over and over again, but that is because it is probably the most controversial point to be made given our current cultural context, and given that it speaks to elements of normal politics that are presently in enormous and bitter dispute. But this dispute—over sexual identity, couples, responsibilities, children, schooling—is properly reduced to the key mortal goods of our existence. These are the goods that, in enduring faith and for the sake of that faith, we must finally let go of in thanks. The paradox of valuing that which is intrinsically transient has stymied especially modern habits of faith and action so deeply as to confuse our common and individual lives to the point of destruction, leading to anxiety, despair, exhaustion, and all the demons of, especially, young life in our era. But the paradox is simply a cognitive tic of the miracle of mortal creation; it is revelatory and hence to be embraced with joy.

Leaving aside its mortal goods, the family was always (and in some minds still remains) the main motor of social stability. A host of traditioned skills linked to the goods of family are laid out within the scriptural tradition— claims of honor, loyalty, self-giving, love, honesty. These were long viewed as taught primarily by members of a family in their varied, if shifting, roles and relationships. Since these skills were also viewed as necessary to the civil sphere, it was also long believed that politics seeks both to preserve and to guard family membership but also to confirm and reflect its skills.

As early modernity developed, however, the family seems to have become, at least in terms of practical civil life, less and less the seat or font of political integrity. With this change, so too did the place of mortal goods as central to the political realm fade. Honor, loyalty, and the rest, after all, are virtues or skills aimed at maintaining the generational energies of short-lived and vulnerable creatures. By contrast, Machiavelli, as an exemplar of this emerging modern attitude, saw the family (with its women and passions) as less useful to the stability required of the virtuous life. Instead, he turned his interest toward the republic's survival as a whole, which he thought was made possible by the realistic wielding of power. His overriding concern with the state's stability seems to have muted, for him, Aristotle's worry over the corrupting influence of concentrated wealth. Artful use of power, after all, was what was needed, in Machiavelli's view, and for such an art, power itself was necessary, not the small stories of family relations.[12] This is one key moment, at least in intellectual theory, of domestic displacement.

But in the next few centuries, as power, in the form of wealth, is distributed in an expanding "middle-class" liberal society—something that blossoms into full flower within modernity—artfulness itself also loses its particular agents, and corruption is more broadly disseminated. No longer is the struggle waged between the democracy of the poor and the oligarchy of the rich, in Aristotle's framework of balance; no longer is there the clear instrument of *vertu* capable of being wielded with focus, as still in Machiavelli. Instead, stability itself is now idolized in terms of wealth production *tout court*. Within the context of the twentieth century's Great Health Transition, whereby the limits of mortality are widely, if only briefly and superficially, mitigated, the relative poor themselves are driven less by the needs of survival (though that too) than by the hunger for and possibility of wealth for themselves. But if the domestic (family) commonwealth—as it was put in the seventeenth century—is thus now but part of this great corrupting search for the achievement of wealth, as the many social parables of the Hearsts and Gettys tell us, it is no surprise if the family's own stability is exposed as existing in some profound tension with today's wealth-ordered life of the liberal middle class. The very value of mortal goods makes no sense here any longer. A true domestic focus, then, must always be ascetic in some fashion; yet that can happen only if the central value of mortal goods permits their suffering.

Thus, we cannot properly release our "goods" unless and until we allow them rightly to inform our faith in a positive fashion. This claim derives from the defining goal of endurance and its catechetical ground with respect to our mortal calling: the family is the primordial and richest source of formational catechesis, given as this is in marriage and child-rearing.[13] In contemporary psychological resilience theory, the family is both the major source of the traumas that threaten existence and also the major source of resiliency's formation. The family is, furthermore, a political entity in Christian terms, even if sui generis, as all political theorists since Aristotle, at least, understood.[14] Christians are therefore not mistaken in struggling on this ground, both in their normal and abnormal politics. The family and its formational life and character are central to Christian politics, insofar as the roughly thirty years of Jesus's life are given their shape in Nazareth.

I am here driven back to the challenge of counseling my children. All this book amounts to, after all, is the message of my passing fatherhood: I have given you life, as has your mother; we have done this only because God has given both us and you a life that cannot even be grasped apart from this grace; these lives are his to give and to take, and so God will; rejoice in this and so order your lives that this giving and taking, this generation and commending, this sense of grace in all things here and now can be a source of rejoicing for others.

When the Christian church and Christians themselves no longer see this great lesson and the teaching of this lesson as their political vocation, then life itself is squandered. The great scriptural admonitions in this regard—Deuteronomy 6:6–7, Proverbs 1:8–9, Ephesians 6:1–4, and the poignant nod to endurance in 2 Timothy 1:5—are testimonies, if only partial, to the great catechetical ordering of Christian existence in this ever-strange world. It is not so much that teaching is the culmination of a peculiarly Christian politics, but it *is* a supreme benchmark for that politics' evaluation. Teaching the faith—through the shape of a patient life, through deliberate catechetical practice, and, most of all, through the engagement of human family and its community of neighbors—is the ground of endurance, both individually and corporately, as believer and as church; and thus the capacity and enactment of Christian teaching in its various forms constitutes the lens through which normal and abnormal politics can be discerned and their engagement judged.

All the elements of a Christian politics we have discussed—thanksgiving, self-offering, and worshiping, with their ascetic, catechetical, and familial concerns—are not idiosyncratically suggested. They have in fact tended, if in perhaps quite different nuances, to inform contemporary interest in one of the major recent orientations of Christian social thinking—that is, "diasporic" politics. George Lindbeck was one of the first major Christian theologians to reflect on this category. More recently, other thinkers have explored this theme from Anabaptist perspectives or from postcolonialist vantages.[15] Such diasporic theory, which deserves careful consideration, is properly located within the category of catastrophe. Hence, the place to study it is just in terms of the character of Jesus's words in a place like Mark 13.

What, after all, is the first catastrophe described by Jesus in this text? The destruction of the temple and Jerusalem. And who are its first participants, victims, and survivors? The Jews. Jewish diaspora, which is embedded in the Scriptures from Genesis on, is thus the great figure of Christian politics, comprehending the sojourning reality of mortal life as well as its vocation. This figure and its details stretch forth to the post-temple eras of imperial Rome, the Middle Ages, and early and late modernity. That experience is the school for Christian politics, and it is only recently beginning to receive the attention it should in political-scientific terms.[16] When it comes to the ascetic, catechetical, and familial dimensions of Christian catastrophic politics, "salvation is from the Jews" (John 4:22 NIV). The logic follows the simple evangelical thread that moves from John 13:1 ("Having loved his own who were in the world, he loved them to the end" [NIV]) through the hinge verse of Matthew 24:13 ("The one who endures to the end will be saved" [NRSV]) and, finally, that locates the originating form of that salvation in the Jews themselves. This was the insight Luther struggled unsuccessfully to articulate, hampered by his own and centuries of vicious anti-Judaism. Yet there it was, waiting to be grasped: the great historical synecdoche of Matthew 24 had properly brought the church finally into the actual fold of Israel, which is precisely that to which the promise of the gospel, in its political dimensions, is aimed. "And Pilate wrote a title, and put it on the cross. And the writing was JESUS OF NAZARETH THE KING OF THE JEWS" (John 19:19). This is where Nazareth "ends," in the sense of its eternal fulfillment.

The great transcendentals that have so preoccupied Christian politics—for example, justice and goodness—therefore do *not* take form in us in any initiating way, nor are they given purely in the external realities of the world. Luther was right about that. They are, rather, fulfilled in God's inhabiting of his created world, an act of generosity that has no purpose beyond its own transfiguring gift. God's forgiveness, thus, is not an empowerment to succeed in our own ameliorative projects. Rather, God's forgiveness is given into a world where things do not succeed in the ways we envisage, desire, and often (wickedly) enforce. God's generosity is its own "effective" force, and we can merely live according to its commanding words, in the obedient form of *avodah*.

The compelling life of the radical disciple of Jesus of Nazareth is one which some are called to in the unpredictable unfolding of our catastrophic existence. I think of someone like André Trocmé and his pacifism, his "conscientious objection," and most famously his leadership of a "normal" Christian congregation, with its normal families and schools, its normal round of preaching and Bible study, its normal visitations and prayers, and then its almost unscripted receipt and protection—in the sudden shift from normal to abnormal—of thousands of Jews seeking survival from the threat of massacre.[17] The shift itself unmasks the divine generosity at the heart of our lives, embodied in the uncertain and strategically inchoate coordination of divine force and human receipt: we dwell here, in the midst of that which God has assumed in order, "effectively," to make his own forever, Nazareth transfigured.

The letter I write to my children is one, I hope, that can point to this "in the midst of" life, a created space that bears the shape of its creation; an intrinsically beautiful space, even in its sheer edges and internal eruptions; and a space that, because we are mortal, thereby belongs to God. Jesus is weaned, taught and nurtured, and dwells in Nazareth. Then comes the moment on the threshold of catastrophe, and he speaks to us: "These things I have spoken unto you, that in me ye might have peace. In the world ye shall have tribulation: but be of good cheer; I have overcome the world" (John 16:33). Be of good cheer, my children, not in another world, but just here in the one we are wondrously blessed to share for a time.

Conclusion

Letter to My Children

Now also when I am old and greyheaded, O God, forsake me not; until I have shewed thy strength unto this generation, and thy power to every one that is to come.

Psalm 71:18

I return now to my own letter. The outline that follows below is one that, in large measure, I drafted a few years ago and in fact sent to my young adult children. Yet there were aspects then that I had not confronted, and questions arose about these unfaced realities in my children's own minds. My counsel seemed too modest, and the world and its needs seemed to over-whelm that modesty. While I have not altered the core of that first letter, I have had to face the hard reality in our day that modesty of vocation needs to be justified, it seems, before the voracious moral imperatives of the modern world. The justifying answer I have given in this book is, in itself perhaps, no more convincing than simply remaining silent on these matters. Still, it strikes me as inescapably true: we are mortal, and the most wonderful essence of our lives, which draws out all desire, counsel, and love, is tied up with this mortality and its gifts. Can young people understand this? They will have to, even if it is in the form of "another [who] shall gird thee, and carry thee whither thou wouldest not" (John 21:18). I tremble before such an imperative thrust upon them, though it comes to all of us in our own way.

As the letter below unfolds, it will touch upon many elements that have come up in this volume, some only in passing or not at all (e.g., friendship and the church), others in ways that form deep foundations to the brief com-ments in my actual counsel. As I have indicated, this book is not meant to be a guide to politics or a systematic treatment of the logic and ethics that ground our politics (normal and abnormal). Rather, I have only wanted to reflect on how the goods of our lives are mortal and how tending to these mortal goods is all that is *required* of us politically, because it is the sum of our grace-filled existence as creatures of God. I have tried to place politics in the context of the service of God—*avodat Hashem*—with God as his own parameter to that service, as it were: our creation by God, and thus our mortality, is the realm of this service, no more and no less. We worship God with our lives and with our deaths both, and the form of our service follows the boundaries of this frame.

From one perspective, not much new, with respect to activity, is offered by this vision of the politics of mortal goods. Indeed, the vision offers far less than the ameliorative politics, variously conceived, that is mostly on offer in our day. At the same time, the outline I am presenting refocuses its narrowed scope to particular areas of existence, wherein the structures of birth, death, generation, and their enduring extension over time are underlined as steering our energies within normal politics, as well as re-fashioning them when the normal shifts into the abnormal. The politics of mortal goods is thus subordinated to that grand dynamism of catastrophe that marks our existence as a whole and that renders the ameliorative dream beside the point and generally vain on its own terms. We live to offer our mortal goods to God in thanks, and thus the virtues of such a life's political interests come down to our patience within the miraculous span of our created time, our teaching of God's grace in making this possible, and the integrity of the fundamental familial networks in which such virtues find their origin and purpose. I have been fortunate in so living that I can at least write the following letter to my children; at least have learned some of its central contents well enough to recognize their truth and share them; at least find joy in this sharing. This good fortune—a decidedly political fortune, with its space, its contours, its tending—is one I pray that others may enjoy as well.

––––––––––

To My Children,

I've been pondering of late the question of what makes for a "good life." I'm not sure why the question has become so important to me. Perhaps just getting older. Or seeing things that were once important to me change so much. Or watching your own lives develop, in both struggles and joys. The last few years, with their pandemic and wars, have certainly pressed this question for most people, given the sudden limitations placed on everybody's choices and, for more than a few, some very real challenges and sorrows. If we said that "the days are evil," we would all probably nod our heads. Whether that acknowledgment is something that brings shudders or encourages turning away, I don't know. You have told me that many of your own peers swing wildly between trying to take our common challenges seriously, finding them overwhelming and despairing, and just turning to the small concerns that are close at hand.

In any case, I sympathize with the sense of emotional push and pull, perhaps exhaustion, in the face of our world. Over these past few years I've certainly seen my views about what makes for a good life change as a result. In particular, they have changed toward a much greater appreciation of the "ordinary," the "normal," the kinds of things that everybody, billions and billions of people, over time and space, have lived and embodied. I've had a growing sense that these are just the places where what is "good" is to be found, rather than in the grand currents of "bettering" things that seem to run out to sea. Seeing things this way is not foreign to me intellectually. A few years ago I wrote a book, *A Time to Keep*, that was about what it might mean, theologically, that we live for just a few years and then die—being mortal. So I've been thinking about all this for a bit.

But the direction that this reflection has taken is in tension with my own inner and mostly unconscious drives, ones that have fueled my purposes and projects over the years. These have too long been aimed at "achievement," "doing something useful," "making the world better," "creating," and so on, all according to my own group's standards, of course, but very much in line with the general push toward "production." Production is what our culture is all about, and I think that, even in the special realms of the intellectual and the artistic, not to mention the moral and the political, it is probably a mistaken value. I'm sorry that I ever bought into it as I did.

I remember one of you used to prod me when we walked through the airport and passed by the guy shining shoes: "That's what I want to do when I grow up," you'd say. "What would you think of that?" It was a bit of a joke at the time, designed to play off my instinctively negative reaction. Well, I can now pretty confidently say that I really don't think it would matter one way or the other. What makes for a good life is lodged elsewhere altogether. The days may be evil. But that truth is wrapped up in a yet larger truth encompassed by the truly good, God's own life itself.

Here is my outline, as I've been thinking about it. It's long, I realize; but I hope you'll read it through. It is filled with allusions and quotes from Scripture because that is where I have found the truth so clearly offered. Thus it's going to be a religious letter. In the end, that's just because this outline is what my Christian faith boils down to. My normal life rises up just here too. This is what I want to share with you.

Avodat Hashem

The main thing that makes for a good life, I believe, is that everything in our life be seen as a "service of God." Judaism calls this *avodat Hashem*. *Avodat* means "service" or "worship"; *Hashem* means "the Name" in Hebrew, which is a way of speaking about God without actually "naming" him literally and allowing God to remain someone beyond us who has yet given us all things. Everything! Jesus's prayer—the Lord's Prayer—speaks of this when he says to his Father, "Hallowed be thy Name." Let God be honored in everything: *avodat Hashem*.

Avodat Hashem is a framework for all of living, and I have found it immensely illuminating. Serving God in all things means receiving every aspect of our life as a gift from God and somehow treating it that way. Sleeping, waking, cooking and eating, dressing, walking, arranging flowers on the table, speaking to a neighbor, shopping in a store, sitting quietly, spending time with someone, writing, working in the garden, playing music, humming, shining shoes or laboring in an office, even being ill or weeping, praying and hoping, grieving and rejoicing, being born and finally dying. Yes, even our deaths are a service to God, since the whole of us belongs to him.

This last point is deeply important, especially as I grow older and realize how I will leave you in this world—or, God forbid, you leave me. I have seen this with parents and siblings; I have considered it when we have, in different moments, taken ill and that frontier that surrounds the light and struggle of our lives seems to be closing in. On the one hand, the prospect of dying—yours, mine, your mother's— fills me with dread and terrible sadness; I don't deny that. Yet even that sadness, which I have experienced more than once, emerges from within the miracle of God's gift of creating us. Love shimmers in this bounded giftedness, and its light drills through all things and across all frontiers somehow. I sense this. Since our life is utterly and in every way a gift from God—we come from God's hands and go to God—everything is something we can and should give thanks for and, as it were, offer back to God. If I live twenty or seventy or ninety years, and my life—whatever it is—has been offered to God in this way, in all the small things that form it, then I have had a good life. In fact, the "best" life.

Jesus says that the poor woman who anointed him with expensive oil while he sat at a dinner wasn't wasting things (others criticized her because she might have used the money for the poor); rather, he says, "she has done a beautiful thing" for him (Mark 14:6 RSV). Every aspect of our life can be such a "beautiful thing" if it is offered up in thanks and, even more so, if that offering somehow comes to define the larger form of our existence so that, when we die, our mortal being has a shape, a thankful shape, however hard it has been to mold it.

What aspects of this larger life, in all its mortal limitations, can and, dare I say, should we offer to God? Here are a few of the major ones.

The Image of God

First, there is the grasping of our selves and our life as being made in the image of God. That is a wonderful promise and reality: every human being, including each of us, somehow reflects the person of God. How does this happen? Jews and Christians see this as located in our interpersonal particularity: "So God created man in his own image, in the image of God created he him; male and female created he them" (Gen. 1:27). It is a startling challenge to think this through: I am because someone else is, someone who is not only not me but is not *like* me. To be a human being is to be a woman or a man and to live this out with the other. A good life seeks to do this.

This is a struggle for many, if not all the time, then some of the time: our fundamental character as a human being is limited by our makeup, our createdness, as a woman or a man, and it is lived out only as this is engaged with the other sex, so different from us in ways we can never really grasp. We do this in a process of struggle and goodness that begins early and goes to the end of life. "The image of God" seems to imply a range of things. I am underlining here only one aspect that is central to its meaning: a man and a woman, coming together and engaging the gamut of the world's other creatures, replenishing this domain of mortal beings whom God has made (Gen. 1:26–28). What a wondrous thing!

"Image" is reception, pure and simple; for there can be no image if there is not first something from which it arises and on which it depends. But, then, why not a "rock"? Indeed! The world as an image of God is not a concept outside of the Jewish and Christian traditions. Still, human beings are "reception that is offered": they offer divine love—not that we love, but he loves and we reflect it (1 John 4:10). Love is generativity, responsibility, struggle, toil, loss, and finally sacrifice. Hence, the image of God is first and foremost the person of Christ, in whose image we are remade. But it is important how one gets to this image of Christ. Its substance contains Adam, as male and female, and this relational identity drives the dynamic of our lives as they are transformed into Christ's own image. Rocks have a history and reflect one; but they do not make their history in the sense of struggling within it.

Learning to love, to be humble, to grow in generosity and in receipt is rooted in this process more than in anything else. How strange your mother and I are to each other! How marvelous! All creation is a wealth of differences, and just these pointed diversities mark our mortal particularities; they are intertwining marks of our life in God's image. From their dependent interplay flows the whole mystery of the human race.

So I am commending marriage to you as a living out and offering to God of this divine image he has made you in. I know that marriage doesn't figure personally in everyone's life, though I think it does or can in an indirect and real way nonetheless. The celibate nun or monk, for instance, lives into the divine image as well, only, in a way, postponing its fruition for the sake of others. And there are, we know, some people for whom, whatever their wishes, marriage doesn't occur. But their very wish is part of the reality we are all grasped by—they suffer their stymied desires (as we all do with most of our desires!), they turn to God in hope, they engage with others whose married lives they support and can be a part of in unique ways, as friends and examples of other goods.

These are important issues for individuals and obviously for our society in its contemporary debates. There is much to be said about the exceptions and disagreements among which, it seems, you have grown up far more immersively than I. But none of that undercuts the reality that we are made in God's image as people who seek the other, in his or her fundamental difference from us, in a primary way. And for those who are married, for all the potential difficulties and burdens marriage may carry (which vary for lots of reasons), the goodness of life is touched in a way that is basic to God's giving us our lives. Take hold of this good, if God leads you there; tend it with all your energies; receive its gifts (gentle and harsh); give thanks. When death comes, you will know you have done your duty in a splendid way (Luke 17:10).

Family

The second part of *avodat Hashem* is found in family. The family is a gift that arises naturally from the blessing of being created in the image of God and, as it turns out, vice versa. Jesus quotes Genesis 2:24 when he says, "For this reason a man shall leave his father and mother and be joined to his wife, and the two shall become one flesh" (Matt. 19:5 RSV). Marriage itself is obviously spoken of here, but more than that. For the context of the woman and the man coming together is the fact that they themselves have parents—a father and a mother from whom they grow and whom they leave in order to form a new family of their own. Furthermore, the "one flesh" that the man and woman "become" speaks not only of their sexual union but—as many have interpreted the verse—of the new life that comes from that. When the two become one there is a re-creation of the image of God in another life, one of the richest blessings of the created world.

It is interesting that another place where the Bible speaks of "bone of my bones and flesh of my flesh" (Gen. 2:23) is in the context not of marriage itself but of family and its generations: when Laban meets his nephew Jacob for the first time, this is what he exclaims (29:14). Israel is a family of peoples, and their relationship is described in terms of the same "flesh" and "bone," joined to their king, David (2 Sam. 5:1). Elsewhere, one's very self can be described in these same terms (Job 2:5). Selfhood, then, is itself procreative at root, and the image of God is given not only in the joining together of otherness but in the new life that this joining brings into the world.

That said, however, family is more than just a woman and a man coming together and having a child. Sometimes—quite a few times, in fact!—there are no children, for instance. In any case, family weaves together generations in more than one direction. One's own father and mother and grandparents and aunts and uncles are a part of one's being, as are sisters and brothers and others who have been made a part of one's common, daily, and shared life. Within the family, the gifts of growth that are so special to the life of a man and a woman together, in their particular life as "two," become gifts that are multiplied—service, patience, affection, generosity, food, forgiveness, working and rest, teaching and learning, singing and asking. The particularities of difference are brought together (not always easily, of course) for the sake of life that moves through time, which is the great gift of God to each of us.

Families are where life takes form in its most central way. So much so that, when ancient Jews spoke of the resurrection, they often conceived of "life after death" in a non-individualized sense, in terms precisely of family and Israel as a whole: we live in and through others into the future, even as we are brought into being by God from their pasts. Family is the fruit of the image of God, the image of the image, one might say, a dynamic that runs throughout our lives. This is why the church—another "image of the image"—is so essential to understanding who we are, and why, when families disappear, so does the church. One might say the same of wider communities and nations. Do not let families become either the optional instruments of self-fulfillment or the focus of your heaviest resentments. They are instead the soil in which you live and where you serve.

There are whole parts of your family that you do not know, from one side or another in the past to present lines that have diverged. You don't know about them because of misunderstandings and estrangements, moving away and losing touch, fatigue, and finally the accumulation of ignorance about who we are. Some of this is inevitable. But a lot of it is not and simply requires attention, and behind that attention a sense of gratitude at the way God orders our lives through our parents and their generations and those that follow. To know their goodness is to know something of the goodness you have been brought into and are now given to nurture in your own life. Here you find the richest fruit of your service of God. When I commend to you the repeated scriptural injunction to "honor your father and your mother" (Exod.

20:12; Deut. 5:16; Matt. 15:4; 19:19; Eph. 6:2), it is not to gain anything from you, but to point to where the world of God touches you from afar and leads you into a future you cannot now see. You are part of the great tree of life in this respect, in the same way that medieval artists drew wonderful and elaborate images of the tree of Jesus's ancestry, growing out of a dreaming vision that David's father, Jesse, beheld in a renewing slumber.

Friendship

Third, there is friendship. Friendship is the gift of life shared between families, a kind of spark that flies wide and lights itself in a new place, so that the image of God can multiply with a kind of spiritual freedom. Sometimes friendships are tentative or short-lived; sometimes they are intense or long-lasting. Each, however, involves a kind of recognition that the blessings of God are far bigger and broader than those of one's own immediate concern. Though they don't always overlap, friends and families "go together" because each is the source of a special growth for the other. *Avodat Hashem* is something taking place in all these areas—in the mutual life of men and women, of families, and of friends—as acts of service, work, engagement, self-giving, and receiving are all grasped as the wonderful contours of the life God gives us.

But the "service" of friendship is particular to itself because it is wholly free and is not tied to the responsibilities of care that marriage and one's own family eventually demand. (And the weight of their "demand" is real and inescapable.) In the service of friendship, all the elements of affection and enjoyment, as well as of sensitive response, are taken up by us only because we see them for the blessings they are, in a kind of unmixed purity. In this, the blessings of friendship remind men and women of the ground of their own love for one another and point families in the direction of their own inner joys, ones that are often only unconsciously recognized and sometimes even forgotten, especially amid the "cares of the world" (Mark 4:19). Furthermore, every friend has a family of his or her own; they are images of us in this way at least. Men and women leave their parents because friendship has made this possible; and friends exist for one another because families have granted each of them the "one flesh" of their particular lives now to be shared.

Couples certainly need friendships with other couples. But the need includes the friendship of single persons also. I am convinced that married persons need friends beyond their marriage and that single people need families within which their friendship can be both a gift and a kind of accountable petition: pay attention to goods of loyal affection! This is one of the great challenges of our present culture's social arrangements, in which I know you have sometimes struggled: there seems to be a clash going on between the values of friendship and family, as if the two cannot share the same space, let alone recognize their dependence on one another. The relationship of friends and families that are not their own is, of course, sometimes complicated. Partners in a marriage do not always share the same friends; friends themselves often prefer to attach themselves to only one person and not take on the baggage of that person's larger family.

It is our mortality, more than anything, that reveals the common root of family and friends, as Job discovered. Despite the inadequacies of what they had to offer, it was Job's friends who came to him as he grieved his children's deaths and suffered his own broken body. It was Job's own difficult life that clarified his friends' understanding of the world. Many readers of the book of Job focus on how his friends gave him all the wrong answers. Not at all! This long book is about the profundity of friendship as much as anything! Their words and arguments, caught up in the hard experience of all the lives they knew, including their own, were the place where the truth of God's creating grace could come into view. Together, in a kind of common work, they dug through the soil to get at the otherwise obscured goods that God had given, reflecting each other's existence with a deepening honesty in the process.

Whatever works to unravel your friendships, even if it is your friends' own limitations (not to mention your own), oppose that and instead find a way to stand firm with your friends. Once you are ensconced in your own family, open it up to single persons who are able to be friends par excellence (that is perhaps their particular vocation). How shall a family endure, if the friends that shore each other up cannot persist in the common tending of each other's lives? And vice versa. "You are those who have stood by me in my trials," Jesus says about his friends (Luke 22:28 NIV). For how else, apart from this loyalty, colored by not a little failure, might they have learned the truth (John 15:15)? And, having learned the truth, offered it up in thanks to God.

Toil

One could imagine the life of women and men together, of families, of friendships, each as a kind of garden. A good life, the best life, takes place within the boundaries of these gardens. But planting, tending, and gathering *are* work, work that is sometimes not easily rewarded, depending on the seasons and their often fickle character. The fact that much of life—its hours and days—is spent in labor for the provision of food, home, and safety can often seem to overwhelm the appreciation of the garden itself. In the biblical story, toil is given as a burden upon human beings and is frequently associated with something "cursed," an existence in which we are consigned to the unending efforts that give rise to the "sweat of one's brow" (Gen. 3:19). As one of you put it, "soul-sucking" labor.

In fact, though, it is the ground that is cursed, not human beings (Gen. 3:17). And the idea here seems to be that a gap in appreciation has arisen between our daily activities and the lives we are given: we are granted a life from the earth (the "dust"), after all, but now all we can see of the earth is that it is our enemy. We forget that dust and spirit are bound to each other—that is the astonishing thing about our lives! "Toil" seems nothing but drudgery or worse, in part because we have lost the ability to see its central place in our service of God. Parents know something about this; they can grasp, as others perhaps cannot, in the often difficult demands of raising and caring for children (or even spouses for one another) how toil is a part of love itself. Even more, I think gardeners are among the closest to rediscovering this ability: they have found joy—as your own mother does—in "working" the soil for its gifts. Gardens are both a tangible symbol and a reality of the blessing of toil.

Work is hardly always fun, nor is it usually "productive" in the way our culture has taught us is important. "Satisfying work" is frequently, in this culture, a code for pleasures of self-stimulation. Work *can* be, however—and indeed it is meant to be—the place where the preciousness of the gifts that order our lives is seen again and again: we are born from the earth, and we return to it. Yet out of it God has given us everything. Attending to our labor—whatever it is—day after day, hour after hour, minute after minute is a kind of "tuning" to the rhythm of giftedness that grounds the other joys that spring up from the garden, whether easily or with effort or for but a moment. All the great monastic traditions, and not only in Christianity, have seen in

labor a place of deep recognition about who we really are in relation
to the life we have been given. Wordsworth wrote his famous poem
"Nuns Fret Not at Their Convent's Narrow Room" to mark the creative
richness of a formal discipline. But he was also pointing to the richness of that discipline's labor. More explicit—and, for all the triteness
time has encrusted on the verses, true enough—is George Herbert's
poem "The Elixir" (set as a hymn you have sung in church—forget
not that blessing!):

> Teach me, my God and King,
>   In all things Thee to see,
> And what I do in anything
>   To do it as for Thee. . . .
>
> All may of Thee partake:
>   Nothing can be so mean,
> Which with his tincture—"for Thy sake"—
>   Will not grow bright and clean.
>
> A servant with this clause
>   Makes drudgery divine:
> Who sweeps a room as for Thy laws,
>   Makes that and th' action fine.

That is why the shoeshiner really *is* no different from the physicist
or doctor, artist or athlete, at least insofar as each is able to offer toil
to God as the place where God's offering of life more fundamentally
is seen and blessed. Among all these persons, the offering is of utterly
equal and infinite value, as the finite creature lifts its gifts—embodied
in family and friends, received from the infinite Giver—back into God's
boundless receipt.

I wish I had known this much earlier in my life. I wish I could
comprehend this now far more deeply than I do. I wish I had taught
you this from the first breath of your existence. Cherish your earthly
toil as the breath of grace.

Neighbors

I realize that all the talk of gardens can sound rather private. Voltaire famously ended *Candide* with a vision of his protagonists now
gathered as a small group of family and friends, living out their lives

and "cultivating their own garden" away from the fury of the world. That's not such a bad thing, either; the prophets promise a time when everyone will live without fear, each under their own vine and fig tree (Mic. 4:4). It's something everyone wants, and we feel deep satisfaction when we receive such quiet security. Indeed, the enjoyment of such security, at least for a while, is one of the great embodiments of created purpose, especially in the political realm. Still, the prophets also speak of a future when just such a vine and fig tree can be shared with our "neighbor" (Zech. 3:10). This is not a member of our family or our closest friend. Our neighbor is the one for whom we have compassion in a way that takes us out into the world and brings the world into our heart. Rabbi Hillel, more or less a contemporary of Jesus, made an oft-quoted remark that links the private garden with the shared fields of the landscape, as it were: "If I am not for myself, who is for me? If I am only for myself, what am I?" He also added a note of urgency about this: "If not now, when?" (*Pirkei Avot* 1:14).

It *is* a matter of urgency to see that God is not only for you (or me), but that God is for others too, and completely so. To recognize how God is completely for others is to recognize the fact that our own lives really are not our own but are God's utter gift, as I have been insisting. The reality of the neighbor (and stranger too, for every stranger becomes a neighbor through the opening of our hearts) is an essential part of our life's giftedness or grace and marks the fifth area of *avodat Hashem*. Neighbors show us that the world is not ours; that our survival is not ours; that work is not ours; that love is, finally, not our own, as if we possessed any of it and could manipulate it and control it just for ourselves. To recognize this essential "not my own" quality of life is not just a personal intellectual attitude; it is an opening up of ourselves to God and to the freedom, joy, and beauty of existence. To say "It's not all about me" is not just a therapeutic exercise; it's a form of deep liberation in the face of the absolute truth of all things.

So while Jesus is clear about the family's central place—"You know the commandments," he says to a young man seeking purpose, "honor your father and mother" (Luke 18:20 RSV)—he also summarizes the law with two phrases from Deuteronomy and Leviticus (in a manner, by the way, that Rabbi Hillel also articulated): "Thou shalt love the Lord thy God with all thy heart, and with all thy soul, and with all thy mind. . . . And . . . thou shalt love thy neighbor as thyself" (Matt. 22:37, 39). In a way, this summary is meant to be a broad description of *avodat Hashem*, as if loving God and neighbor somehow could take in our personal relationships of men and women, family, friends, and work.

Community life (as in even a local block or neighborhood), cities, nations, and the normal politics that keeps these functioning and moving along—all these derive their motive claim upon us from the fact that we are neighbors to one another. And Jesus tells us to *be* a neighbor, not figure out who my neighbor is first, as if we could parcel out God's gifts to others (Luke 10:36–37). "Ye were strangers in the land of Egypt," God tells Israel as a way of both turning them away from self-absorption and reminding them that his love is bigger than each of our small gardens (Lev. 19:34). This reminder is not to burden us with new responsibilities but to reassure us that we can bear the wealth of God's gifts—other people!—in his grace. The dynamic by which the stranger comes close to us and becomes our neighbor is the same one by which we are driven to recognize our lives as divine gifts: we are receivers at the core of our beings.

I think that toil can be transfigured in the context of neighbors, especially. We work simply because we must; we do so also out of love for those we live with and for. But even more than this, we can *share* our work and its fruits (including money) and its formal purposes with others. What constitutes being a neighbor? Not changing the world or righting wrongs or mastering our weaknesses and sins or alleviating guilt. All good, when doable, though often they consist of impossible and repeatedly wrecked attempts. But, more centrally, being a neighbor is characterized by *generosity*, whether small or great in extent. We want our neighbor's good; we desire to be in a position to bring this about; we struggle at trimming, pruning, digging, rebuilding, and reviving, not just our gardens and landscapes but even the terrain of our own habits and inner geographies. We should never forget that, in ordering our own lives—sometimes with the most agonizing strains—we are also serving our neighbors. They inevitably are the recipients of our fruit or failures.

Generosity is not, however, about exhausting ourselves in the battle for the good! I know that some people think this; but they are bad examples whom I have unhappily followed at times, motivated by the common modern notion that the purpose of our lives is to make everything "better." Generosity is freedom, the freest thing a person can ever be or do. Not that it doesn't require some effort! And I am not particularly good at this. Tithing, which generally means giving away

10 percent of what one has (money, mostly, in our day), is a wonderful discipline in grounding generosity, and your mother and I have struggled to follow it, with greater and lesser success at various points in our lives. But this following has *always*—I emphasize this—been a breath of fresh air within the staleness of worrying about ourselves. There is nothing phony or superficial about the gifts of charity that we offer and perhaps can learn to offer regularly; rather, they enclose the thankful treasuring of the mortal gifts that human creatures represent, both those near and those far.

I am being honest when I say that seeing one's own self, when I have been able to sense it for myself as something to share, even in its work and struggle, has opened up light for me: writing, teaching, talking with others as a pastor or simply as a nameless person standing beside another. When we share our work, whatever it is—from simple labor to craft and art, from words or skills or hours of difficult companionship to an experience of our own struggle and perseverance—that deep generosity that lies at the heart of our existence comes into the light. If the Holy Spirit is like a wind, this is where it blows, as it lifts us back to the origin of our life and our death: God's giving. The shoeshiner who converses day by day with those whose shoes he shines is far more generous than the rich person's yearly pledge of money to a good cause.

"Generosity," of course, means many things—mercy, compassion, grace. I suppose the deepest form of generosity is forgiveness itself, which simply makes room for others, even in their failures and wickedness, within one's own life and heart. Would that forgiveness become central to all our days! Oh how I yearn that you might be persons of forgiveness! I have been the joyful recipient of forgiveness, not least from your mother. But it is God who is first generous, we are told: he sends his sun and rain even on the unthankful and the evil, giving them a share of life itself (Matt. 5:45). That is a marvelous truth. A good life—because it recognizes the nature of life itself in this truth—has tasted this and shared it.

Suffering

We open our gardens and share them as we are able. But these places are often overrun, broken down, even blasted and upended by the times, by enemies (who perhaps were even once our neighbors), by our own neglect, selfishness, and weakness. One reason Voltaire recommended that we *deliberately* "cultivate our gardens" is that it is hard to keep them thriving under the best of circumstances. Our lives are filled with suffering, despite our most valiant efforts. The suffering need not be wide-ranging. But when suffering arises, it is always somehow enfolding, burrowing deep, emptying. There is no denying this, the sixth aspect of *avodat Hashem*; and unless we wish to deny the gift of life itself, we must face the reality that a *good* life is filled with suffering, too, as part of its very nature and service.

There are mysteries here that I struggle to understand or even just encounter steadily in my own experience. But if you think about all the things I've mentioned above—being made in a particular way as a woman or a man, living in and with and for a family, cultivating and engaging friends, toiling, opening oneself up to being a neighbor— they all touch upon limits and uncertainties and thus upon disappointments and losses. Sometimes people speak of "catastrophe" as a rare, single, and terminal event. But the word means only "overturning," and in this sense our lives are a constant catastrophe, and our search for stability is just that, always a striving in the face of what we cannot really fix in a permanent way. If we seek to tend our lives like a garden, we realize eventually that the borders of such a garden are constantly being broken down, the plot of land we had carefully laid out but a part of some larger space through which we are forced to move on. These limiting and upending forces are sometimes terribly profound, precisely because they strike at the center of our love and service. I have been mostly spared material and physical suffering; but in other ways I have sensed some of suffering's depth, and, as you know, it has not always been easy to bear. And I know that the suffering each of you has experienced has often seemed heavy indeed.

But just because suffering is most intense as it arises from our love and our hopes, suffering is also their revelation, unveiling their grace. *Avodat Hashem* is often painful because it takes place before, and emerges out of, the very giftedness of our existence as that which God has given us. How to understand this? How to properly grasp it and express it? Our very incapacity drives us to dissatisfaction and sometimes to destructive acts—the kind of cosmic, infantile frustration out of which evil comes to be, from whatever source. God teaches Israel to form their families well, to shape a life with neighbors properly, but also, for all the temporary gardens that we tend, to know themselves as strangers and sojourners who dwell in a land of others, in the wilderness. Where else can it happen? Our inability to accept being the objects of God's generous love, and not the source and master of it, is always and simply felt as pain. It sorrows me that you have had to feel this yourself and will again.

The wilderness, however, is not a bad place to be. Gardens are wonderful; but the wilderness is the greatest, the vastest, space of receipt, where we stand always as those to whom God gives gifts. Remember that the wilderness is but the felt underside of what is in fact the greatest good conceivable: God's creation of you. While I cannot resolve how this is so, I can say with certainty that its embrace—the transfiguring embrace of suffering itself—comes in just the form I mentioned above: generosity, the giving over of one's self, even in pain, to others. Much of the anxiety that is mixed in with my daily breath is fueled by my inability to see things in this way, something I regret. In part, I worry that I have not taught *you* well here, by my example and sometimes unnerved presence. For some kind of deliberate training is essential in navigating this often upended terrain. Suffering well is learned; otherwise it is only brute pain.

Patience, humility, hope, the sharing of what one has learned and lived, and finally forgiveness itself in the face of what others have done—these are obviously all central parts of what is called "the Christian life." For all my failures in exemplifying these attitudes and acts, I am a Christian in part because what I *have* learned in living within just this nexus of suffering and generosity has been absolutely settled: "settled" in the sense of standing firm and stable within our pilgrimage and granted a transcendent beauty. If suffering in love amid and because of the goods God has offered me in my created life—goods that include you yourselves simply in your coming into my existence and mine into yours—*has*, as it were, opened the heavens so as to show me the living God, it is because of what I have heard, read, and seen in the gospel of Jesus, the Son of God, who is God's own self given over in just this astounding way of generous suffering. I am not writing to convince you of this. But I have both sought to endure and in fact have endured as your father because I have been carried along by this knowledge. In any case, do know that my faith in this respect is not an arbitrary matter of taste; it is the fruit, in part, of an ongoing and sometimes difficult process of confirmation of how life—life with you and others—is indescribably beautiful. I have been blessed to know this.

Joy

Perhaps you can sense, then, how suffering and joy are not opposites. Suffering well, the endurance that accompanies it, and the training that shapes and strengthens that endurance all clear the ground for joy. Although not opposites, then, they are not to be confused. The point of "the Good Life" is to enter a light that clarifies how life itself is *a* good and *is* good. But since it is good because it is a gift from God, life's goodness only takes clear form in its orientation to its Giver. A good life, that is, has a direction. I have used the phrase "service (or worship) of God" (*avodat Hashem*) to talk about this, but the phrase can be misleading if it seems to point only to our works, to the things *we* do or feel or live. Our life is given to us, and thus our life is taken from us (so Job says), but not as if it were some kind of object to be thrown about. The Giver takes our life back—for what? For more? For something new? For some reworking? Philosophies and theologies of all sorts have speculated about all this. But I think we can at least say clearly that death is not an absolute end. To us it may seem, in human terms, to be so. Yet the point in being born and dying is precisely that our perspective, that of "it seems to us," is only relative, is only itself given as a gift to help us recognize how our lives are God's to give and sustain. Death marks the clear declaration that we are not our own; hence, death also restores the clarity, somehow, of the One whose we are. The clarity is itself enlivening, uplifting, astonishing, an opening through which light flows and envelops.

Avodat Hashem, which is the shape of a good life, is thus never static. This seventh aspect, joy, is thus more of a moral character than a realm of experience. Our service of God is always on the way to the great clarity and joy of the truth that is God's giving—of our lives, of our selves, of each other, of our toil and service, of God's own self to us. We like to focus on particular moments of pleasure, beauty, thrill, and satisfaction, including those that are bound to and with the people we love. We remember these moments; we sometimes take pictures of them or simply sit and enjoy their savor well past their momentary gleam. All this is rightly an aspect of the joy that can inform our lives. More than that, their accumulation can color times and places with a suffusing glow: "I was happy then," even "I am happy now and here."

But I am speaking of something more than these moments and their numbering, important though they are. After all, we cannot truly measure the goodness of our life mainly according to such quantifi-able variables. The habit itself is distorting, leading to false hopes, to indulgence sometimes, to an almost frightened carpe diem approach to our life's meaning, and certainly to disappointment. Rather, I want to stress how joy is built into our lives more deeply and expresses itself more fully through our ongoing recognition of its giftedness from God, quite simply but also quite comprehensively. Our service of God, which is the whole movement of our lives, is *itself* what joy is all about. The last verse of the poem by George Herbert I quoted above—when talking about understanding our toil as something we do "for the sake of" God as well—makes this clear:

> This is the famous stone
> That turneth all to gold;
> For that which God doth touch and own
> Cannot for less be told.

The sweep of our lives, in our recognition of their moments, ac-cumulations, and exhaustive grasp by God, *is* in itself the carrier of joy. The movement here, which our deaths only give voice to, is a kind of obbligato to all we do, if we could but hear it. I don't mean to sound merely pious about these matters; still, if we could "hum" along with this underlying tune day to day, it would turn into the sound of something glorious. I think music, in general and at least when rejoiced in, is a sign of this movement forward to God. All the virtues that we relate to faith and hope are a part of this singing along. Heaven—and I know that its depiction is a kind of symbol in this case—has always been described in part as a great assembly of song. No masks! Each voice in its own language with all the details of our lives expressed, from shoeshiners to physicists to parents to children. Heaven is also depicted—again, it's a kind of symbol—as an entire world, a new earth, with all its wide vistas, even its deserts and wildernesses, gathered into a new kind of garden where people such as these, you and I, can finally recognize the ordinary as fraught with wonder and joy. The ordinary, which I am trying to celebrate and commend here, has a direction: the gift moves, it comes, it goes and arrives, all because it is created and drawn forward by the One who stamps the ordinary with his image.

The Church

I haven't said anything about the church thus far, despite the fact that I have given much of my life to it, for better or worse. In a way, that is because I have myself often misunderstood what the church is, seeing it as a kind of super-good, something that is "more important" than some other group or endeavor. I don't usually think this way anymore. Instead, I see the church as a comprehensive space rather than a value: the place I have toiled, certainly; the place I have found friends; the place where neighbors were given to me and where I was asked to be a neighbor; the place I have raised my family; the place I encountered your mother and within which we joined together our lives; the place where all the depictions of God's unveiling have been expressed and given a certain dynamic sense. Put this way, this "place" is the whole of God's gift of life, not to the exclusion of this or that part of life but rather to its recognition as just this divine gift. The church is glorious in this sense, but not other than or opposed to the life, limited and mortal but also glorious, that we live in the world.

In the Christian faith we call the church "the body of Christ," and we speak of those who follow Jesus and are baptized as being "members of his body." That has been viewed at times as setting up a contrast between the church and the larger world—who's in and who's out. I think now, however, that the church is more the place of "recognition" where we can realize (over time, on and off, sometimes more, sometimes less, but truly) that the life we have been given by God is actually God's own self somehow, given over to us as pure gift. The body of Christ is precisely God's self-offering to us, and as members of Christ, God's self in the flesh, we are helped to see that our creation and life are not, for all their limited forms and days, a shadow, in the sense of something insubstantial. Rather, our lives really do embody the substance of what is most important, true, and lasting in all the universe: he who made us has come to us just as he has made us, and thus just as we are! There is recognition here but also the deepest energies of the world at work. What we call the incarnation of God in Jesus of Nazareth, which and whom I believe in, constitutes the display and motor of God's life as the gift of our life. All the (overly) complicated theology of the church comes from this simple, if infinitely profound, reality.

I suppose that, in a way, the church is herself a "mortal good," in the sense that, as a space of recognition or revelation, all the elements that make it up—mortal goods themselves—carry us with them, take us up, and open us to God, and their embracing space is carried with them even as that space lifts them up on display. The "body of Christ" that all this embodies has a transfiguring character, as well as a destiny that somehow goes beyond this collection of elements. Here the category of salvation arises, the revelation of mortality's "potential" as being in the hands of God. I have assumed the reality of Christ Jesus here in my reliance upon the Scriptures; but any "natural" theology of mortal goods always comes up short without the epiphany of his being and life, mortal and resurrected. (I am not writing you a gospel, only the letter of a father to his children. A gospel surely lurks here, but that is for another conversation.)

There is a text in the prophet Isaiah that I think is extraordinarily illuminating (and encouraging) on all this. Israel is looking at its life—a long journey from Abraham and Jacob through Moses, through judges and kings, through David and Solomon, wealth, wars, and finally disasters. What did all this amount to? Israel (which is Jacob's name, passed on to a people) is like any person here: "Then I said, I have labored in vain, I have spent my strength for nought, and in vain" (Isa. 49:4). Like any *mortal* person. Here *avodat Hashem* has been a mixed experience at best and seems to have ended in a wretched failure. Surely you and I both have felt this way at times. But then Israel responds to this reality: "Yet surely my judgment is with the LORD, and my work with my God."

Israel's life was never its own in the first place. Nor, therefore, was its service of offering. It was all God's, after all. Is not the "worth" of what God creates thus measured by God's originating grace and not by our small offerings or their failures? "And now, saith the LORD that formed me from the womb to be his servant, to bring Jacob again to him, though Israel be not gathered, yet shall I be glorious in the eyes of the LORD, and my God shall be my strength" (Isa. 49:5). "Not gathered": that is, a life that still seems incomplete, that did not reach its hopes, succeed in its plans, even do its proper duty. A mortal life, a creature's life, our life. But "not gathered" is itself a creaturely way of talking; for the Lord who gives us our life—its relations, families, toil, suffering, and joy—has had its "gathering" from the start in his own eyes, eyes that see all things in the glory of his own being.

After reflecting on this, Isaiah, now speaking God's word, returns to this point again and uses the very image of the central mortal goods I have been enumerating, showing how they themselves originate, in their goodness, within the very heart of God: "But Zion said, The LORD hath forsaken me, and my Lord hath forgotten me. Can a woman forget her sucking child, that she should not have compassion on the son of her womb? Yea, they may forget, yet will I not forget thee" (Isa. 49:14–15). Isaiah then states one of the most remarkable words from God in all the Bible: "Behold, I have graven thee upon the palms of my hands" (v. 16). "Graven" or "inscribed": the word connotes the laws of a great governor—the Governor of the Universe!—written, decreed, enacted. And here that decree is Israel herself, mortal Jacob, who struggled for the Good Life and seemed to have come up short in his own perception, yet turns out to be God's own eternal purpose of creating grace.

This is what the church implies because she, like ("as"!) Israel, and carrying her many Israels—Isaacs, Jacobs, Hannahs, Marys, you and me—is swept into the life of Christ as the great Gift or Sacrifice to God, as "the Good Life" incarnate, the fleshly palms of God into which we are all inscribed. If nothing else—and it is much more, I believe!—this is a beautiful image.

As I said, I bring this up here at the end of my letter because I don't want to leave you with the impression that our service of offering up our lives to God is about simple endings and disappearances. The mortal goods we are given and that we tend, and that we often then extend into the world of politics and the rest, cannot really be "final" goods, even if they are still absolute in their way, "truly good." Each of us will lose all of it "for" something else—unknown for now, but utterly known in God. Only the church has feet in both these worlds—of the truly but not final good, and of the Good that remains veiled in its fullness—not so as to grant the church's worldly claims immortal status in the midst of mortality, but so as to always disturb mortality's satisfactions and fears both. The church is filled with peace and restlessness together.

I would hope and I pray that you can participate in the life of the church. What I would not like you to feel pressed into doing is to be consumed by that life—as, in a way, I have been. I have given myself to what I believed to be the church's "true" politics—preservational endurance-building—in the face of forces that would dissolve this revelatory space. But I now see more clearly than ever the paradoxical nature of this work. I can serve the church only by promoting her survival in the loosest of ways, ways that "lose" all things ("Let goods and kindred go, this mortal life also," as Luther's "A Mighty Fortress

Is Our God" puts it). This is of course built into mortality itself! But the "letting go" is bound to a promise that is here empowered. We will let go—I will leave you, as you will leave me in this life—not so as to efface the goods that make up the Good Life, but to find their "right time," their "timeliness," their place in the great sifting realm of God's gifts. The time of the church is "another time," relativizing so much of what led Israel to bemoan its life as a life lived "in vain." Which is why it is so important to live within the church's time as well as in the moments of our mortal lives.

Just to be clear: even though I feel that I have misunderstood a lot in my service of the church, a service that in a way ended up obscuring the true goods of my service of God, I don't mean to denigrate the church as an institution, with her customs, teachings, and worship. These are central, and they remain so for me. They deserve to be taken seriously and struggled over. But these aspects of the church are simply about the truth coming into view with all its directive force, a truth that "was from the beginning, which we have heard, which we have seen with our eyes, which we have looked upon, and our hands have handled, of the Word of life" (1 John 1:1): a "life"—our life given to us by God, but somehow connected thereby to the One who *is* Life—and a truth that will set us free (John 8:32).

When I began to write this, I wanted to avoid too much religion. But now it seems that this is all I've been able to write about, flowing as it does from the riches of life itself, which seem to be expressed in the Scriptures I hold so dearly. I suppose this is finally because our lives, I am convinced, are not just "things," relationships, activities, and feelings. They are all this and more, but only as they are grasped in their inner spring, their source and goal. In all this, I hold God to be their living presupposition. For many of us—including me, much of the time—God is also always a question, an encounter, a discovery, a struggle, sometimes (too often, perhaps) even a loss and a cry. You never get it "sorted out," nor have I. Still, the "sorting out" is part of the goodness that is bound up in the gift itself. We do see his face in all this. When we do, things click into place, if only for a moment, and we give thanks.

A good life, the best life, is a life that can somehow hold these moments together and thus, in the short arc of our existence, can depict a reception, a thanks, an offering. My great hope is that you be free to do this, something that is possible in any context, in any mode of work, with any amount of money, in the company of any person, in any community and its politics, in any year or age. For neither context, work, money, company, politics, year, or age defines the gift of life that God gives us; neither context, work, money, politics, year, or age makes a person better or worse. The value of life is instead very ordinary, very normal. The elements of *avodat Hashem* I have laid out above are not in themselves the essence of life; no one thing is. Rather, they are the ways that most ordinary human beings have been able to receive their lives from God with thanks. They constitute all that one might ever need in order to give thanks. All.

Which means that I am deeply thankful for this life I have been given with you—though perhaps too slow in seeing it clearly. What I need to do is let you know this, and know that I do not seek more than this gift and all it means.

I write with love for you.

Notes

The following abbreviations appear in the notes:

bk(s).   book(s)
chap(s).   chapter(s)
esp.   especially
FC   Fathers of the Church
frag(s).   fragment(s)
repr.   reprint
sec.   section

Introduction

1. *Avodat Hashem* is a transliteration of the Hebrew. We will discuss *avodah*, or "service," later. *Hashem*—literally, "the Name"—is a normal Jewish way to refer to God that, out of reverence, does so indirectly.

2. Giordano Bruno, *On the Infinite Universe and Worlds* [translation of *De l'infinito universo e mondi*, 1584], in Dorothea Waley Singer, *Giordano Bruno: His Life and Thought, with an Annotated Translation of His Work "On the Infinite Universe and Worlds"* (New York: Schuman, 1950).

3. Jacques Ellul, *The Political Illusion*, trans. Konrad Kellen (New York: Random House, 1967).

4. Karl Marx, "Political Indifferentism," Marxists.org, accessed March 9, 2023, https://www.marxists.org/archive/marx/works/1873/01/indifferentism.htm. The essay, in Italian, was first published in 1874 in *Almanacco Repubblicano per l'anno 1874* and later translated by Bignami from a French version into English in *The Plebs*, vol. 14 (London 1922).

5. William Archibald Dunning, *A History of Political Theories: Ancient and Mediaeval*, vol. 2 (New York: Macmillan, 1910), 154–65.

6. Neil Elliott, "Political Theology and the New Testament," in *T&T Clark Handbook of Political Theology*, ed. Rubén Rosario Rodríguez (London: T&T Clark, 2020), 61–74.

7. Peter L. Berger, *The Many Altars of Modernity: Toward a Paradigm for Religion in a Pluralist Age* (Boston: De Gruyter, 2014).

8. Søren Kierkegaard, *Kierkegaard's Journals and Notebooks*, vol. 8, trans. and ed. Niels Jørgen Cappelørn et al. (Princeton: Princeton University Press, 2015), 165.

9. Matthew Avery Sutton, *American Apocalypse: A History of Modern Evangelicalism* (Cambridge, MA: Belknap, 2014), 295–325.

10. Reinhold Niebuhr, "Barthianism and the Kingdom," in *Essays in Applied Christianity* (New York: Meridian, 1959), 147–50.

11. "The Theological Declaration of Barmen," in *The Constitution of the Presbyterian Church (U.S.A.), Part I: The Book of Confessions* (Louisville: Office of the General Assembly of the Presbyterian Church, 2016), 281–84.

12. Herbert Butterfield, *Christianity and History* (New York: Scribner's Sons, 1950), 146.

13. Michel Mollat and Philippe Wolff, *The Popular Revolutions of the Late Middle Ages*, trans. A. L. Lytton-Sells (London: Allen & Unwin, 1973); Rodney Hilton, *Bond Men Made Free: Medieval Peasant Movements and the English Rising of 1381*, rev. ed. (London: Routledge, 2003); Yves-Marie Bercé, *Revolt and Revolution in Early Modern Europe: An Essay on the History of Political Violence*, trans. Joseph Bergin (Manchester, UK: Manchester University Press, 1987); William Chester Jordan, *The Great Famine: Northern Europe in the Early Fourteenth Century* (Princeton: Princeton University Press, 1996).

14. Here one will find a certain affinity, transposed probably in ways he would not accept, with Donald MacKinnon's notions of "reception" as an essential characteristic of mortal life as "given" by our Creator. See MacKinnon, "Does Faith Create Its Own Objects?," *Religious Studies* 26, no. 4 (Dec. 1990): 439–51.

15. Simone Weil, *The Need for Roots: Prelude to a Declaration of Duties towards Mankind* (London: Routledge & Kegan Paul, 1952).

16. David Cayley, *Ivan Illich: An Intellectual Journey* (University Park: Pennsylvania State University Press, 2021), 346–48.

17. Ivan Illich, *Gender* (New York: Pantheon, 1982).

18. Giorgio Agamben, *Where Are We Now? The Epidemic as Politics*, trans. Valeria Dani (Lanham, MD: Rowman & Littlefield, 2021).

19. C. S. Lewis, *Mere Christianity* (New York: HarperCollins, 2001), 159, 176–78.

20. In a classic depiction of religion as a culturally infantile wish fulfillment, Freud envisages a time of civilizational maturity when religious faith is left behind: "Then, with one of our fellow-unbelievers, they will be able to say without regret: Den Himmel überlassen wir / Den Engeln und den Spatzen. (We leave Heaven to the angels and the sparrows)." Sigmund Freud, *The Future of an Illusion*, trans. James Strachey (1927; repr., New York: Norton, 1961), 50. He is quoting the poet Heine. By contrast, I am leaving heaven to God, in whom I believe completely.

Chapter 1 Letters to Our Children

1. Fannie J. LeMoine, "Parental Gifts: Father-Son Dedications and Dialogues in Roman Didactic Literature," *Illinois Classical Studies* 16, no. 1/2 (1991): 337–66.

2. Dániel Z. Kádár, *Historical Chinese Letter Writing* (New York: Continuum, 2010), 31–70.

3. Eber Carle Perrow, "The Last Will and Testament as a Form of Literature," *Transactions of the Wisconsin Academy of Sciences, Arts, and Letters* 17, no. 1 (1913): 682–753, esp. 692–96.

4. Dilwyn Knox, "Gesture and Comportment: Diversity and Uniformity," in *Cultural Exchange in Early Modern Europe*, vol. 4, *Forging European Identities, 1400–1700*, ed. Herman Roodenburg (Cambridge: Cambridge University Press, 2007), 289–307.

5. Philip Dormer Stanhope (Earl of Chesterfield), *The Letters of Philip Dormer Stanhope, Earl of Chesterfield, with the Characters*, ed. John Bradshaw, vol. 2 (London: Swan Sonnenschein, 1892), 652, 658.

6. Paula McQuade, *Catechisms and Women's Writing in Seventeenth-Century England* (Cambridge: Cambridge University Press, 2017).

7. Dorothy Leigh, *A Mother's Blessing; Or, the godly counsaile of a gentle-woman not long since deceased, left behind her for her children: Contayning many good exhortations, and godly admonitions, profitable for all parents to leaue as a legacy to their children* [. . .] (London, 1616), 3.

8. George Savile (Marquis of Halifax), *Advice to a daughter as to religion, husband, house, family and children, behaviour and conversation, friendship, censure, vanity and affectation, pride, diversions: to which is added The character of a trimmer, as to the laws and government, Protestant religion, the papists, forreign affairs*, 6th ed. (London: M. Gillyflower and B. Tooke, 1699), 1–2, 6.

9. Raoul Vaneigem, *A Letter to My Children and the Children of the World to Come*, trans. Donald Nicholson-Smith (Oakland: PM Press, 2019).

10. James Baldwin, "My Dungeon Shook: Letter to My Nephew on the One Hundredth Anniversary of the Emancipation," in *The Fire Next Time* (London: Michael Joseph, 1963), 21.

11. Maya Angelou, *Letter to My Daughter* (New York: Random House, 2008).

12. Marian Wright Edelman, *The Sea Is So Wide and My Boat Is So Small: Charting a Course for the Next Generation* (New York: Hyperion, 2008).

13. K. J. Dover, *Greek Popular Morality in the Time of Plato and Aristotle* (Oxford: Blackwell, 1974), 167–69, 270.

14. Pope Francis, *Christus Vivit*: Post-Synodal Apostolic Exhortation to Young People and to the Entire People of God, March 25, 2019, https://www.vatican.va/content/francesco/en/apost _exhortations/documents/papa-francesco_esortazione-ap_20190325_christus-vivit.html.

15. Anne Bradstreet, "In Reference to Her Children, June 30, 1659," in *The Works of Anne Bradstreet*, ed. Jeannine Hensley (Cambridge, MA: Belknap, 1967), 232–34 (234).

16. Bradstreet, "To My Dear Children," in *Works of Anne Bradstreet*, 240–45.

17. John Clare, letter to William Hone, April 1825, in *John Clare*, ed. Eric Robinson and David Powell (Oxford: Oxford University Press, 1984), 484.

18. Eric Robinson and David Powell, eds., *John Clare by Himself* (Manchester, UK: Flyfield/ Carcanet, 2002), 4–5.

19. As quoted in Sarah Houghton-Walker, *John Clare's Religion* (Farnham, Surrey: Ashgate, 2009), 223.

Chapter 2 Evil Days

1. "Bertrand Russell's Advice for Future Generations," YouTube (video), accessed March 9, 2023, https://www.youtube.com/watch?v=JtJmnDCoyMo.

2. John W. Dower, *The Violent American Century: War and Terror since World War II* (Chicago: Haymarket, 2017); Stéphane Courtois et al., eds., *The Black Book of Communism: Crimes, Terror, Repression*, trans. Jonathan Murphy and Mark Kramer (Cambridge, MA: Harvard University Press, 1999); Daniel J. Sherman et al., eds., *The Long 1968: Revisions and New Perspectives* (Bloomington: Indiana University Press, 2013).

3. Maddy Reinert, Danielle Fritze, and Theresa Nguyen, "The State of Mental Health in America 2023," Mental Health America, October 2022, https://www.mhanational.org /issues/state-mental-health-america; Alicia Kruisselbrink Flatt, "A Suffering Generation: Six Factors Contributing to the Mental Health Crisis in North American Higher Education," *College Quarterly* 16, no. 1 (Winter 2013), https://files.eric.ed.gov/fulltext/EJ1016492.pdf; Amanda Barroso, Kim Parker, and Jesse Bennett, "As Millennials Near 40, They're Approaching Family Life Differently Than Previous Generations," Pew Research Center, May 27, 2020, https://www.pewresearch.org/social-trends/2020/05/27/as-millennials-near-40 -theyre-approaching-family-life-differently-than-previous-generations/; Stephanie Kramer, "White Evangelicals More Likely Than Other Christians to Say People Should Prioritize Marriage, Procreation," Pew Research Center, December 16, 2021, https://pewrsr.ch/3saYzDv; Aniruddh Prakash Behere, Pravesh Basnet, and Pamela Campbell, "Effects of Family Structure on Mental Health of Children: A Preliminary Study," *Indian Journal of Psychological*

Medicine 39, no. 4 (2017): 457–63, doi:10.4103/0253-7176.211767; C. A. M. Estrada et al., "Religious Education Can Contribute to Adolescent Mental Health in School Settings," *International Journal of Mental Health Systems* 13 (2019), https://doi.org/10.1186/s13033-019-0286 -7; Richard Scheffler et al., "The Anxious Generation: Causes and Consequences of Anxiety Disorder among Young Americans; Preliminary Findings," Berkeley Institute for the Future of Young Americans / Goldman School of Public Policy, Policy Brief, July 2018, https:// gspp.berkeley.edu/assets/uploads/page/Policy_Brief_Final_071618.pdf; "Mental Health and COVID-19: Early Evidence of the Pandemic's Impact: Scientific Brief," World Health Organization, March 2, 2022, https://www.who.int/publications/i/item/WHO-2019-nCoV -Sci_Brief-Mental_health-2022.1.

4. Amanda Barroso, "With a Potential 'Baby Bust' on the Horizon, Key Facts about Fertility in the U.S. before the Pandemic," Pew Research Center, May 7, 2021, https://www.pew research.org/fact-tank/2021/05/07/with-a-potential-baby-bust-on-the-horizon-key-facts -about-fertility-in-the-u-s-before-the-pandemic/; Chris Kohn, "9 Brutally Real Reasons Why Millennials Refuse to Have Kids," *Rooster Magazine*, July 25, 2017, https://therooster.com /blog/10-brutally-real-reasons-why-millennials-refuse-have-kids.

5. On the "nadir" of pessimism, see "A Call for Accountability and Action," Deloitte.com, accessed March 9, 2023, https://www2.deloitte.com/content/dam/Deloitte/global/Docu ments/2021-deloitte-global-millennial-survey-report.pdf, p. 15; Lisa Martine Jenkins and Gaby Galvin, "For Gen Z, Coronavirus and Social Injustice Are the Biggest Issues Facing the World," September 29, 2020, https://morningconsult.com/2020/09/29/gen-z-biggest -issues-polling/; Greta Thunberg, *No One Is Too Small to Make a Difference* (London: Penguin, 2019); Amitav Ghosh, *The Great Derangement: Climate Change and the Unthinkable* (Chicago: University of Chicago Press, 2017).

6. H. G. Wells, "The Star," in *Tales of Space and Time* (New York: Harper & Bros, 1900), 35–57.

7. Stella Ghervas, *Conquering Peace: From the Enlightenment to the European Union* (Cambridge, MA: Harvard University Press, 2021).

8. Joseph Glanvill, *The Vanity of Dogmatizing: Or Confidence in Opinions, Manifested in a Discourse of the Shortness and Uncertainty of Our Knowledge, and Its Causes; With Some Reflexions on Peripateticism; And an Apology for Philosophy* (London: H. Eversden, 1661), 178; see also Richard Foster Jones, *Ancients and Moderns: A Study of the Rise of the Scientific Movement in Seventeenth-Century England* (St. Louis: Washington University, 1961).

9. Simon Patrick, *The Parable of the Pilgrim: Written to a Friend* (London: Robert White, 1665), 508.

10. William J. Fox, "Forwards or Backwards?," *Monthly Repository* 85 (Jan. 1834): 1–7.

11. H. G. Wells, *Mankind in the Making* (New York: Scribner's Sons, 1916), 6.

12. "Baden Powell's Last Message to Scouts and Leaders," The Scouting Pages, accessed March 9, 2023, https://thescoutingpages.org.uk/bps-last-message/.

13. "Big Thinkers, Big Ideas," *New Scientist*, September 16, 2009, https://www.newscientist .com/article/mg20327262-200-big-thinkers-big-ideas/. Cf. Sophie McAdam, "10 Ways to Make Positive Change in the World," True Activist, August 6, 2013, https://www.trueactivist .com/10-ways-to-make-positive-change-in-the-world/.

14. Johann W. von Goethe, *Wilhelm Meister's Apprenticeship: A Novel*, trans. Thomas Carlyle, vol. 3 (Edinburgh: Oliver & Boyd, 1924), 87.

15. Augustine, *De beata vita* 33–34. Latin from Patrologia Latina, vol. 32, at Augustinus Hipponensis, "De Beata Vita liber unus," accessed March 10, 2023, http://www.augustinus.it /latino/felicita/index2.htm. See also *Saint Augustine: The Happy Life, Answer to Skeptics, Divine Providence and the Problem of Evil, Soliloquies*, FC 5 (Washington, DC: Catholic University of America Press, 2010), 81–82.

16. Augustine, *The City of God* 22.22, in *The Works of Aurelius Augustine, Bishop of Hippo*, vol. 2, ed. Marcus Dods (Edinburgh: T&T Clark, 1872), 519.

17. Augustine, *The City of God* 19.4 (Dods, 307).

18. Augustine, *The City of God* 22.30 (Dods, 544–45).

19. Michael Thomas Ford, *The Road Home* (New York: Kensington, 2010), 190.

20. A. G. Long, *Death and Immortality in Ancient Philosophy* (Cambridge: Cambridge University Press, 2019).

21. Aristotle, *Nichomachean Ethics* bk. 10, in *The Basic Works of Aristotle*, ed. Richard McKeon (New York: Random House, 1941), 1093–112. All references to Aristotle's works are to this edition.

22. Aristotle, *Nichomachean Ethics* 1101b (bk. 1.12; McKeon, 949).

23. Aristotle, *Nichomachean Ethics* 1178b (bk. 10.8; McKeon, 1107).

24. Aristotle, *Nichomachean Ethics* 1177b (bk. 10.7; McKeon, 1105).

25. Christopher M. Cullen, SJ, "The Natural Desire for God and Pure Nature: A Debate Renewed," *American Catholic Philosophical Quarterly* 86, no. 4 (2012): 705–30.

26. Blaise Pascal, *Pensées*, frags. 166–69, in *Pensées; The Provincial Letters*, trans. W. F. Trotter and Thomas M'Crie (New York: Modern Library, 1941), 59–60. The enumeration of Pascal's fragments varies widely according to critical editions. The Trotter translation follows the numbering of the critical edition of Léon Brunschvicg.

27. Pascal, *Pensées*, frag. 131 (Trotter, 47).

28. Pascal, *Pensées*, frag. 139 (Trotter, 52).

29. Pascal, *Pensées*, frag. 183 (Trotter, 63).

30. John Andrew Bernstein, *Progress and the Quest for Meaning: A Philosophical and Historical Inquiry* (Cranbury, NJ: Associated University Presses, 1993), 195–200; John Blake, *Children of the Movement* (Chicago: Lawrence Hill Books, 2004).

31. Peter Singer, *The Most Good You Can Do: How Effective Altruism Is Changing Ideas about Living Ethically* (New Haven: Yale University Press, 2015).

Chapter 3 Days of Sojourning

1. Ephraim Radner, *Time and the Word: Figural Reading of the Christian Scriptures* (Grand Rapids: Eerdmans, 2016), 17–43; Sarah Stewart-Kroeker, *Pilgrimage as Moral and Aesthetic Formation in Augustine's Thought* (Oxford: Oxford University Press, 2017).

2. Augustine, *The City of God* 19.17–18, in *The Works of Aurelius Augustine, Bishop of Hippo*, vol. 2, ed. Marcus Dods (Edinburgh: T&T Clark, 1872), 328.

3. Augustine, *Confessions*, trans. Henry Chadwick (Oxford: Oxford University Press, 2008), 175–76 (bk. 9.12.29–30).

4. Martha Nussbaum, *The Fragility of Goodness* (Cambridge: Cambridge University Press, 1986); Bernard Yack, "How Good Is the Aristotelian Good Life?," *Soundings: An Interdisciplinary Journal* 72, no. 4 (Winter 1989): 607–29.

5. K. J. Dover, *Greek Popular Morality in the Time of Plato and Aristotle* (Oxford: Blackwell, 1974).

6. Aristotle, *Nichomachean Ethics* 1.9 (1100a4–9); 1.10 (1101a), in *The Basic Works of Aristotle*, ed. Richard McKeon (New York: Random House, 1941), 946–48.

7. Aristotle, *Politics* 7.1 (1323a–1324a; McKeon, 1277–79).

8. Aristotle, *Nichomachean Ethics* 1.7–11 (1097–1101b; McKeon, 941–49).

9. Augustine, "*On the Predestination of the Saints*" and "*On the Gift of Perseverance*," in *St. Augustine: Four Anti-Pelagian Writings*, trans. John A. Mourant and William J. Collinge, FC 86 (Washington, DC: Catholic University of America Press, 1992), 218–337.

10. David Cayley, *Ivan Illich: An Intellectual Journey* (University Park, PA: Penn State University Press, 2021), 180–84, 191–94, 226–27.

Chapter 4 The Service of God

1. Amitai Etzioni, *The Spirit of Community: Rights, Responsibilities, and the Communitarian Agenda* (New York: Crown, 1993); R. Kenneth Carty and Munroe Eagles, *Politics Is Local: National Politics at the Grassroots* (Don Mills, ON: Oxford University Press, 2005); Rebecca

Winthrop, "The Need for Civic Education in 21st-Century Schools," Brookings Institution, June 2020, https://www.brookings.edu/wp-content/uploads/2020/04/BrookingsPolicy2020_BigIdeas_Winthrop_CivicEducation.pdf.

2. Aristotle, *Politics* 3 (1278b–1288b), in *The Basic Works of Aristotle*, ed. Richard McKeon (New York: Random House, 1941), 1183–205.

3. Aristotle, *Politics* 4.11 (1295a–1296b; McKeon, 1219–23).

4. Daniel H. Deudney, *Bounding Power: Republican Security Theory from the Polis to the Global Village* (Princeton: Princeton University Press, 2007).

5. "Democracy Index 2021: The China Challenge," Economist Intelligence Unit, accessed March 10, 2023, https://www.eiu.com/n/campaigns/democracy-index-2021/.

6. James Hankins, *Virtue Politics: Soulcraft and Statecraft in Renaissance Italy* (Cambridge, MA: Belknap, 2019).

7. E. P. Thompson, *Customs in Common: Studies in Traditional Popular Culture* (New York: New Press, 1993); James C. Scott, *The Moral Economy of the Peasant: Rebellion and Subsistence in Southeast Asia* (New Haven: Yale University Press, 1976).

8. Karl Polanyi, *The Great Transformation: The Political and Economic Origins of Our Time*, 2nd ed. (1944; repr., Boston: Beacon, 2001).

9. James C. Riley, *Sickness, Recovery and Death: A History and Forecast of Ill Health* (London: Macmillan, 1989); Riley, *Rising Life Expectancy: A Global History* (Cambridge: Cambridge University Press, 2001).

10. Edward Banfield, *The Moral Basis of a Backward Society* (Glencoe, IL: Free Press, 1958); Thomas Fleming, *The Morality of Everyday Life: Rediscovering an Ancient Alternative to the Liberal Tradition* (Columbia: University of Missouri Press, 2004).

Chapter 5 The Good Life as Offering

1. Ephraim Radner, *Leviticus*, Brazos Theological Commentary on the Bible (Grand Rapids: Brazos, 2008), 89–90, 161–67.

2. Radner, *Leviticus*, 237–56.

3. For example, James B. Rives, "Animal Sacrifice and Political Identity in Rome and Judaea," in *Jews and Christians in the First and Second Centuries: How to Write Their History*, ed. Peter J. Tomson and Joshua J. Schwartz (Leiden: Brill, 2014), 105–25.

4. Augustine, *The City of God* 19, in *The Works of Aurelius Augustine, Bishop of Hippo*, vol. 2, ed. Marcus Dods (Edinburgh: T&T Clark, 1872), 293–344; Andrew Hofer, OP, "Book 19. The Ends of the Two Cities: Augustine's Appeal for Peace," in *The Cambridge Companion to Augustine's "City of God,"* ed. David Vincent Meconi (Cambridge: Cambridge University Press, 2021), 228–49.

5. Augustine, *De beata vita* 33–34, trans. Ludwig Schopp, FC 5 (1948; repr., Washington, DC: Catholic University of America Press, 2010), 81–82; Latin from the Patrologia Latina edition, vol. 32, at Augustinus Hipponensis—De Beata Vita liber unus, http://www.augustinus.it/latino/felicita/index2.htm.

6. John Clarke, OCD, *Story of a Soul: The Autobiography of St. Thérèse of Lisieux*, 3rd ed. (Washington, DC: ICS Publications, 2013), 266.

7. Augustine, *The City of God* 19.13 (Dods, 319–21).

8. Jean Bethke Elshtain, *Augustine and the Limits of Politics* (1995; repr., Notre Dame, IN: University of Notre Dame Press, 2018).

9. Augustine, *The City of God* 19.23 (Dods, 334–39).

10. Augustine, *The City of God* 19.27.

Chapter 6 The Beauty of Limits

1. Augustine, *On Grace and Free Choice* 6–7, in *Augustine: "On the Free Choice of the Will," "On Grace and Free Choice," and Other Writings*, ed. and trans. Peter King (Cambridge: Cambridge University Press, 2010), 141–84, 153–54.

2. Malcolm Muggeridge, *Something Beautiful for God: Mother Teresa of Calcutta* (New York: Harper & Row, 1971).

3. Christopher Hitchens, *The Missionary Position: The Ideology of Mother Teresa* (New York: Verso, 1995).

4. Muggeridge, *Something Beautiful for God*, 125.

5. Cf. Aquinas, *Quaestiones Disputatae de Veritate* 1.a.1.resp.5; Latin and English by Robert W. Mulligan, SJ, at https://isidore.co/aquinas/QDdeVer1.htm.

6. *Epistle to Diognetus* 5, in *The Apostolic Fathers: Greek Texts and English Translations*, ed. and trans. Michael W. Holmes, 3rd ed. (Grand Rapids: Baker Academic, 2007), 703.

7. Ephraim Radner, "Mortality," St. Andrews Encyclopaedia of Theology, March 8, 2023, https://www.saet.ac.uk/Christianity/Mortality.

8. Ben Thomas, "*Disegno*: Superficial Line or Universal Design?," in *Renaissance Keywords*, ed. Ita Mac Carthy (London: Legenda, 2013), 31–44.

9. Jane Bennett, *Vibrant Matter: A Political Ecology of Things* (Durham, NC: Duke University Press, 2010).

10. Paul A. Lombardo, "The Great Chain of Being and the Limits to the Machiavellian Cosmos," *Journal of Thought* 17, no. 1 (Spring 1982): 37–52.

11. Clive Bell, *Art* (1913; repr., Oxford: Oxford University Press, 1987).

12. Aristotle, *Poetics* 1448b, in *The Basic Works of Aristotle*, ed. Richard McKeon (New York: Random House, 1941), 1457–58.

13. Augustine, *Exposition of Psalm 148*, 10, in Saint Augustine, *Expositions of the Book of Psalms*, trans. A. Cleveland Coxe, in *Nicene and Post-Nicene Fathers*, First Series (Peabody, MA: Hendrickson, 1994), 8:676.

14. John Milton, *An Apology for Smectymnuus*, in *John Milton: Selected Prose*, ed. C. A. Patrides, rev. ed. (Columbia: University of Missouri Press, 1985), 62.

15. Augustine, *The City of God* 19.14, 27, in *The Works of Aurelius Augustine, Bishop of Hippo*, vol. 2, ed. Marcus Dods (Edinburgh: T&T Clark, 1872), 322–23, 342–43.

16. Ephraim Radner, *Leviticus*, Brazos Theological Commentary on the Bible (Grand Rapids: Brazos, 2008), 265–78.

17. Lucy Bregman, *Preaching Death: The Transformation of Christian Funeral Sermons* (Waco: Baylor University Press, 2011).

18. Karl Barth, *Dogmatics in Outline*, trans. G. T. Thomson (New York: Philosophical Library, 1949), 119.

Chapter 7 An Incomplete Life

1. Larry Siedentop, *Inventing the Individual: The Origins of Western Liberalism* (Cambridge, MA: Belknap, 2014).

2. *Rule of Saint Benedict*, trans. and ed. David Parry and Esther de Waal (Leominster, UK: Gracewing, 1990), Prologue, 1–4.

3. Jean-Jacques Rousseau, *The Social Contract*, trans. Maurice Cranston (1762; repr., Harmondsworth, UK: Penguin, 1968), 72–74 (book 2, chap. 3).

4. Kristine Brennan, *Burundi* (Philadelphia: Mason Crest, 2013).

5. Ephraim Radner, "African Politics and the Will to Silence," *Christian Century*, November 7, 1984, 1034–38; republished as "The Will to Silence," *Index on Censorship* 14, no. 4 (1985): 28–31.

6. Sarah Maddison, *Conflict Transformation and Reconciliation: Multi-level Challenges in Deeply Divided Societies* (London: Routledge, 2016).

7. G. W. Leibniz, *Theodicy* [*Essais de Théodicée*, 1710], ed. Austin Farrer, trans. E. M. Huggard (1951; repr., La Salle, IL: Open Court, 1985), passim (e.g., sec. 210, p. 258); Hernán D. Caro, ed., *The Best of All Possible Worlds? Leibniz's Philosophical Optimism and Its Critics, 1710–1755* (Leiden: Brill, 2020).

Chapter 8 The Conditions of Our Offering

1. Aristotle, *Nicomachean Ethics* 1.2 (1094a–b), in *The Basic Works of Aristotle*, ed. Richard McKeon (New York: Random House, 1941), 935–36; Aristotle, *Politics* 7.1–3 (1323a–1325b; McKeon, 1277–82).

2. Thomas Hobbes, *Leviathan*, ed. Richard Tuck, rev. student ed. (Cambridge: Cambridge University Press, 1996), chap. 14, pp. 91–92.

3. Hobbes, *Leviathan*, chap. 15, pp. 109–10.

4. Hobbes, *Leviathan*, chap. 13, p. 89.

5. Hobbes, *Leviathan*, chap. 29, p. 221.

6. Hobbes, *Leviathan*, chap. 28, p. 219.

7. Aristotle *Politics* 3.7 (1279a–b; McKeon, 1185–86); Hobbes, *Leviathan*, chap. 19, pp. 129–38.

8. Jonathan Swift, "The Sentiments of a Church of England Man," in *The Works of the Rev. Jonathan Swift*, vol. 2, ed. Thomas Sheridan et al. (1708; repr., London: J. Johnson, 1801), 352.

9. *The Book of English Songs: From the Sixteenth to the Nineteenth Century* (London: Office of the National Illustrated Library, 1851), 149–50.

10. Hobbes, *Leviathan*, chap. 29, pp. 222, 225.

11. Zohreh Bayatrizi, *Life Sentences: The Modern Ordering of Mortality*, 2nd ed. (Toronto: University of Toronto Press, 2008), 89–123.

12. Hobbes, *Leviathan*, chaps. 42–43, esp. chap. 43, p. 414.

13. Benjamin Hoadly, "The Nature of the Kingdom, or Church, of Christ: A Sermon Preach'd before the King, at The Royal Chapel at St. James's, on Sunday March 31, 1717" (London: Timothy Childe, 1717).

14. Hobbes, *Leviathan*, chap. 42, p. 345.

15. S. G. F. Brandon, "The Origin of Death in Some Ancient Near Eastern Religions," *Religious Studies* 1 (1966): 217–28 (223).

16. See Aaron M. Faust, *The Ba'thification of Iraq: Saddam Hussein's Totalitarianism* (Austin: University of Texas Press, 2015); or the novel by Sinan Antoon, *The Corpse Washer* (New Haven: Yale University Press, 2013).

17. Anne Case and Angus Deaton, *Deaths of Despair and the Future of Capitalism* (Princeton: Princeton University Press, 2021).

18. Richard J. Regan, *Just War: Principles and Cases* (Washington, DC: Catholic University of America Press, 1996).

Chapter 9 Catastrophe—the Container of Our Politics

1. Stephen Kierulff, "Belief in 'Armageddon Theology' and Willingness to Risk Nuclear War," *Journal for the Scientific Study of Religion* 30, no. 1 (March 1991): 81–93 (esp. 90–91, 91n14).

2. Sasha Lilley et al., *Catastrophism: The Apocalyptic Politics of Collapse and Rebirth* (Oakland: PM Press, 2012). See the foreword by Doug Henwood, p. xv.

3. Frédéric Neyrat, "The Biopolitics of Catastrophe, or How to Avert the Past and Regulate the Future," *South Atlantic Quarterly* 115, no. 2 (April 2016): 247–65.

4. Carl Schmitt, *Political Theology: Four Chapters on the Concept of Sovereignty*, trans. G. Schwab (1922; repr., Chicago: University of Chicago Press, 2005).

5. Mathew Barrett Gross and Mel Gilles, *The Last Myth: What the Rise of Apocalyptic Thinking Tells Us about America* (Amherst, NY: Prometheus, 2012).

6. Jared Diamond, *Collapse: How Societies Choose to Fail or Succeed* (New York: Viking, 2005).

7. William H. McNeill, *Plagues and Peoples* (New York: Anchor, 1998); Lester K. Little, ed., *Plague and the End of Antiquity: The Pandemic of 541–750* (New York: Cambridge University

Press, 2007); Daniel T. Reff, *Plagues, Priests, and Demons: Sacred Narratives and the Rise of Christianity in the Old World and the New* (Cambridge: Cambridge University Press, 2005); Alfred W. Crosby, *America's Forgotten Pandemic: The Influenza of 1918*, 2nd ed. (Cambridge: Cambridge University Press, 2003).

8. Nana K. Poku and Alan Whiteside, eds., *The Political Economy of AIDS in Africa* (2004; repr., London: Routledge, 2017); for contrasting analysis, see Alex de Waal, *AIDS and Power: Why There Is No Political Crisis—Yet* (London: Zed Books, 2006).

9. Colin Kahl and Thomas Wright, *Aftershocks: Pandemic Politics and the End of the Old International Order* (New York: St. Martin's Press, 2021).

10. James C. Riley, *Rising Life Expectancy: A Global History* (Cambridge: Cambridge University Press, 2001).

11. Andrew Cunningham and Ole Peter Grell, *The Four Horsemen of the Apocalypse: Religion, War, Famine, and Death in Reformation Europe* (Cambridge: Cambridge University Press, 2000).

12. Walter Scheidel, *The Great Leveler: Violence and the History of Inequality from the Stone Age to the Twenty-First Century* (Princeton: Princeton University Press, 2017).

13. Walter Scheidel, "The Only Thing, Historically, That's Curbed Inequality: Catastrophe," *The Atlantic*, February 21, 2017, https://www.theatlantic.com/business/archive/2017/02/scheidel-great-leveler-inequality-violence/517164/; Scheidel, *Great Leveler*, part 7, "Inequality Redux and the Future of Leveling," 403–44.

14. Scheidel, "The Only Thing, Historically, That's Curbed Inequality."

15. Caroline Zickgraf, "Climate Change and Migration Crisis in Africa," in *The Oxford Handbook of Migration Crises*, ed. Cecilia Menjívar, Marie Ruiz, and Immanuel Ness (New York: Oxford University Press, 2019), 347–64; Alan Riley and Francis Ghilès, "Brexit: Causes and Consequences," Barcelona Centre for International Affairs (CIDOB), October 2016, https://www.cidob.org/en/publications/publication_series/notes_internacionals/n1_159/brexit_causes_and_consequences.

Chapter 10 Visions of Catastrophe

1. Michael Cahill, trans. and ed., *The First Commentary on Mark: An Annotated Translation* (New York: Oxford University Press, 1998), 95–98; James A. Kellerman, trans., *Incomplete Commentary on Matthew (Opus imperfectum)*, Ancient Christian Texts (Downers Grove, IL: IVP Academic, 2010), homilies 48–53, pp. 372–407.

2. Hilary of Poitiers, *Commentary on Matthew*, trans. D. H. Williams, FC 125 (Washington, DC: Catholic University of America Press, 2012), 249.

3. John Chrysostom, *Homily 75*, in *The Homilies of S. John Chrysostom, Archbishop of Constantinople, on the Gospel of St. Matthew*, trans. George Prevost (London: Walter Smith, 1885), 1000. See also *Homily 76*.

4. John Chrysostom, *Homilies 76* and *77* (Prevost, 1007–34).

5. Ambrose, *Commentary of Saint Ambrose on the Gospel according to Saint Luke*, trans. Íde M. Ní Riain (Dublin: Halcyon, 2001), bk. 10.5–45, pp. 317–28.

6. A text of the *Catena Aurea* can be found at https://www.ccel.org/ccel/a/aquinas/catena2/cache/catena2.pdf.

7. One exception is Ambrose, who briefly describes the "end of the world" that has "come upon us" in terms of wars waged by Huns, Alani, Goths, and others (*Gospel according to Saint Luke*, 319).

8. Martin Luther, "Sermons on the Gospel of St. Matthew," in *Luther's Works*, vol. 68, ed. Benjamin T. G. Mayes, trans. Kevin G. Walker (St. Louis: Concordia, 2015), chaps. 19–24.

9. Luther, "Sermons on the Gospel of St. Matthew," 263.

10. Luther, "Sermons on the Gospel of St. Matthew," 278.

11. Luther, "Sermons on the Gospel of St. Matthew," 278.

12. Martin Luther, *Confession concerning Christ's Supper* (1528), in *Luther's Works*, vol. 37, ed. Hilton C. Oswald and Helmut T. Lehman (St. Louis: Concordia, 1976), 301–3, 330.

13. Luther, "Sermons on the Gospel of St. Matthew," 341. On the temporal aspect of synecdoche and scriptural reference, see Ephraim Radner, *Time and the Word: Figural Reading of the Christian Scriptures* (Grand Rapids: Eerdmans, 2016), 163–203.

14. Luther, "Sermons on the Gospel of St. Matthew," 341.

15. Luther, "Sermons on the Gospel of St. Matthew," 274.

16. Andrew Cunningham and Ole Peter Grell, *The Four Horsemen of the Apocalypse: Religion, War, Famine, and Death in Reformation Europe* (Cambridge: Cambridge University Press, 2000).

17. Luther, "Sermons on the Gospel of St. Matthew," 264.

18. Pippa Norris and Ronald Inglehart, *Sacred and Secular: Religion and Politics Worldwide* (Cambridge: Cambridge University Press, 2004).

19. Edward Leigh, *Annotations upon all the New Testament philologicall and theologicall* (London: William Lee, 1650), 63–66.

20. Richard Burton, *Anatomy of Melancholy*, ed. Thomas C. Faulkner, Nicolas K. Kiessling, Rhonda L. Blair, 3 vols. (Oxford: Clarendon, 1989–94).

21. Thomas Burnet, *The Sacred Theory of the Earth: Containing an Account of the Original of the Earth, and of All the General Changes Which It Hath Already Undergone, or Is to Undergo, Till the Consummation of All Things* [. . .], 2 vols. (London: John Hooke, 1719).

22. Thomas Burnet, *De Statu Mortuorum et Resurgentium* (Rotterdam: Johannes Hofhout, 1719).

23. John Woodward, *An Essay towards a Natural History of the Earth and Terrestrial Bodies* [. . .] (London: Richard Wilkin, 1695).

24. See Roy A. Harrisville and Walter Sundberg, *The Bible in Modern Culture: Baruch Spinoza to Brevard Childs* (Grand Rapids: Eerdmans, 2002); Michael Legaspi, *The Death of Scripture and the Rise of Biblical Studies* (New York: Oxford University Press, 2010).

25. Ezra Palmer Gould, *A Critical and Exegetical Commentary on the Gospel according to St. Mark* (New York: Scribner's Sons, 1896), 240–55.

26. Rudolph Bultmann, *Theology of the New Testament*, trans. Kendrick Grobel (1951–55; repr., Waco: Baylor University Press, 2007), 3–32 and passim.

27. John Wesley, *Serious Thoughts Occasioned by the Late Earthquake at Lisbon* (London, 1755); John Wesley and Charles Wesley, *Earthquake Hymns* (Bristol: E. Farley, 1756).

28. Anne-Marie Mercier-Faivre and Chantal Thomas, *L'invention de la catastrophe au XVIIIe siècle: Du châtiment divin au désastre naturel* (Geneva: Droz, 2008).

29. John Wesley, "The General Spread of the Gospel," in *Sermons on Several Occasions*, vol. 2 (London: J. Kershaw, 1825), 157–67; Randy L. Maddox, "Wesley's Engagement with the Natural Sciences," and Deborah Madden, "Wesley as Adviser on Health and Healing," in *The Cambridge Companion to John Wesley*, ed. Randy L. Maddox and Jason E. Vickers (Cambridge: Cambridge University Press, 2010), 160–75, 176–89; Theodore E. D. Braun and John B. Radner, *The Lisbon Earthquake of 1755: Representations and Reactions* (Oxford: The Voltaire Foundation, 2005).

30. Michel Foucault, *"Society Must Be Defended": Lectures at the Collège de France, 1975–76*, ed. Mauro Bertani and Alessandro Fontana, trans. David Macey (New York: Picador, 2003); Catherine Mills, *Biopolitics* (Abingdon, UK: Routledge, 2018).

31. Ben Marsden and Crosbie Smith, *Engineering Empires: A Cultural History of Technology in Nineteenth-Century Britain* (Basingstoke, UK: Palgrave Macmillan, 2005), 246.

32. J. B. Bury, *The Idea of Progress: An Inquiry into Its Origin and Growth* (London: Macmillan, 1920).

33. R. A. Markus, *Saeculum: History and Society in the Theology of St. Augustine* (Cambridge: Cambridge University Press, 1970), 22–44.

34. Arnold Burgen, Peter McLaughlin, and Jürgen Mittelstrass, eds., *The Idea of Progress* (New York: De Gruyter, 1997).

35. James H. Moorhead, *World without End: Mainstream American Protestant Visions of the Last Things, 1880–1925* (Bloomington: Indiana University Press, 1999).

36. J. B. Bury, *A History of Freedom of Thought* (London: Williams & Norgate, 1913).

37. Charles C. Ryrie, *The Basis for the Premillennial Faith* (New York: Loizeaux Brothers, 1953).

38. Marco Mira d'Ercole et al., eds., *How Was Life? Vol. II: New Perspectives on Well-Being and Global Inequality since 1820* (Paris: OECD, 2021), https://doi.org/10.1787/3d96efc5-en.

39. OECD, *How's Life? 2020: Measuring Well-Being* (Paris: OECD, 2020), executive summary, p. 16, https://doi.org/10.1787/9870c393-en.

40. Johan Norberg, *Open: The Story of Human Progress* (London: Atlantic Books, 2020).

41. Steven Pinker, *Enlightenment Now: The Case for Reason, Science, Humanism, and Progress* (New York: Penguin, 2018).

42. Richard J. Estes and M. Joseph Sirgy, eds., *The Pursuit of Human Well-Being: The Untold Global History* (Cham, Switzerland: Springer, 2017), 737.

43. Charles Taylor, *Sources of the Self: The Making of the Modern Identity* (Cambridge, MA: Harvard University Press, 1989), 12–13.

44. "COVID-19 and Well-Being: Life in the Pandemic," OECD, November 25, 2021, https://doi.org/10.1787/1e1ecb53-en.

45. C. P. Snow, *The Two Cultures* (1959; repr., Cambridge: Cambridge University Press, 1998), 27.

Chapter 11 Infinite Finitudes, Desperate Complexities

1. Sophocles, *Antigone* 332–73, in *Sophocles: Antigone and Other Tragedies; "Antigone," "Deianeira," "Elektra,"* trans. Oliver Taplin (Oxford: Oxford University Press, 2020), 26–27.

2. Anselm, *Cur Deus Homo*, in *St. Anselm: Basic Writings; "Proslogium," "Monologium," "Cur Deus Homo," Gaunilo's "In Behalf of the Fool,"* trans. S. N. Deane, 2nd ed. (La Salle, IL: Open Court, 1962), 177–288.

3. Christopher Lasch, *The True and Only Heaven: Progress and Its Critics* (New York: Norton, 1991), 33–34.

4. S. G. F. Brandon, "The Origin of Death in Some Ancient Near Eastern Religions," *Religious Studies* 1 (1966): 217–28; Paul Oslington, "Natural Theology, Theodicy, and Political Economy in Nineteenth-Century Britain: William Whewell's Struggle," *History of Political Economy* 49, no. 4 (2017): 575–606.

5. Erle C. Ellis, *Anthropocene: A Very Short Introduction* (Oxford: Oxford University Press, 2018).

6. Pramod K. Nayar, *Posthumanism* (Cambridge: Polity, 2014).

7. Richard Hooker, *Laws of Ecclesiastical Polity*, Preface VI.1 and 3; cf. Hooker, *Preface to the Laws of Ecclesiastical Polity*, Cambridge Plain Texts (Cambridge: Cambridge University Press, 1922), 41–42.

8. Sean B. Walker and Keith W. Hipel, "Strategy, Complexity and Cooperation: The Sino-American Climate Regime," *Group Decision and Negotiation* 26 (2017): 997–1027.

9. Robert Michels, *Political Parties: A Sociological Study of the Oligarchical Tendencies of Modern Democracy* (New York: Free Press, 1961); Nadia Urbinati, *Representative Democracy: Principles and Genealogy* (Chicago: University of Chicago Press, 2006); Nancy L. Rosenblum, *On the Side of the Angels: An Appreciation of Parties and Partisanship* (Princeton: Princeton University Press, 2008).

10. Alberto Alesina and Enrico Spolaore, *The Size of Nations* (Cambridge, MA: MIT Press, 2003).

11. Dag Anckar, "Small Is Democratic, but Who Is Small?," *Arts and Social Sciences Journal* 2 (2010): 1–10.

12. Roger Keil and Rianne Mahon, eds., *Leviathan Undone? Towards a Political Economy of Scale* (Vancouver: University of British Columbia Press, 2009).

13. Brian Tierney, *Foundations of the Conciliar Theory: The Contribution of the Medieval Canonists from Gratian to the Great Schism*, new ed. (Leiden: Brill, 1997); Antony Black, *Council and Commune: The Conciliar Movement and the Fifteenth-Century Heritage* (London: Burns & Oates, 1979).

14. John Marshall, *John Locke, Toleration and Early Enlightenment Culture: Religious Intolerance and Arguments for Religious Toleration in Early Modern and "Early Enlightenment" Europe* (New York: Cambridge University Press, 2006).

15. Omar El Akkad, *American War* (New York: Knopf, 2017).

16. Neil E. Harrison, ed., *Complexity in World Politics: Concepts and Methods of a New Paradigm* (Albany: State University of New York Press, 2006). See the issue devoted to the topic in *Globalizations* 5, no. 2 (June 2008); John L. Campbell and John A. Hall, *The Paradox of Vulnerability: States, Nationalism, and the Financial Crisis* (Princeton: Princeton University Press, 2017).

17. Richard A. Posner, "Jervis on Complexity Theory," *Critical Review* 24, no. 3 (2012): 367–73 (372); Robert Jervis, *System Effects: Complexity in Political and Social Life* (Princeton: Princeton University Press, 1997); James Bohman, *Public Deliberation: Pluralism, Complexity, and Democracy* (Cambridge, MA: MIT Press, 2000); Andrea Jones-Rooy and Scott E. Page, "The Complexity of System Effects," *Critical Review* 24, no. 3 (2012): 313–42.

18. David Stadelmann, Benno Torgler, and Alex Mesoudi, "Bounded Rationality and Voting Decisions over 160 Years: Voter Behavior and Increasing Complexity in Decision-Making," PLOS ONE 8, no. 12 (Dec. 31, 2013), https://doi.org/10.1371/journal.pone.0084078.

19. Jedediah Purdy, *After Nature: A Politics for the Anthropocene* (Cambridge, MA: Harvard University Press, 2015).

20. Adrian Little, *Democratic Piety: Complexity, Conflict and Violence* (Edinburgh: Edinburgh University Press, 2008).

21. Stadelmann, Torgler, and Mesoudi, "Bounded Rationality and Voting Decisions"; Gabriel Leon, "Bad Apples: Political Paralysis and the Quality of Politicians," *Journal of Public Economic Theory* 15, no. 3 (June 2013): 433–47.

22. John S. Dryzek, Richard B. Norgaard, and David Schlosberg, *The Oxford Handbook of Climate Change and Society* (Oxford: Oxford University Press, 2011), 14.

23. Leopold Kohr, *The Breakdown of Nations* (London: Routledge & Kegan Paul, 1957).

24. "God Helps Those Who Help Themselves," Wikipedia, accessed March 13, 2023, https://en.wikipedia.org/wiki/God_helps_those_who_help_themselves.

25. Hannah Arendt, *The Human Condition* (Chicago: University of Chicago Press, 1958), 247; W. Totschnig, "Arendt's Notion of Natality: An Attempt at Clarification," *Ideas y Valores* 66, no. 165 (2017): 327–46.

Chapter 12 Normal, Abnormal, and Charitable

1. David Osborne and Ted Gaebler, *Reinventing Government: How the Entrepreneurial Spirit Is Transforming the Public Sector* (New York: Plume/Penguin, 1992); Vladimir Tismaneanu, *Reinventing Politics: Eastern Europe from Stalin to Havel* (New York: Free Press, 1992); Moisés Naím, *The Revenge of Power: How Autocrats Are Reinventing Politics for the 21st Century* (New York: St. Martin's Press, 2022); Michael Chessum, Birgitta Jónsdóttir, and Andreas Karitzis, "Reinventing Politics," Open Democracy, July 17, 2017, https://www.opendemocracy.net/en/reinventing-politics/.

2. James Burnham, *The Managerial Revolution: What Is Happening in the World* (New York: John Day, 1941); Willard F. Enteman, *Managerialism: The Emergence of a New Ideology* (Madison: University of Wisconsin Press, 1993).

3. Thomas S. Kuhn, *The Structure of Scientific Revolutions* (Chicago: University of Chicago Press, 1962).

4. "Family-Friendly Workplaces: Policies and Practices to Advance Decent Work in Global Supply Chains," United Nations Global Compact / UNICEF, accessed March 13, 2023, https://www.unicef.org/documents/family-friendly-workplaces-policies-and-practices-advance-decent-work-global-supply; Katherine Gallagher Robbins and Shawn Fremstad, "4 Progressive Policies That Make Families Stronger," Center for American Progress, October 25, 2016, https://www.americanprogress.org/article/4-progressive-policies-that-make-families-stronger/; Josh McCabe, "A New Agenda for the Pro-Family Movement," Institute for Family Studies, June 13, 2019, https://ifstudies.org/blog/a-new-agenda-for-the-pro-family-movement; Serena Sigillito, "A Conservative Case for Pro-Family Policy," *Public Discourse*, February 8, 2021, https://www.thepublicdiscourse.com/2021/02/74009/. Cf. Ephraim Radner, "Figgis, Families, and Synodality," in *Neville Figgis, CR: His Life, Thought, and Significance*, ed. Paul Avis (Leiden: Brill, 2022), 202–19.

5. Gerhard Uhlhorn, *Christian Charity in the Ancient Church*, trans. Sophia Taylor (New York: Scribner's Sons, 1883); J. W. Brodman, *Charity and Religion in Medieval Europe* (Washington, DC: Catholic University of America Press, 2009); Adam J. Davis, *The Medieval Economy of Salvation: Charity, Commerce, and the Rise of the Hospital* (Ithaca, NY: Cornell University Press, 2019).

6. Ivan Illich, "The Seamy Side of Charity," *America* 116, no. 3 (January 21, 1967): 88–91; David Cayley, *Ivan Illich: An Intellectual Journey* (University Park: Pennsylvania State University Press, 2021), 349–87.

7. Office for Social Justice, Archdiocese of St. Paul and Minneapolis, "Major Themes from Catholic Social Teaching," accessed March 13, 2023, https://web.archive.org/web/20060216183419/http:/www.osjspm.org/cst/themes.htm.

8. Russell R. Dynes, "The Lisbon Earthquake of 1755: The First Modern Disaster," in *The Lisbon Earthquake of 1755: Representations and Reactions*, ed. Theodore Braun and John Radner (Oxford: Voltaire Foundation, 2005), 34–49.

9. Franck Damour, *Heureux les mortels car ils sont vivants: Lettres à Larry Page et Sergey Brin* (Clichy, France: Corlevour, 2016); Max More and Natasha Vita-More, eds., *The Transhumanist Reader: Classical and Contemporary Essays on the Science, Technology, and Philosophy of the Human Future* (Malden, MA: Wiley-Blackwell, 2013).

Chapter 13 Nazareth, an Enduring City

1. Rodney Stark, *The Victory of Reason: How Christianity Led to Freedom, Capitalism, and Western Success* (New York: Random House, 2005), 233.

2. Ellen T. Charry, *God and the Art of Happiness* (Grand Rapids: Eerdmans, 2010).

3. "HUD Releases 2021 Annual Homeless Assessment Report Part 1," HUD.gov, February 4, 2022, https://www.hud.gov/press/press_releases_media_advisories/hud_no_22_022; Joshua Meribole, "The State of Homelessness in the Philippines," The Borgen Project, July 2, 2020, https://borgenproject.org/homelessness-in-the-philippines/.

4. Jean-Jacques Antier, *Charles de Foucauld (Charles of Jesus)*, trans. Julia Shirek Smith, 2nd ed. (San Francisco: Ignatius, 2022); René Voillaume, *Seeds of the Desert: Like Jesus at Nazareth*, trans. Willard Hill (Notre Dame, IN: Fides, 1964).

5. Markus Keck and Patrick Sakdapolrak, "What Is Social Resilience? Lessons Learned and Ways Forward," *Erdkunde: Archive for Scientific Geography* 67, no. 1 (January–March 2013): 5–19.

6. Martin Luther, "Sermons on the Gospel of St. Matthew," in *Luther's Works*, vol. 68, ed. Benjamin T. G. Mayes, trans. Kevin G. Walker (St. Louis: Concordia, 2015), 257–59.

7. Luther, "Sermons on the Gospel of St. Matthew," 332.

8. Luther, "Sermons on the Gospel of St. Matthew," 315.

9. Luther, "Sermons on the Gospel of St. Matthew," 267.

10. Luther, "Sermons on the Gospel of St. Matthew," 265, 267.

11. Luther, "Sermons on the Gospel of St. Matthew," 276–77.

12. Mary O'Brien, "The Root of the Mandrake: Machiavelli and Manliness," in *Reproducing the World: Essays in Feminist Theory* (1989; repr., New York: Routledge, 2019), 103–32.

13. Vern L. Bengtson, Norella M. Putney, and Susan C. Harris, *Families and Faith: How Religion Is Passed Down across Generations* (Oxford: Oxford University Press, 2017).

14. Jean Bethke Elshtain, *The Family in Political Thought* (Amherst: University of Massachusetts Press, 1982).

15. George Lindbeck, "Confession and Community: An Israel-like View of the Church," *Christian Century*, May 9, 1990, 492–96; P. Travis Kroeker, *Messianic Political Theology and Diaspora Ethics: Essays in Exile* (Eugene, OR: Cascade Books, 2017); Jana Evans Braziel, *Diaspora: An Introduction* (Malden, MA: Blackwell, 2008).

16. Daniel J. Elazar, "The Jewish People as the Classic Diaspora: A Political Analysis," in *Modern Diasporas in International Politics*, ed. Gabriel Sheffer (London: Croom Helm, 1986), 212–57.

17. Caroline Moorehead, *Village of Secrets: Defying the Nazis in Vichy France* (New York: Harper, 2014); André Trocmé, "Morale chrétienne et objection de conscience" [Christian morality and conscientious objection], *Cahiers de la Réconciliation*, March–April, 1933, 6–11.

Scripture Index

Subject Index